Cross-Cultural
Social Work Practice

Also Available from Lyceum Books, Inc.

Cross-Cultural
Social Work Practice
Purpose and Meaning
Second Edition

Karen V. Harper-Dorton

West Virginia University

Jim Lantz

LYCEUM
BOOKS, INC.
Chicago, Illinois

© Lyceum Books, Inc., 2007

Published by

LYCEUM BOOKS, INC.
5758 S. Blackstone Ave.
Chicago, Illinois 60637
773+643-1903 (Fax)
773+643-1902 (Phone)
lyceum@lyceumbooks.com
http://www.lyceumbooks.com

10 9 8 7 6 5 4 3

ISBN-13: 978-0-925065-76-6

Library of Congress Cataloging-in-Publication Data

Harper-Dorton, Karen V., 1942–
    Cross-cultural practice : social work with diverse populations / Karen V.
Harper-Dorton, Jim Lantz. — 2nd ed.
        p. cm.
    Includes bibliographical references and index.
    ISBN-13: 978-0-925065-76-6 (alk. paper)
    ISBN-10: 0-925065-76-5 (alk. paper)
    1. Social work with minorities—United States. 2. Minorities—Counseling of—United
States. I. Lantz, James E., 1943–2003. II. Title.
HV3176.H37 2007
362.84—dc22
                                                                    2006020807

This book is dedicated to Jim Lantz (1943–2003),
coauthor and inspiration behind this book.

Contents

Tables and Figure

Preface

AS THE PROCESS OF GLOBALIZATION CONTINUES TO TAKE PLACE EVER more quickly, social work and other helping professions are increasingly faced with the challenge to address the need for excellence in cultural competence. Expanded by dimensions of culture, ethnicity, gender, race, disabilities, education, and much more, human diversity is individual as well as collective. Not unlike the populations we serve, social workers, too, are diverse in their worldviews, images of helper attractiveness, needs for control, respect for rites of initiation, and hope for the future. These cross-cultural curative factors are common to humankind and informed by experiences of living in the world. Uncovered through naturalistic research, cross-cultural curative factors are close to the core of being, of human needs, and of human potential to discover meaning and purpose in living. Our opportunities for discovering meaning and purpose are influenced by the cultural practices and social influences in our present life situations. For the worker, the challenge is providing empathetic understanding and empowering those in search of meaning and purpose in their life experiences.

Cross-Cultural Social Work Practice: Meaning and Purpose is intended to increase the cross-cultural competence of the social work practitioner. The book is consistent with generalist practice yet provides information critical to clinical practice in helping clients search for meaning and purpose in daily living. Social work students and helping professionals will benefit not only from an understanding of cross-cultural curative factors and the four helping elements in the worker-client relationship, but also from the wealth of information provided on the social, political, and economic forces in the social environments of several diverse populations.

More than a decade has passed since the publication of the first edition of this book. Although we had originally intended to write only one edition, in response to numerous requests for a second edition from colleagues who continue to use *Cross-Cultural Practice* in graduate and undergraduate social work classes, we set out to extensively update and revise the text. Since the writing of the first edition, social work education and practice addressing cross-cultural competencies for working with diverse populations have expanded immensely. This second edition provides a framework to guide the helping relationship that utilizes cross-cultural curative factors to increase practitioners' understanding and build their cross-cultural competencies.

The second edition also has two new chapters on cross-cultural helping from an existential perspective and the role of cross-cultural concerns in competent social work practice, as well as updated information on the diverse populations discussed in the first edition. The new and expanded discussion of the existential perspective will help the social worker who is competent in cross-cultural practice move beyond assessing cultural differences to develop awareness of processes that people use in meeting their needs and solving problems in uniquely meaningful ways. Culturally relevant case studies incorporating the cross-cultural curative factors show how the four elements of helping can be used to guide intervention. The expanded chapter on traumatized clients provides a current discussion of trauma, whether observed or experienced. Expanded and updated with more than four hundred references, the second edition will help practitioners increases their understanding of the experiences of immigrants, refugees, trauma victims, and clients from diverse backgrounds who seek meaning and purpose in their lives. It is my hope that the reader will come away with the understanding that helping to empower those we serve to discover meaning and purpose in each life experience at every stage of living is critical to being, to living, and to contributing to civility in the world.

I want to express my gratitude to those individuals who have provided support over the past year. I appreciate the work of Geraldine Dawson, James Forte, Victoria Jackson, and Shirley Hall, who not only assigned the book to their students but also wrote valuable and detailed critiques of the first edition and of the manuscript for this edition. Steven Hartsock read many chapters and offered helpful feedback. Amy Trusheim, MSW graduate assistant, reviewed chapters, assisted with library research, and provided editorial assistance. Holly Whitlock, MSW graduate assistant, helped organize the final draft. Linda Grandon managed my schedule and provided encouragement to Amy and Holly. My son, Chris, provided editorial help. My husband's patient encouragement made all the difference.

While his untimely death prevented him from helping to finish this edition, Jim Lantz was the inspiration behind this book as well as much of the movement of logotherapy in the United States. I am thankful for Jim's wisdom and excellence in clinical practice and for Viktor Frankl's teachings and encouragement. I extend my appreciation to our clients and students.

Karen V. Harper-Dorton

1

Cross-Cultural Curative Factors

CULTURALLY COMPETENT SOCIAL WORKERS, COUNSELORS, AND OTHER human service professionals are critically important in the multicultural world of the twenty-first century. The ability to interact professionally with clients who are culturally different requires great cultural awareness, sensitivity, and empathy for the human experience of living in the world. The premise of this book is that social workers and other professionals can help individuals and families discover and experience a sense of meaning and purpose in their everyday lives through culturally sensitive and meaningful helping relationships.

Every culture has processes, healers, medications, and prescribed practices that define healing and wellness. It is from observing instances of healing activities, and then recording and observing them again, that people understand and share phenomena. Healing or curative factors have emerged through the discovery of natural and sanctioned helping in the world. Qualitative naturalistic studies identifying cross-cultural curative factors help inform social workers and counselors about basic intervention methods that are often useful in working with clients of differing ethnic background, gender, race, class, or socioeconomic status (Lantz, 2000b; Lantz & Pegram, 1989).

NATURALISTIC RESEARCH AND CROSS-CULTURAL CURATIVE FACTORS

This overview of naturalistic research presents the emergence of eight cross-cultural curative factors as they have been collected, recorded, and understood from the voices of people living throughout the world. Researchers observe instances of human activities and then record and observe them again, so that phenomena become shared and understood.

Naturalistic research is a form of qualitative research that occurs "in the field," using a "flexible human instrument" to gain and evaluate data (Hancock, 1998; Lincoln & Guba, 1985). Naturalistic research is done in the field so data can be observed and evaluated in terms of connection with the social environment. Conducted in natural settings, naturalistic research is different from experimental research, as experimental research flows from theory and confirms or disconfirms theory. Naturalistic research flows from data observed in the field, with the result that theory is created from the data observed. Theory evolving out of naturalistic research is called "grounded" theory, as it is grounded in the themes that emerge during observation in the field (Corbin & Strauss, 1990; Strauss & Corbin, 1990, 1998). Some authorities state that classical experimental research uses deductive analysis, while naturalistic research uses inductive methods of analysis (Lincoln & Guba, 1985). Developing theory inductively from data in an environment allows information and themes to emerge with some consistency. Seeking and understanding perspectives and voices of those studied are critical in generating data for comparison and interpretation for theory development. The connection of relationships among concepts contributes to "conceptual density," which is necessary for theoretical formulation that is both systematic and believable (Strauss & Corbin, 1998). Four stages of naturalistic research have been outlined by Kirk and Miller (1986): the invention stage, the discovery stage, the interpretation stage, and the explanation stage.

During the invention stage of naturalistic research, the field worker begins to develop a relationship with the culture to be studied and identifies individuals or organizations who can introduce the worker to members of the culture. These individuals can then help the worker gain entry into that culture. Kirk and Miller (1986) report that in this stage of naturalistic research, the research worker focuses primarily upon "getting in" and "getting along."

In the discovery stage, the field worker concentrates upon collecting data. Such data collection should be systematic, organized, and prolonged, and the field worker should use maximum variation sampling methods to obtain rich thick data. The field worker is taught to recognize that the data collection stage is nearing an end when data collection stops bringing in new facts, new associations, and new relationships among data (Kirk & Miller, 1986; Lincoln & Guba, 1985).

In the interpretation stage, the field worker attempts to identify data themes that emerge and reemerge from the collected data base. The field worker uses qualitative research methods such as data triangulation, member checking, audit trails, and peer debriefing to ensure that these themes have dependability and credibility (Greenlee & Lantz, 1993; Kirk & Miller, 1986; Lincoln & Guba, 1985). The major task of the field worker in the interpretation stage is to consistently and validly interpret themes and meanings, with careful attention to acquire an objective understanding of findings from the field.

In the explanation stage, the field worker exits the field, returns home, and writes the research report. In this stage, field workers must terminate their relationships with those they have been observing in the field. The focus of this stage is closure for all persons involved. The field worker should leave the field in a way that minimizes harm to the subjects of the research (Kirk & Miller, 1986). The explanation stage is characterized by leaving the field in a way that is fair to those who were there previously and will remain behind. The preparation of the research report marks the field worker's return home to his or her own culture and is a milestone of great importance, both for the project and for the field worker.

EIGHT CROSS-CULTURAL CURATIVE FACTORS

Cross-cultural curative factors uncovered through naturalistic research have great relevance to the practice of social work with varied populations. Their application in cross-cultural practice can aid the worker in developing helpful and culturally appropriate intervention activities with special populations and clients from different cultural backgrounds. Cross-cultural commonalities reflect basic human needs as well as culturally consistent processes for meeting these needs. Each culture's helping processes incorporate culturally significant sources of help or problem solutions.

The basic processes of human existence are similar for all persons in all cultures. All persons need to eat, to have clothing and shelter, to learn, to grow through the life cycle, and to experience a sense of meaning and purpose in their existence (Frankl, 1988; Krill, 1978; Lantz & Gyamerah, 2002a). These basic aspects of human existence have long been identified in social work literature as "common human needs" (Towle, 1952). Although all people throughout the world have the same common human needs, different cultural environments and ethnic backgrounds instill different ways to meet those needs (Lantz, 2000b). People are both different and similar. Only by respecting the sameness of our common human needs and the uniqueness of our different cultural methods of meeting these needs can a person begin to become a competent cross-cultural social work practitioner (Lantz, 2000a; Lantz & Harper, 1989; Lantz & Pegram, 1989)

Cross-cultural curative factors are believed to be common to the human experience of living in the world. These factors have been found to be helpful in many different cultures with many different kinds of clients in a variety of helping situations (Lantz, 2002; Torrey, 1986). Cross-cultural curative factors provide a gateway, a portal of common understanding, for helpers to intervene in the lives of clients. The eight cross-cultural curative factors believed to be common to the human experience that must be understood and embraced by competent cross-cultural social workers and other helping professionals working with diverse client populations are worldview respect, hope, helper attractiveness, control, rites of initiation, cleansing experiences, existential realization, and physical intervention.

Worldview Respect

The experience of living in the world (i.e., being in the world) includes understandings of existence in society, family, and interpersonal relationships. People hold positive and negative beliefs and values about religion, art, politics, and science in the immediate world. One's worldview encompasses the need to understand and have trust in the world and is a lens for constructing an image of cultural reality in the world. The ultimate questions in life—Who am I? Where am I? What's wrong? What's the remedy?—are answered from one's personal worldview (Walsh & Middleton, 1984).

Worldview respect (i.e., having respect for other worldviews) is the most important factor in gaining cultural competence as a social work practitioner. Anthropologists and experienced cross-cultural social work practitioners consistently point out that nonmedical, verbal, and psychosocial healing do not work unless the healing methods used are compatible with the client's worldview (Frankl, 1973; Jilek, 1982; Lantz, 2004; Lantz & Pegram, 1989). The following case material illustrates worldview respect in cross-cultural social work practice.

Mrs. A and the Root Woman

Mrs. A requested social work intervention at a nearby mental health center because she wanted to leave her husband but said she couldn't. Mrs. A was a thirty-eight-year-old African American who lived in a ghetto neighborhood. She had no children and did not feel dependent upon her husband for financial security. She wanted to leave her husband because he beat her. She reported that she could not leave him because he had "hired a root woman to hex me." Mrs. A believed that the hex was keeping her in the marriage.

Mrs. A was provided with supportive social work services but out of respect for Mrs. A's worldview, the social worker at the mental health center put Mrs. A in contact with a local folk healer with whom the staff had worked in the past. The healer used a ceremony to remove the hex, thus enabling Mrs. A to leave her husband.

The social worker in this case was able to provide competent cross-cultural services by putting the client in contact with a healer who shared her worldview (Lantz & Pegram, 1989).

Hope

Anthropologists, social workers, and other cross-cultural practitioners also consistently report that hope is an important curative factor in all cultures and societies (Jilek, 1974, 1982; Lantz, 2001; Lantz & Lantz, 2001; Torrey, 1986). The more hope the client has about the power or potential for help in the healing relationship, the greater the chance that the healing process will be effective. Most successful healers, cross-cultural social workers, and other kinds of mental health workers understand this concept and decorate their offices or sacred huts with a variety of artifacts symbolizing their effectiveness and healing power (Lantz & Pegram, 1989; Torrey, 1986). For example, many social workers hang certificates and awards on their office walls. Helping professionals often display licenses to practice and service awards for contributions they have made to their communities. Such certificates and awards are important symbols of achievement and credibility. These credentials help clients have faith in the social worker and the helping process. Folk healers and non-Western helpers also use symbols of healing power to help clients have more hope in the healing process. For example, an Ojibway healer (called a "Roadman" and who was known to Jim Lantz) collects crutches from patients who have been healed of lameness. These crutches are shown to new clients who request help. Representing the healing experiences of others, these leftover crutches are important symbols of hope for those seeking recovery.

A third example comes from Lantz's private practice. Since he was an existential social worker, Lantz asked new clients to read Viktor Frankl's book *Man's Search for Meaning*. This book describes Frankl's experiences in a German concentration camp during World War II and how existential principles helped him even in such a terrible situation as a German death camp. New clients are asked to read this book because, after reading it, they often feel that if existential concepts can be helpful even in a World War II death camp, then existential social work may be useful to them (Lantz, 1987, 1993).

Helper Attractiveness

"Helper attractiveness" is a term coined by Carl Rogers (1980) to mean the client's perception of the practitioner's ability to help. Rogers points out that helper qualities that clients find attractive in the United States are warmth, kindness, competence, concern, integrity, genuineness, and empathy. These qualities support human needs for compassion and caring. Beliefs in healing and healers vary across cultures, and there are as many different images of helpers as there are different ethnic, regional, and religious groups and subcultures worldwide.

Sandner (1979), Torrey (1986), and Jilek (1982) are all transcultural psychiatrists who point out that Rogerian helper characteristics are important in non-Western healing and folk healing as well. Field research has consistently found native healers to be ethical, responsible, warm, kind, mature, and committed to the ethics and standards of their healing profession. Sandner has pointed out that Navajo healers spend approximately twenty years learning the chants, rituals, and sand paintings that are a part of their healing profession. The length and intensity of the Navajo healer's training help to ensure that the healer will demonstrate ethical behavior; integrity; and sincere, self-transcendent commitment to helping others. A study of AIDS patients in Thai families found ethnomedical practices to produce hope even in situations where families affirm their belief in modern medicine (Nilmanat & Street, 2004).

The qualities of helper attractiveness identified by Rogers (1980) are important in social work intervention regardless of the cultural context. When informed by culture and worldview respect, helper attractiveness facilitates healing and supports the curative factor of hope (Lantz & Harper, 1989, 1990; Lantz & Pegram, 1989).

Control

In Western helping practices, it is considered important that the client learn something from the helping intervention and that what has been learned be used after termination to prevent problems in the future. For example, it is believed that the experience of recovering from an illness teaches people something about mastery and control so that they can better manage or even avoid similar illnesses in the future. In social work practice, the process of helping clients develop a sense of control is often identified as "empowerment" (Saleeby, 1999). Empowerment practices in social work are activities that help clients, groups, and communities build and restore their social functioning. Empowerment occurs as vulnerable and oppressed groups gain control of their own lives.

Social workers and other helping professionals hold theoretical psychological perspectives that inform their beliefs about human behavior, and it follows that these perspectives then inform their practices with their clients. In other words, what clinicians, social workers, and folk healers believe about psychological and social behavior shapes intervention. Psychoanalytic practitioners help clients develop and use insight to master problems (Lindy, 1988). Cognitive practitioners help clients learn to identify and challenge irrational "self-talk" to solve problems. Behavioral practitioners teach clients to use learning theory principles for "self-management and self-control." Community organizers help clients learn to "join together" to change oppressive social conditions.

On a more individual level, folk healers teach clients methods of mastery and control (Edwards, 1996; Eliade, 1964). Torrey (1986) shows that the Balian healer teaches the client to pray correctly, that a Mexican-American *curandero* may teach the client a water purification ritual, and that some Arab healers teach clients to write out verses from the Koran. These are all techniques of mastery and control. Similarly, Sandner (1979) points out that considerable time and effort go into teaching the client "methods to control evil" during Navajo healing. Eliade (1964) shows that folk healers consistently use rites, symbols, and oral repetition of creation myths to teach individuals to master cultural tasks throughout each stage of life cycle development. Helping the client develop a sense of mastery and control is an important curative factor in many cultures and is extremely important in social work practice. It is believed that a sense of control helps the client reduce frustration and anxiety (Caple & Salcido, 1995; Sue & Sue, 2003).

Rites of Initiation

Rites of initiation are methods of mastery and control that almost universally involve two elements: movement toward chaos and symbolic death, and movement toward new life or rebirth (Eliade, 1964). In a rite of initiation, the person going through the initiation is expected to change old behaviors (symbolic death) and then accept or learn new behaviors (rebirth). A rite of initiation symbolizing this process of death and rebirth is found in almost every major helping orientation or program directed toward helping people change.

A Western initiation ritual that many clinical social work practitioners have experienced is the training program, or psychotherapy ritual. In this ritual the social worker who wants to learn to practice a new orientation to therapy is required by the training institution to undergo the particular type of therapy either prior to his or her acceptance into the training program or concurrently with the training program. Such a process involves confrontation and disruption of the social worker's old methods of intervention and personal methods of adaptation (movement toward chaos and symbolic death). After this disruption has occurred, the social worker is guided into new practice methods or personal skills in social functioning (the rebirth experience). Such a process may be observed in many psychoanalytic, Gestalt, and family therapy training institutions. This process of symbolic death and rebirth is ritualized and celebrated in the certificate of completion and ceremony of graduation (Lantz, 2004; Lantz & Pegram, 1989).

A second example of a Western rite of initiation occurs in the twelve-step work of Alcoholics Anonymous (Eliade, 1964; Holmes, 1991). The alcoholic is expected to confess inappropriate past behavior, make restitution for such behavior, and engage in new behaviors (sobriety and helping others). Group support, the help of a sponsor, and a request for assistance from a higher power are parts of the rite of initiation and process of symbolic death and rebirth in Alcoholics Anonymous.

A non-Western example of the death and rebirth rite of initiation is described by Eliade (1964), who reports that some shamans become healers because they experience a "calling" after a personal near-death experience. Such a calling is often signaled by a dream and is accepted by the tribe or community when the future shaman recounts the dream in a community rebirth celebration.

Some social workers, family therapists, and other professional counselors sometimes use rites of initiation, or ordinary culturally congruent rites of passage, to help individual clients and families who are experiencing problems in moving from one stage of life to the next. Consistent with a cross-cultural practice point of view, intervention must help the social work client develop a meaningful celebration, ritual, or ceremony if life transitions are to be successfully mastered (Lantz, 2000b, 2002).

Cleansing Experiences

Frankl (1959) and Yalom (1980) have both pointed out that guilt is a universal human experience. People constantly experience limitations, mistakes, and failures, as human nature is imperfect. No matter how intense the effort to succeed, most people continue to fail in living up to all their challenges and responsibilities. The cleansing experience appears to be a universal method for dealing with the fact of human imperfection (Eliade, 1964; Lantz & Pegram, 1989; Norwich, 1966).

A good example of a Native American folk healing/cleansing process is "sweating." In this experience the client is placed in a closed hut or tent where water is thrown upon hot rocks to produce steam. The healer works to purify the client, both physically and spiritually, while the client sits in the steam for many hours. Water purification rituals are used by folk healers in many cultures to help clients overcome feelings of guilt, sadness, and depression (Eliade, 1964; Lantz, 1987; Tick, 1989; Torrey, 1986). The cleansing experience is sometimes used by folk healers in a rebirth ritual to help the person being initiated remove spiritual impurities of past behaviors and role performances in preparation to enter a new role or stage of life. Eliade makes the observation that in such rituals, the physical act of sweating takes on a symbolic function and is extremely effective in helping the client to feel spiritually clean and pure.

A Western helping activity that is also a purification or cleansing ritual is called restitution. In restitution, the client performs an act, ritual, or service in an attempt to make up for a past mistake or transgression or to turn the mistake into something of value and meaning (Lantz & Pegram, 1989). The story of Mr. and Mrs. C provides an example of how social work clients can use restitution as a cleansing experience.

Mistake in the C Family

Mr. and Mrs. C requested clinical services after the death of their son from an AIDS-related illness. Mr. C indicated that he was having problems sleeping because his conscience was bothering him. Mrs. C stated that she was worried about her husband. Mr. C explained, "I kicked my son out of the house three years ago when he told me he was gay." He added, "Learning my son was gay was a big shock. . . . I didn't handle it well." Mrs. C reported that her husband and the son eventually reconciled, and that their son had lived at home for the last three months of his life. Mr. and Mrs. C both said they felt proud that they were there for their son when he was dying.

The couple felt that they had been "fools" to kick him out of the house and that they would always feel guilty about their ignorance. They stated that they had lost a year and a half with their son because of their ignorance. Now that their son was dead, they would give anything to get that time back.

In this situation the social work practitioner initially encouraged the couple to talk about their tragedy and their feelings about it. The social worker was careful not to give advice and simply listened to the couple until they felt comfortable that their worker had some understanding of their feelings. When trust had developed, the social worker asked the couple how they might feel about giving talks about their mistake to other parents—those who had recently discovered their son or daughter was gay or lesbian. Mr. and Mrs. C initially felt uncomfortable with this idea but as time went on decided that it was a good idea. The couple felt that this suggestion gave them a way to help others and help turn a mistake into something useful. Mr. and Mrs. C were linked with a

GLBT organization for volunteer work and were also provided support and training in public speaking. They have now shared their mistake in over forty speeches. Mr. C no longer has difficulty sleeping.

Another cleansing experience that occurs in Western social work is called catharsis. In catharsis the client expresses strong feelings that have been hidden, repressed, or denied. Clients frequently report emotional relief after expressing these feelings. Catharsis often results in insight and frequently helps clients improve their self-esteem and reduce overly intense feelings of guilt (Frankl, 1973; Lantz, 1993; Rogers, 1980).

Existential Realization

Existential realization occurs when a social worker, therapist, shaman, or native healer helps a client discover, create, and experience meaning or meaning potentials in everyday life. In existential helping and in many forms of cross-cultural helping, the major motivational dynamic is understood to be the human search for meaning. Frequently the primary difficulty that clients experience is a disruption in their search for meaning and purpose in life (Lantz & Lantz, 2001). When social work clients are unable to discover or create meaning, they experience a "meaning" or "existential" vacuum (Frankl, 1967, 1975; Lantz, 1993, 2001). The disruption, denial, or repression of meaning awareness triggers the development of an existential vacuum and its associated symptoms.

In a metaphorical sense, the filling of an existential vacuum is like air rushing in to fill a physical vacuum. An existential vacuum may be positively filled when one develops a sense of meaning and purpose in life. On the other hand, an existential vacuum frequently contains negative factors from the development of symptoms and problems, such as anxiety, depression, or substance abuse. An existential vacuum produces a sense of loss of meaning and direction in life. The social worker's job in cross-cultural intervention is to use questions, comments, suggestions, activities, empathy, and sincere personal interest to facilitate a kind of reflection that expands meaning awareness and challenges the client's existential vacuum (Frankl, 1959; Lantz, 2000a, 2000c; Lantz & Gyamerah, 2002a).

A concept in shamanic and folk healing therapy that is very similar to Frankl's existential-meaning vacuum is "soul loss" (Eliade, 1964). Both Eliade and Jilek (1982) have pointed out that healing rituals performed by shamans to call back the client's "fugitive soul" help the client discover or reestablish a connection with meaning. For Eliade, the folk magician, healer, yogi, shaman, and guru are all existential psychotherapists working with basic processes of meaning and existence. Eliade reports that the basic helping factor in both existential and shamanic soul-loss intervention is an existential attempt to rediscover "sacred meanings" camouflaged in the client's life.

Physical Intervention

Physical intervention is a process in which the helper provides the client with physical treatment such as massage, medication, or surgery. In many non-Western and so-called primitive societies, medications and surgery are provided for symbolic, sacred, or cathartic reasons (Eliade, 1964). Our Western knowledge about the symbolic, sacred, and cathartic uses of physical intervention is limited in depth and scope (Murguia et al., 2003; Nilmanat & Street, 2004; Torrey, 1986). In Western society, medications and surgery are frequently provided by physicians to correct biochemical imbalances or to repair damaged tissue. Physical intervention in the modern Western world rarely extends beyond the scientific application of commonly accepted techniques, and little attention is given to personal, social, or existential meanings. Carefully honed by repeated investigation, sterile procedures, and empirical research, physical intervention in the Western world is sterile and mostly impersonally administered by specialized technicians. Belief in science and information informs Westerners' acceptance of modern scientific procedures and frequently clouds personal symbolic but sacred meanings.

RELEVANCE OF CROSS-CULTURAL CURATIVE FACTORS TO SOCIAL WORK INTERVENTION

The eight cross-cultural curative factors that consistently emerge in many naturalistic studies of helping processes are critical in cross-cultural competence and professional practice regardless of the theoretical framework or methods used in the approach to intervention (Lantz & Harper, 1990). Gaining awareness of meaning in daily living and finding new meaning potentials in living in the world are essential in cross-cultural pursuits of meaning and purpose in life. These curative factors have great potential to facilitate clients' meaning awareness and discovery of new meaning opportunities within the social environment.

Minority clients, special populations, and other vulnerable clients consistently confirm the need for cross-cultural intervention to help overcome experiences of oppression and social injustice. Such experiences include prejudice, racism, oppression, economic deprivation, inadequate medical care, disconnection from family and network supports, and disruptions in familiar coping strategies. These same factors help define values and strengths as well as those things in life that are celebrated and shared with family, social networks, and community. Curative factors identify strengths important in empowering clients at all levels of social systems—individual, family, group, community, and society.

The broadly accepted ecological model of social work practice calls for cross-cultural competence. The balance of people and social systems throughout the world evolves and changes through transactional processes and shifts in power. Minority populations, politically disenfranchised groups, and other vulnerable people experience oppression and exclusion for one reason or another. Human beings suffer from harsh culturally informed transactions and sanctions in the face of political oppression, dictatorships, and civil wars. From an ecological perspective, competent cross-cultural social work practice can effect change at a variety of social work levels. The goal of this book is to increase cross-cultural understanding of people and provide examples of intervention with individuals and families who share common human needs that are informed by each individual's unique worldview.

SUMMARY

For the social worker, cross-cultural curative factors are gateways to understanding a client's worldview and response to cultural and social beliefs and practices. The eight curative factors identified in this chapter are critical to competent cross-cultural practice and are demonstrated in case examples throughout the remaining chapters as people from diverse backgrounds explore their feelings of pain and trauma in search of new purpose and meaning in life. Examining emotional pain and sharing painful experiences in a supportive helping relationship bring trauma and other personal experiences into the interactional world of the social work relationship.

2

Cross-Cultural Concerns and Competent Social Work Practice

JUST AS MEANINGS OF HUMAN DIVERSITY ARE SOCIALLY CONSTRUCTED IN each period of time in each culture, so are processes for helping. Evolving out of early philanthropic movements, social work's mission of service reaches individuals, families, groups, organizations, and communities. Serving poor, disenfranchised, and minority populations, social workers are instrumental in developing social welfare policy for the protection of oppressed populations. Exploitation and oppression target less powerful populations of people on the basis of color, native origin, religion, gender, age, and resources. These populations are particularly at risk of being blamed for their vulnerability while being denied access to services and privilege.

Social welfare organizations grew in nineteenth-century America mostly in response to problems of poverty, homeless and dependent children, and delinquent youth (Dubois & Miley, 2005). Social work has a long history of involvement with immigration and resettlement, including the early settlement house movement of the late 1800s. Social and political advocacy as well as social services to immigrants and their families and to vulnerable ethnic and racial groups were instrumental in bringing about change through the settlement house movement. Families of different national origin, language, religion, and race lived and worked in proximity with each other in the early settlement houses. Some of the most destitute clients of the 1800s were the families of sailors. Seamen's mission houses, like the settlement houses, provided shelter and food along with many other social services (Harper, 2000b; Popple & Leighninger, 2002). With husbands and fathers at sea for many months, wives and children of early sailors lived in extreme poverty and had no way to communicate or receive financial support.

Social work is a profession with a mission to serve those in need of human and social services, particularly poor and disenfranchised persons. Preventing harm and empowering others to overcome oppression and social injustice are central to the profession's mission. Social justice is identified as a core value for the social work profession and requires social workers to "seek to promote sensitivity to and knowledge about oppression and cultural and ethnic diversity" (NASW, 2000, p. 5). Social workers work to prevent oppression, discrimination, and social injustices due to "race, ethnicity, national origin, color, sex, sexual orientation, age, marital status, political belief, religion, or mental or physical disability" (NASW National Committee on Racial and Ethnic Diversity, 2001, p. 5). Barker (2003) defines oppression as "the social act of placing severe restrictions on an individual, group, or institution. Typically, a government or political organization that is in power places these restrictions formally or covertly on oppressed groups so that they may be exploited and less able to compete with other social groups. The oppressed individual or group is devalued, exploited, and deprived of privileges by the individual or group who has more power" (pp. 306–307).

DIVERSITY: SOME TERMS AND CONCEPTS

The multifaceted population mix of the twenty-first century is vastly more diverse than the more homogeneous population of previous centuries. A nation of immigrants since its discovery, America's history is riddled with discrimination and oppression of various minority groups alongside national values of equality, justice, and freedom. While giving voice to democratic traditions and a stated national philosophy of welcoming persons who are different and who come from distant shores, the transformation of America's population has not been without stress and trauma. Many have experienced discrimination, hatred, and violence in their efforts to succeed in the United States. Minority members often celebrate and embrace the majority culture despite the struggle to cope with various forms of oppression and social injustice.

The early twenty-first century witnessed great coexistence and interactions among different racial and ethnic groups in the United States. It is not uniformly easy for members of special populations or minority groups to live in the United States. The country is no longer one of differences just in color, religion, and gender. Within-group minorities emerge where ethnicity cuts across factors of age, race, gender, sexual orientation, disabilities, religion, education, and profession, (Healey, 2003; Popple & Leighninger, 2002). Skin color continues to be a factor that makes many people vulnerable to racism and discrimination. While members of various ethnic groups may blend in with the majority group in appearance, for others, color is a distinguishing factor that places them at risk of oppression and social injustice in a white-dominated society (Lum, 2004).

Some terms and concepts relating to human diversity are used frequently in social sciences literature. Understanding these terms is a prerequisite for gaining competence for working with others. Perhaps even more important, practitioners who are ethnically sensitive are aware of their own ethnic values and keenly aware of clients' cultural and ethnic backgrounds. What follows are some common terms and concepts that one must know in order to gain cultural competence for social work practice in a diverse society.

Minority Groups

A minority group is defined as a group of people who (1) have a history of in-equality of power and/or resources; (2) share a differentiating trait or characteristic of cultural or physical dimensions such as language, religion, or race; (3) have a self-conscious social unit separate from the dominant group that contributes to group identity of lower social status; (4) have ascribed membership (acquired at birth); and (5) marry within their own groups, for example, within their own race or religion (Healey, 2003).

Divested of power, minorities are vulnerable to oppression, discrimination, racism, social injustice, violence, and victimization (Dubois & Miley, 2005). Feelings of subordination, anger, and inferiority increase their vulnerability and make it necessary for them to develop coping behaviors for avoiding harm and for their physical and psychological survival. The histories of Native Americans and African Americans demonstrate the harm minority populations can experience at the discretion of a dominant and powerful majority. Such harm includes being denied freedom, property, land, roots of national origin, the right to vote, and equal participation in a wage economy.

Ethnicity

Ethnicity is defined as having a common identity, sense of belonging, and membership in a cultural group with similar traits and customs. Ethnicity includes social and cultural differences such as religion, language, culture of origin, national background, and tribal membership. Additionally, the culturally informed values, beliefs, and behaviors of population groups with shared traits and customs reflect the groups' ethnic and cultural heritage. Identification with one's cultural heritage establishes identity and membership, and sometimes even prejudice against those outside the group. For whatever personal or social reasons, individuals identify with their ethnic and cultural heritage differently. Some people choose not to share their values and beliefs, while others share openly. Some evidence strong feelings about past oppression and injustices done to the group. There are some people who believe that their ethnic beliefs should be of importance to everyone. The position of having feelings of ethnic superiority is termed *ethnocentrism* (Barker, 1999, 2003). Ethnocentrism involves believing that one's culture is the best and that others should adopt similar beliefs and practices. When taken to the extreme, strong ethnocentric beliefs have led to wars and atrocities, such as the mass execution of European Jews.

Race

Racial characteristics defining groups of people provide meanings of identity, membership, and belonging and may link to culture and ethnicity. The modern concept of race has many meanings that go beyond biological definitions. Schriver

Table 1. Population groups in the United States: Actual and projected

Population	% of total— 2000	Projected % of total— 2025	Projected % of total— 2050
Non-Hispanic Whites	71%	62%	53%
African Americans	12%	13%	13%
Hispanic Americans	12%	18%	24%
Asians and Pacific Islanders	4%	6%	9%
Native Americans, Eskimos, Aleuts	<1%	<1%	<1%
TOTAL POPULATION	275,306,000	337,814,000	403,686,000

Source: U.S. Census Bureau (2000a). *Projections of the resident population by race, Hispanic origin, and nativity.* Retrieved July 15, 2006, from http://www.census.gov/population/projections/nation/ summary

(2004) discusses race as a sociopolitical construct representing a range of consequences including oppression, identity, social inclusion or exclusion, and power.

Characteristics of skin color, facial structure, hair type, and combinations thereof are traits of comparison of populations. The U.S. Census Bureau identifies groups for purposes of reporting population characteristics. For example, Hispanic Americans, Asian Americans, and Native Americans are identified as distinct groups living in the United States. Census data project that racial minorities will represent about 50 percent of the population in the United States by mid-century (table 1).

While the United States currently is a predominantly White society, many countries around the world are not. Multicultural and multiracial backgrounds are common in today's global society. Montague (1964) makes a case for understanding race as a socially defined phenomenon influenced by the evolution of cultures and the long history of humankind. Racial membership is only one factor of diversity and cuts across different religions, ethnicities, ages, gender disabilities, and sexual orientations. Race, age, and gender are among the first characteristics most people notice when meeting or seeing a new person. There is a broad continuum of race and age where skin and hair colors and textures blend, as do facial structures. Social definitions often make racial membership subjective and laden with issues of power. "Racial identity is a definition of self that is constructed during socialization, not a simple or direct function of one's genetic heritage" (Healey, 2003, p. 19).

Cultural Pluralism

Cultural pluralism involves respect between individuals and groups for others' mutual culture, beliefs, and traditions and implies an absence of prejudice (Schaefer, 1998). In a culturally pluralistic society, minority group members can express their culture without fear of repercussion. Minorities can freely maintain their own identity alongside the dominant or mainstream culture while respecting the overarching culture. There is freedom for people to celebrate or rediscover their roots and ethnicity and to choose to protect their cultural identity by maintaining practices and celebrations consistent with their cultural orientation. Pluralistic societies provide opportunities for groups to maintain their cultural and social differences in meaningful and rewarding ways (Healey, 2003).

Not all societies around the world embrace pluralistic values. Unlike cultural pluralism, cultural ethnocentrism devalues individual differences and values mainstream culture as the preferred culture, a standard against which other ethnic, racial, and religious groups are judged or compared (Chau, 1990). Nevertheless, traditional cultural images are becoming less distinct as globalization continues and the mix of diverse cultures increases.

Sociocultural Dissonance

"Sociocultural dissonance occurs when ethnic minorities seek to cope with their life situations while under pressure to conform to dual, often conflicting or incongruent requirements of both minority and dominant cultural systems" (Chau, 1990, p. 126). Affective exploration of individual characteristics between what they think they are and how they are valued by others can create feelings of confusion, guilt, anger, and low self-efficacy. Individuals may internalize prejudice and devalue themselves as a result of such comparisons. Being confronted by conflicting beliefs and practices that are different from those of one's ethnic culture can produce stress and dissonance. Feelings of dissonance may result in efforts to conform and change or may become the impetus for social action or other efforts for change.

MINORITY RESPONSES TO A DOMINANT CULTURE

The identification of coping strategies used by minority group members in the face of oppression, social injustice, discrimination, and even hatred and violence is important, as having an understanding of these strategies can protect the practitioner from labeling minority coping strategies as pathology or mental illness. Identification of ways in which minority group members respond to the dangers of living in the United States is extremely important information for the practitioner of cross-cultural social work (Greenlee & Lantz, 1993).

Assimilation into a new culture involves a process ranging from preserving one's cultural practices and worldview to shedding some practices and traditions and eventually adopting those of the new culture. Assimilation can be a lengthy process, especially for those with strong ties to their native culture. It is impossible to identify all the adaptive strategies used by minority group members in their efforts to cope with social injustice and societal oppression. A few of the adaptive coping strategies that some minority group members use in the face of racism, hatred, violence, prejudice, and disrespect help maintain a personal sense of meaning and purpose in the world. Traditional, acculturation, transitional, and hybrid coping strategies are common coping strategies of minority groups.

Traditional Coping Strategy

Traditional minority culture group members attempt to maintain their traditional values, norms, and methods of experiencing meaning while living in an alien cultural situation (Healey, 2003; Sue & Sue, 2003). The traditional minority culture group member resists acculturation and attempts to interact with representatives of the dominant culture as seldom as possible. Feeling close to their own culture and in touch with the meaning they hold of themselves in their cultural world, traditional minority culture group members are not highly vulnerable to experiences of loss of meaning in life or worldview confusion because they maintain the values and meaning rituals of their past (Jilek, 1982). For some, this is a response to living in a country or society where they feel excluded from participation.

The traditional coping strategy may work better for first-generation members of minority groups or special populations because of the difficulty of their relocation. Many traditional minority culture group members often experience with sadness the realization that their children may not wish to maintain the family's traditional ways. Often this realization leads to considerable intergenerational conflict. The traditional minority culture group member will seldom volunteer to be a client of practitioners who represent the dominant culture. However, at times, the traditional minority culture group member will request treatment in instances of intergenerational conflict. Generally, such requests come reluctantly as a last resort for managing stress and conflict in the family (Lantz, 1993; Lantz & Harper, 1989).

Although the traditional minority culture group member is not highly vulnerable to disruptions of meaning in life, he or she is very vulnerable to economic and political exploitation. Because the traditional minority group member wants to avoid interaction with the dominant culture and attempts to resist acculturation, he or she remains somewhat unfamiliar with the legal and political strategies of the dominant culture and often is not prepared to use these strategies for self-protection (Caudill, 1963). Native Americans, African Americans, and Appalachians are three fairly traditional groups who have had natural resources such as land, timber, and coal taken from them by dominant culture representatives, partially because of their traditional coping style (Lantz & Harper, 1989). The traditional coping strategy works fairly well for members of various minority cultures unless they own mineral-rich land or some other valuable resource that is coveted by members of the dominant culture. Resource ownership tends to require greater interaction with the dominant culture and may limit the effectiveness of traditional coping strategies.

In his classic work on assimilation, Gordon (1964) identified three stages of assimilation. First, acculturation involves learning the dominant society's culture, language, and values. In this initial stage, new members begin to understand customs and values that define living in the culture. In this stage it is likely that the social structure may be poorly understood. As assimilation progresses, minority group members enter their community's formal organizations and then eventually clubs and informal groups and organizations. Many gain powerful positions, and some even develop their own successful businesses. Understanding the societal organizational structure of tasks, institutions, and communications enables new members to link with individuals and organizations within the social structure. The third stage, marital assimilation, extends beyond the earlier cultural and structural assimilation. Assimilation is a developmental process that spans time and even generations. When one has some sense of belonging within the societal structure, greater acceptance of customs and values is likely to follow in the process of acculturation (Healey, 2003; Zastrow, 2004).

Acculturation Coping Strategy

The acculturated minority group member successfully learns, accepts, and internalizes the norms, values, and methods of discovering meaning in the dominant culture. Such individuals are often very willing to become the client of a dominant culture representative, sometimes viewing such a relationship as symbolic of successful acculturation. The acculturated client who has been successful in learning the dominant culture's methods of discovering meaning is still somewhat vulnerable to the experience of meaning disruptions and worldview confusion (Lantz, 1993). If racism and discrimination did not exist, the acculturation coping strategy would be quite effective, and the minority group member attempting acculturation would not be so vulnerable to cultural confusion or meaning disruption (Jilek, 1982; Williams, 1987).

Unfortunately, racism and hatred do exist. Many minority group members who have adopted the norms and values of the dominant culture find their experience of acculturation to be confusing and sometimes isolating. In instances of loss of meaning and sociocultural dissonance, minority group members sometimes choose to embrace their traditional values, norms, and old ways of discovering and experiencing a sense of meaning and purpose in life. Such a return to the past can result in a hybrid form of acculturation that successfully incorporates both old and new experiences of belonging culturally. Finding comfort in traditional values and meaning experiences serves as a bridge to embracing the values and norms of the dominant cultural group. This bridge is often extremely effective in protecting the minority group member from experiencing meaning disruptions or confusion and a lack of direction in life (Jilek, 1982; Spindler & Spindler, 1971). This hybrid coping strategy is discussed later in this chapter.

Transitional Coping Strategy

The transitional minority culture group member is the most vulnerable to cultural confusion and loss of direction or meaning in life. He or she is in the process of giving up traditional methods of discovering and experiencing meaning in an attempt to learn the methods of finding meaning that are used by the dominant cultural group (Lantz & Pegram, 1989; Spindler & Spindler, 1971). During this process of change, the transitional minority culture group member is especially vulnerable because traditional values, beliefs, and practices that have been meaningful in the past are being replaced, or at least reshaped to match the new majority culture. Initially uncomfortable and unfamiliar, the majority culture's beliefs and practices may not fit well with the individual's basic strengths and methods of personal adaptation. Many transitional minority culture group members experience confusion and frustration, especially soon after geographic migration (Lantz & Harper, 1990). Such transitional meaning disruptions are described in detail by Billingsley (1969), Fabry (1979), Frankl (1959), Jilek (1974, 1982), Krill (1978), and Lifton (1973).

Important life changes can happen as a result of societal relocation or migration, both prior to and following migration. Loss of social networks, separation from family supports, and loss of social role or avocation are great stressors that contribute not only to meaning disruption and worldview confusion, but also to emotional distress severe enough to affect mental health. Cultures have traditional aspects that protect against mental health problems. As acculturation processes take place, earlier protective cultural beliefs and traditions lessen and sometimes result in greater vulnerability requiring transitional coping such as reliance on family and familiar helpers, and sometimes folk healers (Vega & Alegria, 2001).

Hybrid Coping Strategy

In the hybrid coping strategy, the minority culture member successfully integrates elements of the dominant culture with elements of his or her traditional ways. If a successful integration occurs, the minority group member is able to utilize the legal and political strategies of the dominant culture for self-protection yet maintain the values, norms, and rituals of the minority tradition to enhance a sense of personal identity and meaning in the face of discrimination and hatred by the dominant cultural group (Jilek, 1982). Hybrid cultures and coping strategies have always existed as one group of people dominate another, and eventually an amalgam or hybrid emerges. Canclini (1992) views hybrid cultures as having evolving or changing processes rather than a static state. Hybrid cultures respond to political processes that reshape and reorganize cultural space and meaning. Art, literature, music, dance, and cultural rituals may appear with nuances of different forms.

Just as cultures produce hybrids over time, individuals evidence hybrid coping strategies as well. Examples of such hybrid coping strategies in the United States include the Black Pride movement (Sniderman & Piazza, 2002; Williams, 1987; Zastrow, 2004), the gay rights movement (Galliano & Lissotta, 2004), the feminist movement (Hanmer & Statham, 1989; Williams, 2004), the Vietnam veterans' self-help movement (Appy, 2003; Lifton, 1973), and the reemergence of shamanism as a form of native healing in the Pacific Northwest (Edwards, 1996; Jilek, 1974; Torrey, 1986). Exclusionary practices can fester and flourish in "absolute" cultures. Interaction, not duplicity, is characteristic of synergistic cultures that continue to grow and change in a state of "hybridity" (Portella, 2000).

The recent Black Pride, gay rights, feminist, and Vietnam veterans' self-help movements have all produced change and continue to shape the multicultural society we live in. This kind of hybrid coping strategy is similar to what is referred to as "empowerment." Individual empowerment in social work practice is an internal process where strengths are identified and greater self-esteem is fostered through experiences of support and effective behaviors (Herbert & Harper-Dorton, 2002). Empowerment is enabled through mobilization of client strengths and reflected in social change and political action brought about by client participation. Personal empowerment can become a bridge leading out of helplessness and victimization (Saleeby, 1999; Wiley & Rappaport, 2000). As individuals become empowered, confidence, new behaviors, and greater participation became evident. Coping and interacting within cultural and subcultural contexts represent hybridity and have led to positive changes in contemporary multicultural society, where diverse populations and cultures coexist.

SOCIAL CONSTRUCTION OF DIVERSITY

The construction of social values and social roles defines minority positions in a society. The dominant class or power-holding majority defines statuses for the less powerful minority. Socially constructed definitions of race, class, and gender roles create hierarchies and social value. Discrimination, domination, oppression, and social statuses have given rise to demonstrations, crises, and wars in struggles of domination versus freedom.

Cultural diversity is integral to the very fabric of values and practices that define the United States in the global society. Nevertheless, fears of differences became apparent in situations of terror and trauma like the terrorist attacks on New York's World Trade Center. Political, economic, and social forces at national and international levels create additional uncertainties. Membership in today's global society causes many people to assess their own cultural beliefs, practices, mores, and prejudices as they consider what is to be kept, replaced, or denied expression.

Many minority culture group members experience what can be called the cross-cultural double bind. In the cross-cultural double bind, a member of a minority culture is encouraged by the dominant culture to change, adapt, and accept the values, norms, and methods of experiencing meaning used by members of the dominant culture. Institutions of the dominant culture develop laws, rules, and procedures making it difficult for minority culture group members to maintain their traditional methods of experiencing meaning. At the same time, the institutions of the dominant culture that encourage acculturation also begin to develop rules, proce-dures, and laws prohibiting the minority culture client from experiencing the re-wards of acculturation. In such a double-bind situation, the member of a minority culture cannot utilize either the old or the new to create a sense of meaning in the new cultural environment (Lantz, 2000b; Spindler & Spindler, 1971). Cross-cultural double binds produce feelings of alienation, powerlessness, and loss of meaning in life and are part of the life experiences of many minority culture groups that have come to the United States.

NEXUS OF COMMON CROSS-CULTURAL CURATIVE FACTORS AND CROSS-CULTURAL CONCERNS

Six common cross-cultural concerns frequently experienced by cultural mi-norities and other minority populations are economic deprivation, inadequate medical care, social injustice and prejudice, racism, disconnection from family sup-ports, and disruption in coping methods. People outside the majority or main-stream culture frequently report that these concerns cause serious oppression and great injustice in their lives. These common cross-cultural concerns are not new ex-periences of living in society and, as reflected in table 2, enter into the daily experi-ences of those who are vulnerable. Minority groups and others in disadvantaged or oppressive circumstances are especially vulnerable to these concerns.

Some minority culture members successfully cope with and adapt to main-stream cultural and social pressures around them without stress, while others ex-perience considerable confusion and even trauma. Trauma, unhappiness, depres-sion, loss of meaning in life, and fearfulness are common reasons why people seek help from helping professionals such as social workers and counselors.

Common cross-cultural concerns represent social injustices and acts of op-pression and discrimination that less powerful population groups have experienced. Sociopolitically constructed meanings of race, ethnicity, society, culture, minority, and majority have labeled groups and obfuscated individual differences.

It is possible that the cross-cultural curative factors discussed in chapter 1 evolved in response to felt or expressed needs and solutions to problems defined by particular cultural contexts. Each culture identifies culturally congruent rites of passages, celebrations, privileges, suffering, loss, and behaviors in general. The reality of living in the world involves commonalities of cross-cultural curative fac-tors that can be discerned as strengths for coping with traumas arising out of cross-cultural concerns.

Common cross-cultural curative factors and cross-cultural concerns form a ma-trix of potential strengths and potential problems, as shown in table 2. These cross-cultural curative factors are relevant to social work practice with diverse popula-tions, where culturally consistent helping requires problem solving and treatment skills that are compatible with clients' cultural mores. Individual interpretation of

Table 2. Cross-cultural curative factors and concerns matrix

Cross-cultural concerns ⇒	Cross-Cultural Curative Factors							
	Worldview respect ⇒	Hope ⇒	Helper attractiveness ⇒	Control ⇒	Rites of initiation ⇒	Cleansing experiences ⇒	Existential realization ⇒	Physical intervention ⇒
Economic deprivation								
Inadequate medical care								
Social injustice and prejudice								
Racism								
Disconnection from family supports								
Disruption in coping methods								

meaning in living is informed by and connected to cultural and social beliefs. This is true for clients as well as social workers and other helping professionals. While much social work literature addresses problem identification and problem solution for individuals and families struggling with problems in their daily lives, meanings associated with these solutions are not always explored. Social workers and other helping professionals must be personally and professionally aware of cultural differences in order to gain cross-culturally competent skills. Cross-cultural practitioners who incorporate common cross-cultural curative factors in their treatment activities can be very helpful to clients who have different cultural backgrounds and worldviews, particularly when they experience one or more of the common cultural concerns.

CROSS-CULTURALLY COMPETENT SOCIAL WORK PRACTICE

From a holistic perspective, competent cross-cultural social work practice with diverse populations requires social workers to understand the realities of human experiences and diverse worldviews at all levels of social systems and individual emotional, spiritual, and physical well-being. Having a greater awareness of self, learning about other cultures and lifestyles, and understanding interpersonal behavior and communication are part of being competent to practice cross-culturally. Realities of human experiences and diverse worldviews expand as the profession serves growing populations of people of different races, ethnicities, age, social class, gender, religions, sexual orientation, and family structures, as well as people with disabilities.

Culturally competent practice requires that social workers understand terms and definitions concerning human diversity. A definition of culturally competent social work practice is "the ability to transform knowledge and cultural awareness into health and/or psychosocial interventions that support and sustain healthy client-system functioning within the appropriate cultural context" (McPhatter, 1997, p. 261). Understanding individual coping strategies, adaptive processes, and ways that ethnic and racial groups relate to others and to their own environment enhances the lens through which human behavior is viewed.

SUMMARY

The sad truth is that no one can simply construct for themselves "an identity." Culture is both inherited and has to be recreated through experience so that it may reside within the individual in memory and feeling. It is the product of experience and history represented in individuals through our internalized parents and by the values and traditions they have passed on to us.

Andreou, *Inner and Outer Reality in Children and Adolescents* (p. 147–148)

The multicultural mix of people in the nation and around the globe has evolved not by divine intervention, social construction, or modeling. Instead, culturally diverse populations evolve as a result of human endeavors to survive, to interact, and to find meaning in existence. Being neither unitary or undifferentiated, nuances of differences are preserved in varying and individually constructed fashions so that each group is indeed diverse and unique.

This chapter calls for competent social work practice in the midst of cross-cultural concerns and human strengths and interpretation of meaning in a multicultural world. Diverse worldviews intersect with the dominant society, often where the social work practitioner interfaces with client systems. Potentially explosive, this intersection requires that the social worker understand forces such as oppression, realities of poverty, and differences of race and ethnicity. Part of gaining knowledge is gaining awareness of oneself and others. This increased awareness requires that social workers and other helping professionals become informed by expanding the boundaries of personal experiences, even if only to vicariously explore experiences of others through literature, music, and narratives of lives lived differently.

3

Social Work Practice: Helping Cross-Culturally from an Existential Perspective

EXISTENTIALISM AND SOCIAL WORK PRACTICE

According to Krill (1979), social work practice informed by an existential perspective does not require workers to delve into the profound depths of existential philosophy. Krill found the existential perspective to offer order and direction useful for working in cross-cultural contexts, where human diversity, individuality, and self-awareness are so important. Existential psychology brings attention to spiritual, personal, social, and cultural environments as important spheres of human existence. An existential perspective is helpful in providing cross-culturally competent intervention that is sensitive to clients' beliefs and worldviews. Helping clients gain a sense of individual freedom and responsibility to identify experiences of loss, grief, harm, social injustice, and emotional traumas is empowering and healing (Lantz, 1999, 2000d; Mengel, 2004). Existential philosophy and literature do not replace theories of biological, cognitive, or psychological development.

Social work intervention from an existential perspective is useful in various cross-cultural contexts, including working with Vietnam veterans (Lantz, 1993, 2000a, 2000b; Lantz & Greenlee, 1990a), Appalachian clients (Lantz, 1992a; Lantz & Alford, 1995; Lantz & Harper, 1992), older adults (Lantz, 1998; Lantz & Raiz, 2004), migrating families (Lantz & Frazer, 1996; Lantz & Harper, 1990), and families and individuals experiencing trauma, illness, and disability (Lantz, 2000c; Lantz & Gyamerah, 2002b; Lantz & Lantz, 2001). It is imperative that social workers, counselors, therapists, and other professionals understand the importance of cross-cultural curative factors relevant to life experiences. Each client brings cultural and personal values informed by his or her individual experiences. This chapter provides an introduction to basic concepts of existential intervention and identifies four elements for helping in cross-cultural social work practice.

The existential movement reaches back in time and offers a holistic approach to the human condition of living in the world, which includes the spiritual, psychological, and social realms of global existence. Existentialism does not replace religion, psychology, or psychiatry. "Existentialism is philosophy derived from man's immediate experience of the world in which he lives—a confrontation with the realities of the human condition and the establishment of a personalized meaning from them" (Krill, 1976, p. 730). While early writers like Søren Kierkegaard and Fyodor Dostoevsky questioned salvation and conveyed despair, contemporary existentialism is a philosophy of life influenced by writers like Martin Heidegger, Paul Tillich, Michel Foucault, Ludwig Binswanger, and Rollo May (Krill, 1979; Lantz, 1999) Authentic living in the world requires awareness, commitment, responsibility, love, and freedom as well as suffering (Binswanger, 1963; Krill, 1976). Individual reality as constructed by the individual calls for awareness and interpretation of experiences in daily living. Mengel (2004) suggests that it is necessary to understand people's lives as having some personal order and orientation toward meaningful living. Beyond finding order and meaning in living in the real world, having a sense of freedom and responsibility is necessary. Attaining authenticity occurs through encounters with others, and through relationships that enable self-awareness and self-realization. Authentic living is not a phenomenon of isolation (Binswanger, 1963; Frie, 2003).

The existential perspective is rooted in philosophical, psychological, and spiritual understandings of human existence—the living, being, and dying of the individual and of others. (Frankl, 1973, Heidegger, 1962; Marcel, 1952, 1963, 1973; May, 1986; May & Yalom, 2005; Tillich, 1952). One simple definition of existential psychology is that it is a psychology of the existence of actual people living in the real world, where thinking, acting, feeling, and doing occur in the context of their cultural experiences (Wong, 2004). Individuals organize their lives within the world in which they live and respond—influenced by their values, their understanding of *what* and *how* they are in their world. Each person has a mind, a soul, a body, and personal fears and joys regarding living, dying, and being in the world. It is the juncture of *what* and *how,* the nexus of one's culturally informed perceptions of needs and solutions, that affords opportunities for meaning in life and for intervention.

Social work intervention from an existential perspective is an approach in which problems, meaning, and meaning potentials in daily living are important. Individuals need to find meaning in life that is consistent with their personal beliefs and values. Exercising freedom in being and responsibility in living is empowering in the reality of existence (Frankl, 1984; Langle, 2004; Lantz, 1996, 1999). It is the task of the social worker or counselor to help the client discover, actualize, and make use of meaning potentials and opportunities found in daily living (Lantz, 1996, 2002).

The client-worker relationship is the medium for intervention and is an essential component in helping individuals, families, couples, and groups work through issues and concerns in search of meanings and responsibilities in life. The worker is an external agent, a facilitator or co-explorer, in the voyage to reduce emotional pain and find opportunities to gain new meaning in life. It has been said that "Family therapy is a family telling its story over and over again with input from the therapist, until it comes out in a way that makes sense to them and they can live with" (Brown, 1990). Individual therapy is similar in that the end result has to be compatible with the client's worldview; in other words, outcomes must be consistent with one's beliefs about problem resolution and reduction of pain or discomfort.

Individuals and families alike can recover and make meaning of their lives that is compatible with their worldview. Cross-cultural curative factors serve as a lens for viewing and understanding diverse beliefs, values, and problem solutions. After all, existential psychology is about real people in the real world (Langle, 2004; Mengel, 2004; Wong, 2004). There are four existential helping elements that offer a structure for intervention.

COMMON CROSS-CULTURAL CURATIVE FACTORS AND EXISTENTIAL HELPING ELEMENTS FOR SOCIAL WORK INTERVENTION

Having service as their primary responsibility, concerned social work practitioners discover and use interventions and activities for practice application with heterogeneous population groups. The existential helping elements of holding, telling, mastering, and honoring chart a process, a pathway, to help clients develop and utilize internal and external resources in the face of problems and personal difficulties. These elements inform practice situations ranging from generalist practice to very specialized psychotherapy depending on the expertise of the practitioner (Lantz & Gyamerah, 2002a, 2002b).

Existential helping elements offer a useful process for helping clients work through existential concerns and existential pain. Existential helping elements are *holding, telling, mastering,* and *honoring.* These four elements are particularly useful with minority-culture clients, for whom oppression, social injustice, and disrespect for human diversity are realities in everyday life (Lantz, 1993, 2000b, 2001, 2004; Lantz & Raiz, 2003). The existential element of holding in the helping relationship allows existential concerns and pain to come into awareness from the "storehouse" of the past. Telling provides the opportunity for the client to explore the existential pain, perhaps reshaping it so that it better fits the client's here and now. The existential element of mastering occurs as coping skills develop and concerns and responses are handled more effectively in daily living. The fourth and last element of honoring happens during the healing process, when meaning potentials for the future can be actualized from painful experiences in the past. In this stage, clients become able to honor their past trauma experiences. Honoring trauma and pain is believed to be central to gaining safety, self-esteem, insight, and capacities to actualize meaning potentials and celebrate new meanings from those things deposited and stored in the past (Lantz, 2000b; Lantz & Gregoire, 2003; Lantz & Gyamerah, 2002b).

Figure 1. Common cross-cultural concerns, cross-cultural curative factors, and existential helping elements for social work intervention

Common cross-cultural concerns
Economic deprivation
Inadequate medical care
Prejudice
Racism
Disconnection from family supports
Disruption in coping methods
↓
Vulnerability, disrupted meaning, and trauma pain
↓
Cross-cultural curative factors
Worldview respect
Hope
Helper attractiveness
Control
Rites of initiation
Cleansing experiences
Existential realization
Physical intervention
↓
Existential helping elements for social work intervention
Holding
Telling
Mastering
Honoring
↓
New meaning and meaning opportunities in daily living

Existential elements provide a structure for accessing individual reality and meaning in daily living. As described in chapter 1, the eight cross-cultural curative factors serve as lenses for understanding discovered and interpreted meanings as clients explore meaning opportunities and actualize meaning potentials. Cross-cultural curative factors are crucial interpreters of meaning, values, and beliefs. The four existential helping elements provide a structure for the social worker and other professional counselors in helping clients hold, tell, master, and honor their experiences of trauma and pain in contexts of socially and politically defined cultural concerns with respect for personal values and beliefs informed by cross-cultural curative factors. Figure 1 shows the relationship of cross-cultural concerns and curative factors as they relate to helping clients find and make meaning from experiences of vulnerability and trauma pain.

Existential helping elements are relevant to the practice of social work with varied populations. Their application in cross-cultural social work practice can aid the worker in discovering helpful intervention activities with special populations and clients with different cultural backgrounds.

Holding

The first and most important existential element is holding. Holding refers to helping to hold the client's painful experiences so that they may be remembered and understood on a conscious level of awareness. Holding is sometimes described as catharsis. As the client is helped to bring painful experiences to conscious awareness, there is often a release of pain that reduces the client's suffering (Lantz, 2002; Lantz & Gyamerah, 2002a, 2002b). As the client holds his or her pain, the trauma experience is remembered and reexperienced. As the client remembers and lets go of some of the pain, the therapist must be empathetically available to help bear the painful experience. Holding can produce a supportive atmosphere in which there are reduced levels of anxiety and increased feelings of safety (Lantz & Raiz, 2003).

In addition to creating increased feelings of safety and emotional support, the existential element of holding the client's pain provides for the emergence of hope, an important cross-cultural curative factor. Hope for the future is a powerful force in healing and recovery and is grounded by individual worldview. The story of Mrs. B, a Vietnamese immigrant, is a good illustration of holding and worldview respect.

Mrs. B: A Vietnamese Immigrant

Mrs. B was suffering from manic depression and needed medication. She refused to take medication, however, because medication did not fit into her worldview about the cause of her troubles. Mrs. B was able to take the medication after the social worker at the mental health center obtained the services of a Vietnamese shaman, who blessed the medical staff providing the medication. Mrs. B improved considerably after she started taking the medication. The worker's ability to hold Mrs. B's emotional pain helped the worker provide Mrs. B with helper attractiveness in the form of a shaman and with worldview respect.

Helping a client hold painful experiences requires the development of empathic availability by the helper (Lantz & Gregoire, 2000a). Empathic availability is a basic and powerful component in the helping process that affords the therapist an opportunity to gain a profound understanding of the client's worldview or frame of reference. Empathic availability requires the worker's committed presence to the client and openness to his or her worldview. It is important for the helper to remember that although the client's cultural context serves as a lens through which pain may be defined, it is the suffering, the condition of being human and in pain, that receives empathy. For instance, in the context of their cultural experience, Appalachian families describe helpers' empathic availability as "loyalty" and at times as "integrity" (Harper, 1996; Lantz, 1993, 2004). Empathic availability provides clients with the emotional support they need to tell their stories and to feel understood.

Empathic availability is probably not occurring unless the helper begins to experience some painful emotional feelings that are similar to the client's feelings. If the helper is really helping the client to hold his or her pain, the helper will begin to personally experience some elements of the client's pain. Frankl (1984) emphasized an ability to experience the pain of others without losing a sense of oneself as critical in the helping relationship. The therapist's willingness to hold and share the client's pain allows the client to remember, reexperience, and openly tell the therapist about his or her pain.

The existential element of holding is particularly helpful in facilitating a deeper awareness of worldview respect and hope, both of which are cross-cultural curative factors. Since most nonmedical emotional problems result from social, interpersonal, existential, or symbolic difficulties, the healing or holding method used to help must be compatible with the client's cultural beliefs (Lantz, 2004; Lantz & Pegram, 1989; Torrey, 1986). The element of holding by the helper facilitates the helper's understanding of the client's biopsycho-social situation and is an opportunity for the helper to understand the client's worldview and situation in life.

Telling

Openly talking about the client's pain is the second existential element. Telling trauma pain makes internal pain available to interactional experiences and for support in the helping relationship. Seen as a critical component for change in intervention, the client-worker relationship provides communication, support, and empathy in the human encounter of counseling or therapy (Krill, 1979; Rogers, 1980). Once the story is brought into the interactions of the worker-client relationship, gaps can be filled, and the story can be changed so that it can become less painful and even have a better ending or purpose (Lantz & Raiz, 2003). Paradoxically, telling about emotional pain makes it possible for the helper to hold the client's pain. Telling of pain powerfully facilitates the development of empathic availability and the ability to hold client pain. Telling is helpful to clients in all cultures, as it places their painful experiences in the interactional world of encounter, where the relationship between the client and helper can be used to process the trauma under conditions of increased support and empathy (Lantz, 1993, 2001; Lantz & Gyamerah, 2002b; Lantz & Lantz, 1991).

The existential helping element of telling is facilitated by the empathic avail-ability of the helper. Helper attractiveness is a cross-cultural curative factor in which the helper is identified as a healer and someone who can be trusted. Cultural beliefs and sanctions for helping increase the helper's abilities to confront defenses and give the client encouragement for expression through the helping element of telling (Lantz, 1993; Lantz & Gyamerah, 2002b). In spite of the fact that telling is a critical element, it is important to remember that different cultural groups have different ways of telling and different time patterns for telling or letting others understand their pain (Lantz, 1993). Rogers (1980) identified helper attractiveness as a process wherein empathic helping was facilitated through trust and positive regard.

The telling stage is grounded upon the development of empathic feelings be-tween the therapist and the client and the therapist's willingness to confront pat-terns of defense used by the client to avoid awareness of emotional pain. Ackerman (1966) describes this confrontive method as "tickling the defenses." Tickling the de-fenses disrupts the process of repression and facilitates telling in the here and now (Lantz & Gyamerah, 2002b). The following interview segment illustrates the pro-cess of tickling the defenses during the telling stage of cross-cultural practice with Appalachian parents who experienced depression after the loss of a child.

Appalachian Parents' Loss

Helper (to husband): Every time we get close to talking about your daughter's death, your wife puts on that "I'm strong, I can take it" smile. You look away, and talk stops. You think she does that to protect her feelings or yours?

Husband: (Starting to cry) I'm not sure. Probably to protect both of us.

Helper (to husband): I wish she'd stop it!

Wife: (Starts to cry)

Husband: (Reaches over and holds wife's hand)

Helper: Good. That seems a lot more natural. More like a couple facing something awful together.

An important function of telling is the unloading or "cleansing" experience in which telling the trauma pain becomes a form of healing. The existential element of telling is facilitated by empathic availability, holding, and helper attractiveness. Support became possible once the pain was told. Having held the trauma, the helper facilitated the telling so that the couple could share each other's pain and provide mutual support. Sharing the pain proved to be a cleansing experience, a cross-cultural curative factor that can bring guilt, embarrassment, and other human emotions into interactions of the helping relationship.

Mastering

The third existential helping element is called mastering (Lantz, 1993, 2001; Lantz & Gyamerah, 2002b). Reflection and experimentation in mastering the trauma are healing activities and help uncover individual and family patterns used in processing and mastering trauma experiences. Individuals and families can find and share messages about the trauma experience. In the stage of mastering, hidden meanings are frequently revealed as clients take control of their trauma experiences. Activities useful in helping clients to master or gain control of trauma pain include role-playing, drama, art, games, and culturally relevant music or story-telling. Mastering tests the "can" dimension of existence, which houses freedom, choices, and opportunities for mastery that are sanctioned with respect to responsibilities for oneself and others within a cultural context. Once the trauma pain is mastered, a client is able to return to a state of control, a cross-cultural curative factor in which boundaries and acceptable control behaviors are culturally defined. For example, one's cultural values and beliefs may define prayer or ancestor worship as appropriate means for mastering feelings of anger, isolation, or despair. On the other hand, mastering feelings of depression may be cause for administration of psychotropic medications, depending upon the determination of contemporary healers such as psychiatrists.

Mastering trauma is a process that helps the client gain control over trauma pain. New behaviors or rituals may be initiated and transitions may be celebrated when new techniques of mastery are learned. Some social workers, family therapists, and other specialists use rites of initiation and transition to help individual clients and families who are experiencing problems in moving from one stage of life to the next (Lantz & Pegram, 1989; Moon, 1990). Divorce, retirement, and the empty-nest syndrome are all common examples of frequently under-ritualized and under-symbolized events. As a result, many providers treat clients who are newly divorced, considering retirement, or alone once child rearing and midlife duties are accomplished. Consistent with a cross-cultural practice point of view, intervention must help the client develop a meaningful celebration, ritual, or ceremony if life transitions are to be successfully mastered.

Honoring

The fourth existential element consistently reported in transcultural healing literature is called honoring (Lantz, 2000a, 2004; Lantz & Frazer, 1996). Honoring is a healing process during which meanings in the trauma situation are identified and meaning potentials are actualized. Some people believe that honoring is the spiritual part of social work practice (Lantz & Gregoire, 2000a; Lantz & Lantz, 2001). The cross-cultural curative factor of existential realization is an objective of the element of honoring. The worker helps the client experience meaning, so that as meaning awareness builds, the existential meaning vacuum shrinks.

Mr. and Mrs. E: Rediscovered Meaning

Mr. and Mrs. E were referred by Mr. E's physician, an oncologist. Mr. E suffered from throat cancer and could no longer eat solid foods. His feeding process was considerably less than dignified. Mr. E reported that he obsessed about solid food, and Mrs. E reported that it bothered her that he could not enjoy his food. For over forty years the members of the E family had been sitting down at the dinner table and dining together. The family abandoned this activity once Mr. E lost the ability to eat solid food.

The E family had always used the family dinner as an opportunity to signal, share, and experience meaning. With the loss of this ritual, the family experienced emptiness in their daily lives. They experienced an existential vacuum. The social worker's task was complex. One part of the task was to help the family create a new ritual that they could use to share and experience meaning. When the E family replaced the lost dinner ritual with a card-playing ritual, Mr. E reported that he was no longer obsessing about solid foods.

Honoring occurred when a social worker helped the E family rediscover meaning through a ritual for honoring and existential realization. Healing processes involved in honoring identify and use meaning potentials and meaning opportunities from the trauma experience. Bringing embedded meanings into awareness and making use of meaning opportunities and potentials are growth experiences. Getting in touch with empathic understanding of trauma pain is part of the healing process, a pathway toward being able to honor the experience.

Frankl (1969, 1997b) found honoring trauma pain to be the best way to overcome pain. The experience of honoring trauma and its pain provides opportunities for self-transcendent giving, a form of giving to the world and others so they can experience joy, avoid pain, or gain empathic understanding from another's painful experience. The existential element of honoring requires the therapist or social worker to help the client honor actualized meanings from the past. Stored away and often not in daily awareness, these meaning opportunities remain significant and are potentially helpful.

Honoring trauma pain helps the client experience existential realization, one of the cross-cultural curative factors. The cross-cultural factor of physical intervention is not necessarily linked to honoring or intervention from an existential perspective. However, the tendency for cultures to revere healers and to practice culturally consistent techniques of physical intervention is a function of honoring the concept of healing. Honoring trauma pain sometimes brings about actual physical sacrifice on the part of clients. For example, clients may volunteer time or engage in physical activities such as marathons or memory walks as ways of honoring trauma pain from past experiences in their lives.

Sergeant G: Honoring Her Husband's Sacrifice

Having recovered from depression and once again active in military duty, Sergeant G attended a ceremony in which four benches were dedicated to the memory of soldiers lost to duty. Sitting on a bench and facing the marble memorial, she commented that her husband, killed in service to his country, would have appreciated the structure of the memorial. She said, "He loved the military, the marching, the order; and he'll know which way I face and that I can find my way. I think I'll stay a few more minutes in honor of his sacrifice and mine."

SOME CONCEPTS THAT INFORM SOCIAL WORK PRACTICE FROM AN EXISTENTIAL PERSPECTIVE

Time in Life

People live in the reality of the time and place they occupy and are influenced by their social and cultural environments. Health and illness, functioning and inability to function, and meaning in life and loss of meaning are all interpreted in daily living. Each person has constructions of living in the world that are informed by cultural definitions and socially and personally constructed realities. Each culture's helping practices incorporate culturally significant sources of help or problem solving (Lantz & Pegram, 1989; Torrey, 1986). Experiences and simple memorable events occur in daily living and become facets of each person's life—sometimes remembered, sometimes celebrated, sometimes forgotten.

Living in the world, or reality in the present, relates to the concept of time. Frankl identifies the past as the collector or storehouse of meaning potentials that have been real or "actualized." The past is real, a part of existence, and is important to successful intervention. The present, or here and now, is a time to act in order to realize meaning in life—in other words, to actualize meaning potentials. It is from the present that meanings are deposited and stored in the past. The future is anticipated and is an opportunity to actualize meaning potentials that are available in living. Interaction in the helping relationship allows the client to explore meanings from past and present experiences and anticipate or find meaning opportunities in the future (Frankl, 1959, 1967, 1984; Lantz, 2000b, 2000d).

Frankl utilizes the concept of time in his work in helping individuals and families discover, actualize, and make use of meaning potentials and opportunities in daily living (Frankl, 1997a, 1997b; Lantz, 1995, 1997). Phenomenological reflection is closely connected to the concept of time—the past, present, and future. Phenomenology was first described as a rigorous research method used to discover the meaning and spirit of human existence and of meaning or "essence" of human life

(Stein, 1964). Phenomenological methods are part of the effort to understand the human experience beyond the physical world and to enter the spiritual or "meaning" world through more scientific inquiry (Lantz, 2000d).

Frankl's existential psychotherapy fits within the phenomenological movement, in which the method of phenomenological reflection involves workers and therapists helping clients to explore and discover meanings and meaning potentials deposited in their storehouse of the past. Then as co-explorer or facilitator, the worker or therapist helps the client find new meanings that help shrink the existential meaning vacuum, or meaning void in his or her life. As co-explorer, the worker or therapist utilizes the helping relationship to support the client's exploration or "scientific" search of past experiences and deposited memories so that their meaning potentials can be noticed, actualized in the present, and honored for the future (Krill, 1979; Lantz, 2000a, 2000c; Wertz, 1982).

Realization of outcomes of new meaning is often an experience of emotional and sometimes spiritual growth. Such realization and experiences are consistent with Frankl's own experiences and philosophy and are reflected in the titles of his world-renowned books, particularly *Man's Search for Meaning* and *The Will to Meaning*. These works set forth the premise that meaning in life is essential to the human struggle to survive in the world.

Making Meaning and Meaning Potentials

The client's search for meaning and meaning potentials is a phenomenological struggle to find and actualize meaning from potentials in life. This reflection and inquiry of self, meaning, meaning potentials, and actualization of identified potentials pushes exploration into scientific consideration where subjective realities are explored. These activities fit within the phenomenological movement in that knowledge can be gleaned through a qualitative approach, thus discounting empirical and positivist accounts of reality. Frankl's life and work bring the struggle of survival, suffering, and the will to meaning in life to the forefront of intervention.

Some consider logotherapy, Frankl's methodology, to be a branch of humanistic/existential psychotherapy (Fabry, 1994; Wong, 2004). Logotherapy incorporates client choice, responsibility, humor, and purpose in life into treatment processes and outcomes. Meaning and meaning potentials are thought to be the most powerful and important force for most human behavior, even more than needs such as survival, security, sexual gratification, or achievement (Frankl, 1967, 1997b; Lantz, 2000a, 2000d; Lantz & Harper, 1991). While many practitioners use existential psychotherapy and logotherapy interchangeably, Frankl's approach is more spiritual and focuses on the strength of the human spirit, its mysteries, the power of meaning in life, the freedom of will, and responsibility in living (Frankl, 1984; Wong, 2004).

Two Different Worldviews: Essence and Existence

Every person has some concept of his or her immediate world, his or her world-view. Two broad worldview philosophies in existential psychotherapy differ widely but serve to inform an understanding of human existence. Essence-oriented and existence-oriented approaches to psychotherapy stem from the philosophical and existential debate of which came first—the concept of humankind followed by creation, or existence followed by definition (Marino, 2004). Heidegger wrote extensively about death imagery and concepts of being and dread and other responses to being in the world (Heidegger, 1962; Lantz, 1999). His work influenced many others, including Frankl (Lantz, 1995) and May (1986).

The perspective of counseling or therapy with individuals and families from an orientation grounded in the philosophy of essence emphasizes "consistencies, rules, and patterns of the world which govern the manifestation of human life" (Lantz, 2004). Many counselors, social workers, and therapists approach individuals and families from a philosophy of essence, which is the most common or mainstream approach to understanding human existence and behavior in the world. In this perspective, helper involvement, scientific knowledge, and empirical practice stand the tests of validity and reliability and inform intervention. In an essence-oriented approach, it is generally thought that identifying and disrupting the nature and sequence of problems are the responsibilities of the therapist.

Various approaches to working with individuals and families fit well with the philosophy of essence. Here the worker or therapist diagnoses or identifies the problems and makes recommendations for change or wellness. The burden of change is on clients to accommodate to recommendations for more acceptable behavior or more positive statements about life as they see it. It follows that intervention is more likely to be helpful once more functional behaviors and problem-solving capacities are adopted (Grove & Haley, 1991; Lantz, 2004; Yalom, 1980).

Approaching individuals and families from an orientation grounded in the philosophy of existence takes into account creativity so that "human beings can shape and/or respond to the material facts, limitations, rules, predictabilities, and essences to be found in human life" (Lantz, 2004). While not the majority perspective, the philosophy of existence offers a worldview in which exploration of practical and everyday dichotomies of good and bad, joy and sorrow, love and hate, and justice and injustice helps to explain the mysteries and paradoxes of life. The philosophy of existence approach fits well with interventions consistent with an existential perspective. Focused upon flexibility, intentionality, freedom, and adaptability, the philosophy of existence approach allows for a broad range of human responses. Creativity, hope, spontaneity, resistance, and disagreement are some ordinary problems encountered in response to daily living (Lantz, 2004).

Based upon the philosophy and worldview of existence in the world rather than the essence or capacities of human existence, existential trauma therapies are applicable to a wide range of problems. Existential trauma therapy can help clients change and increase their understanding of courage, freedom, responsibility, and creativity. Existentially informed intervention builds heavily upon a participatory relationship between the therapist and client in which the richness and depth of meaning are essential to change. This client-therapist relationship facilitates client awareness, meaning, and actualization of meaning potentials. The perspective of existence is evident in the existential approach to intervention, in which the client engages in problem resolution or purpose in life through internal awareness and motivation. Intervention emphasizes responsibility, freedom, opportunities for growth from crises and trauma, and finding and honoring meanings and meaning potentials in life (Lantz, 1999, 2004; Marcel, 1963; Wright, 1985).

Three Dimensions of Existence

In his dimensional ontology, Frankl (1959, 1969) identified three dimensions of existence: *of* the world, *in* the world, and *for* the world. Any or all three dimensions of existence can be disrupted by trauma and stressful events in everyday life. Existential helping elements are especially helpful in situations of trauma and trauma pain. Trauma is a condition or happening powerful enough to disrupt personal existence and meaning in life on one or all three dimensions of existence—of the world, in the world, and for the world (Lantz & Gyamerah, 2002b).

Existence of the world is defined as the physical and biological "musts" such as food, shelter, and water. Existence in the world refers to the "can" dimension, where freedom, choices, and opportunities are found often by intentions or expectations and in respect for responsibilities for oneself and others. Existence for the world is the "ought" dimension, defined as meaning and purpose in life, even in self-transcendence. Honoring is the element in which existence in the world is manifested in the "ought" dimension (Lantz, 2000c; Lantz & Gregoire, 2000a).

Disruption to one's sense of meaning and purpose has the power to produce a meaning vacuum in which symptoms and anxieties can grow (Frankl, 1984; Lantz, 2001). Intervention helps disrupt the sense of loss of meaning that occurs when individuals and their families repress and avoid their traumas (Lantz & Gyamerah, 2002b). Individuals and their families have the ability to act, to create, and to make choices. The existential perspective offers social work professionals additional tools with which to help clients actualize meaning potentials and meaning opportunities from experiences of trauma and pain in their lives.

SUMMARY

This chapter identified elements of existential intervention that offer structure and pathways for viewing influences informed by one or more of the eight cross-cultural curative factors in clients' lives. Intervention from an existential perspective is particularly useful in understanding clients' worldviews, which are shaped by their cultural experiences, beliefs, and values. Underlying the configuration of individual worldviews, the eight cross-cultural curative factors serve as lenses for understanding client worldviews and as pathways to meaning and actualization of meaning potentials in life.

Existential helping elements are the phases of intervention in a helping relationship. The four elements of holding, telling, mastering, and honoring are processes of intervention that can be useful in helping clients in the context of their social and cultural realities. Cross-cultural curative factors represent human commonalities worldwide, reflecting human diversity in living and being in the world. Meeting common human needs consistent with an individual's cultural origins and experiences requires attention to the uniqueness of the individual in the world of human experiences.

A social worker who is competent in cross-cultural practice moves beyond assessing cultural differences and develops awareness of behaviors and efforts that people use in meeting their needs and solving problems. Such awareness is not merely a question of determining adaptation or acculturation of client to culture but also involves the task of determining the match between the client's life patterns and the problem-solving methods in his or her culture.

This chapter provided an intervention perspective useful for working with clients from the broad range of social and cultural diversity. The following chapters address specific minority groups and special populations and offer examples of intervention in response to client concerns. Case studies illustrate various applications of intervention from an existential perspective in the context of cross-cultural practice. Practice applications from the work of Dr. Viktor Frankl are also provided.

4

Hispanic American Clients

HISPANIC AMERICANS BECAME THE LARGEST AND FASTEST-GROWING MI-
nority population in the United States on July 1, 2003, at 39.9 million people,
representing a growth rate of 13 percent over the previous thirty-nine months
(Bernstein, 2004). Having a wide range of race and ethnicity, Hispanics and Latinos
have come to the United States from Mexico, Spain, South and Central America, and
the Caribbean—particularly the Dominican Republic, Cuba, and Puerto Rico. Hispanic Americans are broadly diverse; the largest groups are Mexican Americans,
Cuban Americans, and Puerto Ricans. Mexican Americans have heavy European and
Native American heritage. Puerto Ricans have more White and Black ancestry than
they have Native American ancestry (Healey, 2003).

"Hispanic" and "Latino" are terms that generally connote Spanish origin but
cloud the ethnicity, language, geographic location, and cultural heritage of members of this large and diverse population. Long-standing controversy surrounds the
terms "Hispanic" and "Latino." Either term can cause anger if used to label or classify minority populations. Social and political controversy about geographic location, ethnicity, and social justice have been part of the history of the people and
identifiers of this large minority.

The term "Hispanic" is used by the United States government to count and classify people of Spanish heritage in census surveys. In the 1970s, "Hispanic" referred
to Spanish-speaking people from Mexico, Puerto Rico, Cuba, and Central and South
America. Usage of the term "Hispanic" extends beyond the purpose of census counting, and it is generally used to refer to people of Spanish origin, particularly those
now living in the United States (Burgos-Ocasio, 2000; Perez-Stable, 1987). Many
Hispanic people are bilingual, with Spanish as their native language. However, English is the primary or perhaps only language of those whose families have lived in
the United States for many generations. Efforts to standardize nomenclature for
purposes of ethnic and social classifications of any population are dangerous and
generally fail to serve the interests of those minorities being counted. Generic terms
such as "Hispanic" and "Latino" can lead to stereotyping, identity losses, and political or social divisiveness. For example, the term "Hispanic" does not account for national origin or ethnic diversity and thus risks stereotyping and homogenizing this
diverse population.

"Latino" is a more indigenous designation and is viewed by some as more politically and socially correct. Perceived as being more neutral, "Latino" generally refers to people of Spanish origin living in the United States, with the exception of Spaniards and Filipinos (Hayes-Bautista & Chapa, 1987). Thought by some to be a less biased term, Latino includes Puerto Ricans and Cubans, but not Mexicans and Colombians. While "Latino" and "Hispanic" are nongendered terms, the term "Latina" refers to women with roots in Central or South America or from the Caribbean (Burgos-Ocasio, 2000).

Most people are opposed to using labels that could potentially homogenize the collage of national origin, ethnicity, and racial diversity represented by the broad population of people of Spanish origin. In the 1980s the use of the term "Hispanic" provoked furor as the Reagan administration was accused of applying the term without regard to individual preference or diversity. Demographic data reporting national origin and race provide important information concerning populations, yet classification systems are challenged often for correctness and inclusivity.

Census survey questions about Hispanic origin, while not even in existence before 1970, have lacked adequate choices for reporting national origin. Respondents have written in numerous responses such as Mexicano, Central American, South American, or "other" (Moore & Pachon, 1985). Taking account of the broad range of responses, more inclusive categories of national origin are now utilized. The 2000 census followed federal guidelines defining Hispanic or Latino people as Spanish/Hispanic/Latino, Mexican/Mexican American/Chicano, Puerto Rican, Cuban, or other Spanish/Hispanic/Latino origin (Grieco & Cassidy, 2001; Guzman, 2001).

Not unlike national origin, race varies greatly among the large population of Hispanic people. Neither Hispanic nor Latino denotes race. Census surveys have caused considerable confusion, as earlier census questions asked persons of Spanish origin to select one of four racial categories—White, Black, American Indian/Aleut/Eskimo, and Asian or Pacific Islander. Refusing to be constrained by such categorization, people frequently classified themselves as "other" and wrote in geographic locators. The 2000 census questions on race were changed in an effort to accommodate individual differences while gathering as much accurate information as possible. Racial categories used in the 2000 census were White, Black or African American, American Indian and Alaska Native, Asian, Native Hawaiian and other Pacific Islander, and other (Grieco & Cassidy, 2001).

Identifying one's race from a choice of limited categories can potentially confound race and color. The Native American, Spanish, African, European, and Asian heritages of Latin Americans contribute to a broad spectrum of skin color. Various shades of skin colors evolved as miscegenation resulted from long histories of migration and resettlements in and across continents. Even though members of this group may share the same national origin and ethnicity, Hispanic and Latino people experience prejudices of dark-skin bias and white-skin envy. Phenotyping, or the societal processes of color prejudice, produces social, political, and personal orientations to color (Montalvo, 2004). White, black, and shades of both are properties of color that are socially constructed and valued. Personal and social concerns such as personal regard, societal opportunities, status, and self-image are affected by color prejudice both within groups and in the dominant culture.

Power and privilege are reflected by shades of color among Hispanic and Latino people. Fair-skinned females have historically been valued above their darker sisters in Latin America and Mexico. Social class and esteem have been so linked to color that families once celebrated the births of light-skinned newborns far more than those of their darker babies. While discrimination and oppression of people of color occur in Latin America and Mexico as well as in the United States, social processes are very different in terms of how people of color are valued. Being socially constructed within different cultural contexts, racial status and social accommodation have been differently defined: "'One drop of Spanish blood' raised one above a slave status in Latin America, while in the United States whiteness was defined by hypodescent (hypodescence), the absence of any trace of slave heritage implied by not having 'one drop of African blood'" (Montalvo, 2004, p. 104).

While many continue to disagree about the terms Hispanic and Latino, some use both as nearly interchangeable designations (Burgos-Ocasio, 2000). Hispanic seems to be the most commonly accepted and more inclusive term. For purposes of this book, the term "Hispanic" is used to refer to the large and diverse population of mostly multilingual people of Spanish origin.

The convergence of the large Hispanic population is probably no greater elsewhere than it is in the United States. Efforts to classify this diverse group by race and ethnicity have been confusing and even harmful at times. As in any attempt to classify people, divergent terms and preferences emerge. People of Spanish origin who have immigrated to the United States have a widely diverse heritage and place great value on cultural roots. Given opportunities to self-identify, people may identify themselves as Latino or Hispanic, but most likely by national origin or perhaps as American, Mexican American, Chicano, Puerto Rican, or Cuban American. Competent cross-cultural practices call for providing Hispanic clients with opportunities to self-identify, particularly in view of the importance that their worldview has in treatment or helping relationships.

THE MULTICULTURAL HISPANIC POPULATION IN THE UNITED STATES

Hispanics represent broadly diverse national origin, ethnicity, race, religion, education, and cultural assimilation. It is necessary to understand that the Hispanic population is composed of very different subgroups with rich and different histories of immigration to the United States as well as a variety of ethnic and cultural beliefs and traditions. Hispanics strongly value family ties that often go beyond the nuclear family. Family members help other relatives and gather to celebrate holidays, baptisms, birthdays, weddings, and graduations. Catholicism is generally the religion of choice. Hispanics value their appearance and frequently dress very well for formal occasions such as church and community events.

Having historically lived and worked in hot climates, many Hispanics continue the practice of enjoying a mid-day main meal followed by a brief rest period, *la siesta,* before returning to their job or chores. This native practice is much less frequently observed among those now accustomed to America's five-day work week of thirty-seven-and-a-half hours, or for those who hold more than one job and work many more hours. Nevertheless, many maintain a bicultural mix of language, food, dress, customs, and culturally pluralistic lifestyles.

The three major subgroups comprising the Hispanic population in the United States are Mexican Americans, Puerto Ricans, and Cuban Americans. Other Hispanic groups together comprise about one-fourth of this minority population and include individuals from the Dominican Republic and numerous nations throughout South and Central America.

THE BURGEONING HISPANIC POPULATION IN THE UNITED STATES

Growth of the Hispanic population in the United States since 1990 has been phenomenal. This population is comprised of Mexicans (58.5%), Puerto Ricans (9.6%), Cubans (3.5%), and others, including Spanish, South and Central American, and Dominican populations (28.4%) (Guzman, 2001). It is estimated that the Hispanic population will reach 47.8 million, representing about 15.5 percent of the population in the United States, by 2010. Growth projections for 2050 estimate that 24.4 percent of the United States population will be Hispanic and that the nation's population will be about equally divided between White and nonWhite populations (U.S. Census Bureau, 2000b). The growth of the Hispanic population has been accelerated by the number of babies born to Hispanics in America. These babies are outnumbering new immigrants (Cohn, 2005).

Overall, the Hispanic population is relatively young compared to the aging non-Hispanic population, particularly the vast number of aging baby boomers. Thirty-four percent of Hispanics in the United States were under age eighteen in 2002, nearly 10 percent higher than those under age eighteen in the non-Hispanic White population. At the other end of the population, only 5.1 percent of Hispanics were over age sixty-five, as opposed to 14.4 percent of the non-Hispanic White population. Based on federal income thresholds, about 21.3 percent of Hispanics lived in poverty in 2002, compared to 7.8 percent of non-Hispanic Whites (Ramirez & De la Cruz, 2002).

This large Hispanic population has the potential to change the racial and ethnic mix of the United States forever (Burgos-Ocasio, 2000). No longer clustered in only a few cities or migrant farm areas, persons of Hispanic descent live and work throughout the United States. There are sporadic increases in the flow of persons from Latin America who are seeking better lives or who wish to join relatives who have come to the United States. A willingness to work is characteristic of recent immigrants, who are mostly young and bilingual, and frequently below the average level of education for their age group in the United States. If assimilation experiences of this population are like those of most other immigrant populations, many Hispanic people will become employed based on their skills, while others will obtain additional education and training.

Mexican Americans

The first Spanish-speaking population to become a minority group in the United States as the frontier of the United States pushed westward was of Mexican descent. Territory conquered in the war with Mexico added land, oil, and gold to the American Southwest. It has been estimated that about 75,000 people lived in this territory, mostly in New Mexico. These people experienced great ethnic and racial violence in the southwestern United States in the early 1900s as Anglos rapidly increased in number in New Mexico, California, and Arizona. Life in Mexican communities in the southwestern United States was characterized by great oppression of those who had once occupied the region under Mexican rule (Becerra, 1988).

Being extremely hard working, many Mexican Americans achieved economic security even though forced relocation produced severe oppression. Native customs and rituals are less visible among those in second- or third-generation families as Mexican American families become more Americanized (Moore & Pachon, 1985). These families are smaller in size than those of their ancestors; many families are female headed, and many are middle or upper class.

Mexican women who migrate to the United States often have very different experiences than their male counterparts. Without education and employment, Mexican women are likely to hold low-paying and low-status jobs. Experiencing discrimination and oppression, Mexican women endure many social injustices. Not unlike their White sisters, Mexican American women must negotiate systems of health care, education, day care, and public assistance for their children. For the Mexican American woman, these social systems are threatening in unfamiliar settings and a sometimes hostile society (Burgos-Ocasio, 2000).

Migrant farmworkers continue to cluster in the Midwest. Working long hours and at low wages, transient workers and their families lack housing, transportation, and just about every social service, including health care and education or day-care facilities. Others have moved away from migrant labor in rural, agrarian settings to work in various industries and service jobs in urban areas throughout the United States. Nevertheless, the stream of immigrants crossing the border perpetuates poverty for undereducated, unskilled, and often monolingual newcomers (Burgos-Ocasio, 2000; Moore & Pachon, 1985).

The Mexican American population in the United States has grown at unprecedented rates over the last decade and is the largest subgroup in the Hispanic population, now close to 60 percent of the Hispanic population. Assessing the rate of Mexican American assimilation is difficult due to the fact that there are always newcomers crossing the border. So even though Mexican Americans are often in visible political and professional roles, their status as "real" Americans has often been challenged, a situation that has lasted longer for Mexican Americans than for any other ethnic group (Rodriguez, 2005).

Having a long and well-known history of crossing the United States border without proper authorization, Mexican immigrants have been victims of serious forms of discrimination and violence. There are problems concerning authorities patrolling country borders, identifying undocumented immigration activities, and monitoring illegal immigration status. Demands for employment, services, health care, and immunization and education of children born to illegal immigrants overload service programs, particularly in America's southwestern states. Undoubtedly, many immigrants experience considerable stress in their daily lives as they live in fear of being sent back to their native country.

Puerto Rican Americans

Puerto Ricans began emigrating from their native homeland in the early 1800s in search of better lives and livelihood. The United States annexed the island at the end of the Spanish-American War in 1898 and granted citizenship to the Puerto Rican population in 1917 (Sue & Sue, 2003; Torres, 2004). Large numbers of Puerto Ricans came to America during the early 1940s and then continued to occupy poor housing and work low-paying jobs after World War II ended. Despite their unique history of citizenship, Puerto Ricans have experienced personal and cultural devaluation by the majority population.

Puerto Ricans mostly moved in or near New York or New Jersey, where many found low-wage jobs. While these states continue to have concentrations of Puerto Rican families, Texas and Florida now have large Puerto Rican populations as well (Mapp, 2005). Personal networks, extended families, congenial family relations, and a sense of fatalism characterize the daily lives of many. Puerto Ricans frequently live in urban ghettos where unemployment, poverty, crime, and violence are rampant. Many lack education and employable skills. About 40 percent of Puerto Rican families in the United States are single-parent households, of which approximately one-third live below federally established poverty levels (Colon, 2001).

The Puerto Rican population reflects racial mixes including Indian, White European, Spanish, and African heritage (Burgos-Ocasio, 2000). Discrimination experienced by Puerto Ricans in the United States targets race and skin color as well as ethnicity. Puerto Ricans span the full range of skin color and experience more discrimination based on skin color after migration. On the island, discrimination by social class is very serious and a greater cause of discrimination than skin color.

Experiences of migration are very different for Puerto Ricans than for other

Hispanics. Puerto Ricans are naturalized citizens, free to come and go between the island and the mainland as they choose. Common citizenship allows Puerto Ricans living in the United States to maintain extended family ties, to not need a work visa, and to live in two cultures. Unlike Mexicans and most other immigrants, Puerto Ricans are separated from the States only by an expanse of water without any real borders. Although naive initial perceptions of living cross-culturally are probably going to be shallow, biculturalism does indeed seem plausible in this context of fluid boundaries and fluid citizenship.

Judith Ortiz Cofer (1990) writes eloquently of her experience of being raised by Puerto Rican parents in an American home. Traditional food, music, language, and ethnic practices and beliefs allowed the family to maintain a distance from the Anglo culture. Her father, a navy man, had his children practice English and taught them that education was a way out of their ethnic neighborhood.

Cofer's account of her bicultural experiences demonstrates the difficulties of living between two cultures. Encountering extreme heat and large clusters of relatives in small houses during the family's frequent visits to Puerto Rico caused confusion and fright and seemed foreign to her Americanized comfort and customary personal space. In America, her second culture, she avoided embarrassment by hiding ethnic food, dress, and traditions and trying not to speak English with a Spanish accent. Living on the edge of both cultures produced identity and membership conflicts. Always there were the struggles of blending in and belonging and of protecting ethnicity. "As a Navy brat, shuttling between New Jersey and the pueblo, I was constantly made to feel like the oddball by my peers, who made fun of my two-way accent: a Spanish accent when I spoke English; and, when I spoke Spanish, I was told that I sounded like a 'Gringa.' Being the outsiders had already turned my brother and me into cultural chameleons, developing early the ability to blend into a crowd" (Cofer, 1990, p. 17).

With their unique citizenship, Puerto Rican Americans consider themselves to be Americans and take great pride in their ethnic roots. Personal achievement and success are evidenced in educational accomplishments and upward mobility. There are at least first-, second-, and third-generation Puerto Ricans educated in and living in the United States. Nevertheless, lifestyle changes have been slow for some who continue to live in urban ghettos although they may hold college degrees and have other education and training (Burgos-Ocasio, 1996).

Cuban Americans

The 1959 revolution of Castro's regime opened up the pathway for Cuban immigration to the United States. Three major waves of Cuban immigration ensued under the dictatorship of Fidel Castro. First, beginning in 1959 and ending with the Cuban missile crisis in 1962, about 200,000 people left Cuba when land and economic resources were redistributed as capitalist enterprise gave way to socialist restructuring. This first wave of professional, affluent, and somewhat Americanized immigrants represented human capital but did not bring material wealth with them. Leaving their middle- to upper-class social status behind, these immigrants fled the political and economic strife of their homeland. Well educated and often having professional or technical skills, most Cubans in this first wave of immigration were readily employable in the United States. While most came as nuclear families, it would soon be learned that returning to visit or to bring extended family members out of Cuba was forbidden. The second wave spanned 1965 through 1973, when 340,000 working-class immigrants came to Miami (Healey, 2003). The third wave did not occur until seven years later in a very difficult exodus from Cuba.

In 1980, about 100,000 of the 125,000 refugees who entered the United States by boat came from the Cuban port of Mariel. Referred to as the "boat refugees" and named after the port of departure, the *Marielitos,* or the third wave of Cuban immigrants, were labeled "undesirables." This group was thought to include many felons and individuals who were mentally ill, disabled, or uneducated. This group arrived in the United States under dire circumstances after leaving Cuba, more in response to economic conditions than to political or social changes. As boatloads of refugees reached Florida's coastlines, some lost their lives at sea when their overloaded boats capsized. Early efforts to deport the boat refugees only brought more suffering and violence. Many were jailed for years—some without trial or convictions. Castro's deportation of criminals and mentally ill people is unprecedented.

Many established Cuban Americans express dismay at the images of street people, ex-prisoners, and social outcasts associated with the Mariel boatlift (Moore & Pachon, 1985; Torres, 2004). While some were felons and criminals, others were destitute, and a few were in search of family members who had been deported from Cuba at an earlier time. Rising above their initial struggle for survival, many who arrived under these unfortunate circumstances have become productive U.S. citizens.

A population of 803,226 Cuban Americans was counted in the 1980 census in the United States (Szapocznik & Hernandez, 1988). This number increased to 1,242,000, according to 2000 census data, an increase of about 155 percent, or .4 percent of the population in the United States (Healey, 2003). Mostly city dwellers, Cuban Americans are heavily represented in Miami and surrounding areas. Cuban Americans represent 3.5 percent of Hispanics in the United States. Cuban Americans have acculturated quickly and obtained considerable social and economic security. It is possible that their early assimilation into dominant cultural patterns may be a factor of social class, as many are well educated, successful, and upwardly mobile. A second factor in the economic success of Cuban Americans is that most are fair skinned and face little racial discrimination. One study of race and assimilation of Cuban Americans defines this population as 37 percent White, 11 percent Black, and the remainder of mixed race. Findings suggest that the earnings of non-White Cuban American males remain about 15 percent behind those of their White counterparts. Many Americans forget that Castro called for an end to racial awareness, a "race blind" society. So while dark-skinned Cuban Americans fare less well than those who are lighter in color, questions remain unanswered as to whether or not experiences under Castro, including the loss of wealth and possessions, have any continuing effect on economic success or assimilation (Zavodny, 2003).

In the first decade of the twenty-first century, Cuban Americans came together against the travel restrictions imposed by President Bush's administration. These restrictions are part of national security efforts in response to fears of terrorism in America and around the world. These travel restrictions prevent Cuban Americans from seeing and helping their families on the island. Law-abiding citizens feel the impact of restricted travel and have asked that restrictions be lifted. Cuban Americans, once permitted to visit their families and their homeland once a year, are now restricted to one visit every three years. The outcome of this remains under review and negotiation. However, throughout history, restrictions have been placed on minority populations at times of national disputes. While many have objected in the spirit of human rights and freedom, restrictions remain in place as a means of limiting economic support for Castro's regime. Regardless of political and economic issues, human issues are important to everyone, and painful to those affected.

Cultural Assimilation of a Diverse Population

Smaller groups of Latin American immigrants, including Dominicans, Colombians, Guatemalans, Salvadorans, Nicaraguans, and Chileans, have entered the United States more recently and have joined established Hispanic communities. Undocumented refugees face hardship, poverty, and even deportation. While the future of politically sanctioned entry of immigrant groups is unknown, the likelihood of continuing immigration to the United States is high. In addition to continuing immigration, The Hispanic population in the United States continues to increase, not only because of immigration, but also due to the generally high birthrate among recent immigrants and low-skilled or low-income families. Some of these families experience language barriers and have little access to health care (Burgos-Ocasio, 2000).

Acculturation and assimilation are processes that define adaptation to new cultural environments. These processes occur gradually and involve individual acceptance of new and old, of familiar and unfamiliar cultural practices and beliefs, and perhaps bicultural identity. The growing multicultural context of the United States places greater value on human diversity than ever before.

Multicultural values have replaced images of melted and blended cultures that destroy cultural roots and are contrary to bicultural or multicultural practices. Such "melting pot" concepts are passé in the twenty-first century. When native culture is given up, and new practices and norms are absorbed, cultural diversity is not protected. The route to cultural diversity is not linear along an acculturation continuum but is a varied path along which the valued practices of both cultures accumulate. Multiculturalism allows for mutual respect of different groups and diverse heritages in a culturally pluralistic society (Healey, 2003). While there are many differences among groups within the Hispanic population, there are many similarities and common practices.

SIMILARITIES AND COMMONALITIES AMONG HISPANIC PEOPLE

Various ethnic groups come from different nations of origin and geographic regions, but they share many similarities nevertheless (Gloria, Ruiz, & Castillo, 2004; Moore & Pachon, 1985). Hispanic people are linked by language, values, and many beliefs and traditions. While Spanish is the native language, many Hispanics speak at least one other language. Some Hispanic Americans who are fluent in English prefer to use Spanish, particularly when talking about sensitive or personal issues.

In addition to language, religion is strongly valued by Hispanics, among whom Protestant denominations are common to only a small percentage. Catholicism is widespread, and many are Roman Catholic as a result of the spread of Christianity by early Spanish missionaries. While this is true of many Hispanics, religious beliefs and practices certainly vary within the large Hispanic population. In view of these similarities and differences, assuming that everyone is the same in this heterogeneous population is dangerous. Social workers and other helping professionals need to be aware of commonalities but anticipate differences as well. Certainly, clients and their families can identify their national origin as well as their individual beliefs and lifestyles. In addition to language and religion, many other common values and practices seem to be characteristic of Hispanic families. Commonly held values and practices include *familism, machismo* and *marianismo,* systems of mutual support, dignity, and respect.

Familism is a strong orientation to family and kinship systems found throughout Hispanic populations. *Familism* exists even in circumstances where family members are separated by entire continents. The extended family includes blood relatives, nonblood-related family members, and others who are related by marriage. Extended family networks sometimes include others connected by other meaningful and long-lasting relationships. *Familismo* implies lasting bonds of unity, loyalty, and family honor (Burgos-Ocasio, 2000; Colon, 2001; Gloria et al., 2004). Children are protected and become part of the larger system at birth. The *padrino* and *madrina,* godfather and godmother, ensure that children needing care will be looked after by persons who are part of their extended family—not necessarily blood relatives (Burgos-Ocasio, 1996).

Gender roles have been slow to change for much of the Hispanic population. Increased education and employment outside the home have brought pressure for change for both men and women. Hispanic males have traditionally been seen as courageous, masculine, and dependable providers for their families (Moore & Pachon, 1985). Authority, traditionally resting with the male head of the family, allows males to define gender roles and to demand tolerance for whatever transgressions may occur on their part. *Machismo,* the tradition of the strong, virile, independent Hispanic male, is seen in the roles of breadwinner, autocratic head of household, provider for immediate and extended family members, and romantic and protective husband and father. Historically, males have been raised to be husbands first, and women to be mothers first.

Women frequently assume submissive and dependent roles with their husbands and serve as caregivers to children, parents, and others in the extended family system in various Hispanic populations. *Marianismo,* or the role of wife and mother, is sometimes expressed as subservience and self-sacrifice. *Marianismo* is generally expressed as complementary roles in the traditional families. In less traditional families, *Marianismo* is less pronounced, depending on levels of acculturation, age, education, and employment of the family members (Colon, 2001; Yee, 1990). Changing roles of Hispanic women continue to reflect lifestyle changes including single-parenthood and professional education and employment. Traditionally, Hispanic women were to be protected, to be mothers and homemakers, and to be appreciated for their beauty. The reluctance of many young women to remain in subservient roles or to perform domestic duties in extended families, particularly domestic chores for a mother-in-law, has resulted in changes in gender roles for both women and men (Becerra, 1988; Colon, 2001; Mayo, 1997). Like *marianismo,* the concept of *machismo* or male dominance often softens for many second- or third-generation Mexican American families with contemporary lifestyles.

Mutual support is expected within extended family systems, perhaps because of long histories of poverty and hardship experienced by Hispanic subgroups. The importance of the family is evidenced by patterns of mutual support that are buttressed by informal helpers and helping systems. Family needs supersede individual needs and sometimes require members to divert time and resources away from individual pursuits for the benefit of the larger family system. Long-standing systems of mutual support can result in the Hispanic person seeking help from family rather than from formal institutional helping systems. This reliance on informal systems is particularly strong for older Hispanics (Gloria et al., 2004).

Values of *dignidad* (dignity) and *individualismo* (individualism) are intrinsic to Hispanic heritage and are closely linked to respect for individuals and interpersonal relations. Interpersonal relations, *personalismo,* are valued and tend to be expressed through hugging, free expressions of emotions, and exchanges of friendship. Respect for others is highly valued in the Hispanic culture and is not based on material accomplishments. Respect conveys honor and consideration for other persons, particularly for parents and grandparents in the family structure. The cultural value of respect places constraints on the display of hostile or angry feelings between spouses or toward parents (Colon, 2001).

Respect for the elderly is another widely held common value. Within family structures, the elderly are respected and cared for. Elderly relatives often live in intergenerational households, where they are respected, as older age ranks above younger age in the hierarchy of authority in Hispanic families. Elders are teachers for younger generations, and bearers of cultural traditions. Believing that states of physical and mental illness or wellness have spiritual qualities and causes, elders tend to self-treat, to practice folk remedies, and to believe in the teachings of their *curandero,* a native faith healer or shaman. Older Hispanics and those living in larger ethnic communities often retain ethnomedical practices for treating various illnesses. These practices may seem strange and foreign to health providers who are unfamiliar with ethnomedicine.

Recent research reports that care is often sought from combinations of folk healers, spiritual healers, and folk remedies in addition to Western health-care providers. It is possible that there can be counterindications in certain combinations of prescribed medications and herbal and ethnic remedies and practices (Colon, 2001; Murguia, Peterson, & Zea, 2003). Quite often elderly, rural, or poor people familiar with home remedies and folk medicine continue these ethnomedical practices to the exclusion of preventative health care or Western medicine.

African, Latin American, and European cultural practices have been handed down through generations. Cures by folk healers, spiritualists, and *curanderos* are part of the spiritual worldviews of those influenced by ethnomedical practices. Health is about the balance of good and bad influences responsible for balance or equilibrium among spiritual beliefs, God, cultural traditions, and physical and mental health. Interrelationship of mind and body is based on beliefs in God's ability to heal. Spiritual beliefs and native healing practices can provide emotional comfort to those faced with serious illnesses, including mental illnesses.

At the risk of overgeneralizing, and despite geographic and cultural variations, Latin American families are in many ways both similar and different. Some have attained a bicultural identity and enjoy their native culture along with that of the place in which they have resettled. Such bicultural experiences provide meaning in their lives from a dual perspective. For the social worker, awareness of some commonly held values often found among various cultural subgroups can be helpful in cross-cultural practice.

Mr. D: Caregiver

Mr. D, an eighty-one-year-old bilingual Mexican American, retired after selling his locksmith business to his son. His wife, age seventy-nine, was diagnosed with Alzheimer's disease two years ago. Married for sixty years, the couple have one son who lives nearby. Their son is recently divorced and the caregiver for his only child, a teenage son. Two daughters live out of state, each of them about a day's drive away. In apparent good health, Mr. D is becoming increasingly depressed, as he fears not being able to care for his wife, whose physical and mental states are diminishing. Her agitation, sleeplessness, and need for constant supervision are overwhelming.

He says his children are busy with their own lives, and although his son picks up groceries and medications, it would be too embarrassing to ask him to help bathe or dress his mother. Tearfully he admitted to skipping baths and not changing soiled underwear sometimes because he hopes it will be the last day for both of them. He prays for eternal life "where there is no suffering and where my wife will not have this awful disease." Believing that a "good death" happens at home among family and that "God will not let suffering go on but will keep us together in eternity," Mr. D refused to consider hospice care.

Mr. D has a firm belief in family, religion, eternal life, human dignity, and his responsibility for his family. While not willing to accept hospice or nursing home care, Mr. D did agree to daily visits by nursing aides. Even in this difficult situation, he took great pride in honoring his wife's wishes for him to be with her and for them to be together in the home they had enjoyed for so long.

BEING COMPETENT IN CROSS-CULTURAL SOCIAL WORK PRACTICE

Competent cross-cultural social workers and other helping professionals recognize the importance of client identity and worldview. There are broad differences in national origin, race, language, religion, immigration experiences, citizenship status, and cultural assimilation among Hispanics. It is appropriate to ask clients to share their national origin, ethnicity, the languages they speak, religious preference, racial identity, and how they prefer their name to be spoken and written. In instances involving families or concerns about the safety of children, learning who is considered to be part of the extended family is important. It is essential that social workers and other helping professionals who work with Hispanic clients gain a broader understanding of this culturally diverse population.

Immigration, discrimination, and stereotyping are common experiences of Hispanic immigrants. Referred to by the politically constructed term "Hispanic," this minority population represents rich diversity in so many ways. Racial and cultural factors often become stressful when combined with socioeconomic demands that can produce frustrated coping efforts at the interface of personal characteristics and hostile social environments. Some may feel set apart even from other Hispanic groups by ethnically defined boundaries such as family rituals and gender roles. Environmental stressors such as poverty, discrimination, relocation, isolation, and language are painful and traumatic. These traumatic experiences often result in symptoms such as anger, depression, feelings of shame and guilt, and various somatic complaints (Lantz & Gyamerah, 2002b; Lantz & Lantz, 2001).

Cultural differences produce perceptions, coping styles, and belief systems that may appear strange or irrational to many social work practitioners. For example, Torrey (1986) notes that traditional Mexican Americans often believe in three main causes of illness—natural, emotional, and supernatural. The influence of cultural orientation is reflected in these descriptions of illness. In other words, the way a person defines the world is influenced heavily by that individual's point of reference. Therefore, it becomes evident that making meaning of being in the world is informed by one's referent culture. In this case, the Hispanic culture is the powerful point of reference.

In addition to cultural differences, barriers to help include cost of services, language differences, and a preference to seek help within extended family networks. Mexican Americans may avoid seeking formal help from Anglo psychiatrists, social workers, or counselors. Culturally congruent and consistent with the religiosity of this population, native healers such as *curanderos* and spiritualists are familiar and less threatening (Moore & Pachon, 1985). Spiritual healers can help minority clients reduce their sense of meaninglessness or loss of direction in life (existential vacuum) in response to living in the middle of a dominant culture. For others, typical mainstream helping networks are acceptable but need to be tailored to be especially sensitive to strains produced by cross-cultural life experiences.

Concern with environmental stressors and appropriate social action are essential for helping in instances of stress that may be culturally induced. Processes of cultural assimilation and bicultural identity have far-reaching implications for social work practitioners who are about to intervene with a Hispanic client. Sue and Sue (2003) discuss the importance of identifying the extent of a client's biculturalism to help in determining the skills social work practitioners or counselors must have to intervene appropriately. Professional helpers can avoid assumption pitfalls by understanding the worldview perspectives of clients, particularly in instances of diverse Hispanic heritage. Clients at one extreme in the Hispanic Anglo continuum do not identify themselves as bicultural and prefer to be viewed and treated like any other mainstream client. At the other extreme, clients who self-identify strictly within their ethnic group may demand a Hispanic social worker and reject help from the dominant culture.

EXISTENTIAL HELPING ELEMENTS AND CROSS-CULTURAL CURATIVE FACTORS

Intervention from an existential perspective is known to be helpful with families and clients who are struggling to find meaning and direction out of confusion and existential meaning vacuums in their lives. Providing opportunities for testimony to notice or to hold and tell their trauma pain has the power to reduce confusion or mystery in life and increase awareness of stressors or problems (Lantz, 1999). Existential helping elements of holding, telling, mastering, and honoring are particularly effective in helping individuals and families take control of disruptions in their sense of meaning and meaning opportunities due to experiences of trauma, including experiences of relocation or immigration. Three dimensions of existence can be disrupted through experiences of immigration, relocation, and cultural assimilation. First, existence *of* the world refers to being in the world, living or dying by meeting basic needs for survival. This is the dimension of physical vitality. Second, existence *in* the world refers to making choices in reaction to difficulties and opportunities. Being in the world represents the "can" dimension of existence and involves responsibilities and freedoms. The third dimension, existence *for* the world, is the "ought" dimension referring to meaning and self-transcendence and involves a sense of direction and purpose in life (Frankl, 1969, 1997a; Lantz & Gyamerah, 2002b; Lantz & Lantz, 2001). Loss of control and direction can produce a sense of meaninglessness, or "meaning vacuums," such as those caused by relocation or immigration. Such trauma is powerful and can result in worldview confusion and inability to find meaning opportunities in daily living.

Respecting the eight cross-cultural curative factors in working with clients of Hispanic heritage provides a perspective for understanding meaning and meaning potentials in their lives. The eight cross-cultural curative factors are easily identifiable throughout cross-cultural social work practice with Hispanic populations. The factors of worldview respect, hope, helper attractiveness, control, rites of initiation, cleansing, existential realization, and physical intervention are important in cross-cultural contexts. Hispanic people share and celebrate various aspects of their daily realities of being in the world by including family, respect, religion, and beliefs in ethnic and spiritual practices and healers.

The following case presents a wide variety of cross-cultural concerns experienced in the life of a Mexican American young woman in her desire to transition from a traditional ethnic background into college and other activities in the dominant culture. Feelings of anger and guilt cloud her desire to be a college graduate. A child of migrant workers in the Midwest, her concerns reflect pain and confusion related to the bicultural world of her native family and adopted American community. Respect for cross-cultural curative factors and use of existential helping elements are shown to be helpful in the case of Ms. N.

Ms. N's Conflicting Roles as Daughter and Student

Meeting her advisor and professor for the first time, Ms. N is twenty-one years old and a college freshman planning to major in social work. She is experiencing problems in pursuing her life course in opposition to her family of origin. The youngest of six children, Ms. N has four sisters and one brother. Her father died when she was nineteen, and now she lives with her mother and brother. Her family continues to follow a traditional hierarchy of authority. Her brother is now the figure of authority in her family. Ms. N tearfully expressed fear that her brother would make her leave college if he found out that she enrolled.

Born in Mexico, Ms. N's parents picked vegetables in the southwestern United

States and traveled with the crops at harvest time as far north as Canada. Ms. N talked about feeling small, as she entered one elementary school after another, so insignificant and alone. She told of moving with her family, picking tomatoes, living in shacks in the summer months, and her family's celebration when her father found a job as a laborer in a factory in the midwestern United States. She was happy that she had not had to change schools since the ninth grade, where she learned "good" English and stopped speaking Spanish.

She expressed anger toward her brother because of his attempts to "be my father and run my life." Ms. N explained that her brother wanted her to stay at home to care for their mother, do housework, and cook for him and his friends. She adamantly stated that she would "cook no Mexican foods for those bums!"

In the case of Ms. N, the worker used existential helping elements while respecting her client's cross-cultural experiences. The pressure she feels from her family to cling to traditional cultural beliefs and practices is stressful and involves demands for caregiving and female submission in the family. For Ms. N, these expectations further constrain her acculturation and assimilation processes and cause undue anxiety and guilt. The existential helping processes of holding, telling, mastering, and honoring go beyond observation and provide opportunities for testimony and reflection.

The four helping elements of holding, telling, mastering, and honoring were used to help Ms. N hold up her pain. Holding allowed her to bring repressed feelings and conflicts concerning expectations associated with her Mexican heritage into awareness. She described herself as "cheap and unthankful," a "sister shunned by my brother." When asked whether her brother had stopped talking to her, Ms. N paused before replying, "I have been so mad at his ugly face that I forget to ask him anything."

By exploring her feelings and telling of her pain caused by her father's death and her family's efforts to maintain traditions in his memory, Ms. N gained an increasing sense of belonging and respect for her family. She told of how proud her father was of his American job far from the vegetable fields. Telling of how her father celebrated his own bicultural membership provided comfort and allowed her to name her own bicultural orientation. Also, this was an opportunity for the worker to provide empathic support for Ms. N's feelings of loss and pride surrounding her father. An increased sense of worldview respect emerged as Ms. N told of her appreciation for the religious values in her family and the customs they observed while still enjoying celebrating American holidays. Recognizing the best of both worlds gave Ms. N a new sense of mastery and meaning in her life.

It is important to note that the social work educator here encountered ethical concerns of dual relationships and responsibilities. Although acting in a helper role, the social worker was primarily a social work educator. Ms. N was encouraged to join the student social work organization, where she was introduced to two other Hispanic students—one Puerto Rican and the other Mexican American. She attended an orientation about the women's center on campus. She and several of her Anglo friends eventually joined an assertiveness training group. Ms. N's expanded social network provided opportunities where the cross-cultural curative factor of existential realization could occur as she discovered and created new meanings in a safe social network.

Personal and professional milestones marked Ms. N's progress in college, but she continued to mourn the loss of her brother's friendship. Ms. N finally decided that she was ready to speak with her brother. She and her brother met in the presence of the family priest, a person whom she respected and who represented hope and healing (cross-cultural curative factors of hope and helper attractiveness) for her and her brother. The priest was able to help brother and sister hold their pain and share hurt feelings and concerns for each other. The cleansing effect of their testimony with their priest became evident as Ms. N's relationship with her brother improved. She proudly reported one day that it is "possible both to be true to myself and still have a special place in my family" (honoring).

Ms. N's new sense of meaning and direction was evident the day she walked into the social worker's office and announced that she would show the school how to make money for the student social work organization. She had decided to organize a Mexican bake sale and to have no "pale Anglo cookies." Ms. N was mastering her pain and honoring her rich bicultural heritage in keeping with the cross-cultural factor of worldview respect. For Ms. N, worldview respect involves strong values of family and expressions of cultural heritage symbolized by ethnic food. In a sense, she provided an initiation experience (a cross-cultural curative factor) for her classmates to sample her cooking.

Ms. N began to enjoy her renewed sense of belonging in her family and relished the respect she received from her relatives for her accomplishments as a student. She began volunteering at a preschool attended by Hispanic youngsters, where she helped them with new words and read them stories by Hispanic and Anglo writers. She helped the youngsters bridge the two main cultures in their lives, an accomplishment that she too was achieving. Ms. N was able to honor her cultural heritage and her own broadening worldview through her volunteer work.

At her graduation, she was flanked by her mother, four sisters, four brothers-in-law, six nieces and nephews, her new boyfriend, and her brother. All applauded her success. She was especially proud of her brother's congratulations and attentiveness. Ms. N told the social work educator that she was able to accept both her heritage and her differences with her heritage. Ms. N said that her social work professor's listening skills helped her to get things off her chest (holding and telling) and that being part of a student association helped her feel more powerful as a person from two cultures (mastering).

SUMMARY

The term "Hispanic" refers to a wide and rich group of people with great diversity and many different strengths. Cross-cultural social work practice with Hispanic people must include an awareness of both similarities and differences. To be effective and competent, social workers and other professionals should practice from a stance of openness, willingness to learn, and basic confidence in cross-cultural curative factors as a lens for understanding another's cultural context and worldview. Existential helping elements are helpful methods that can be used in cross-cultural helping. This approach can be useful with people who are experiencing and remembering trauma pain while searching for meaning and meaning potentials in life.

5

Traumatized Clients

MANY OF THE POPULATION GROUPS DISCUSSED IN THIS BOOK HAVE SUF-
fered extreme violence and cruelty as a result of pathogenic cultural patterns of
prejudice, discrimination, and outright hatred. Regardless of ethnic, racial, cultural, or religious background, adults and children experience trauma from painful
experiences such as illness and death; experiencing or observing severe injury from
accidents, abuse, war, or terrorism; economic deprivation; and migration and immigration. Threats of death or serious injury can result in feelings of fear or helplessness and risk for psychological disability later in life, particularly if the terror
event involved human remains (Hanscom, 2001; Miller, 2003).

Estimates from nearly two decades ago reported that close to 50 percent of all
people living in the United States have suffered from the effects of violence (Figley,
1990). This estimate seems minuscule after the terrorist strikes on September 11,
2001. The devastation and terror of this horrible event were observed on live broad-
casts, and many continue to experience trauma from the terrorist attacks on that
fateful September morning. Altman and Davies (2002) claim that this traumatic experience changed people's perceptions of the world more than it changed the realities of the world itself. Change can be seen in new levels of security: airport inspec-
tions of one's person, clothing, and belongings; new identity checks for college
admission, driver licensing, new employment; and new concerns for how to identify children over their lifetime through technological advances in forensics. These
changes are constant reminders of this and possible terrorist attacks in the future.
The struggle of how to deal with posttraumatic stress from acts of terrorism, how to
reduce the threat of future terrorist attacks, and how to live with threats of terrorism over time has become the reality of the American people.

Many people in the United States experience post-traumatic stress in response
to initial trauma, even from trauma that occurred years before. Experiences of
trauma can cause symptoms that greatly distress survivors and their friends and
families. Depression, sleeplessness, flashbacks, shame, fear, guilt, low self-esteem,
somatic complaints, and rage are common symptoms of post-traumatic stress disorder (PTSD) (Bell, 1995; Koenen, Stellman, Stellman, & Sommer, 2003; MacPherson, 2001). Trauma that is expressed as rage and anger brings frightening experiences to awareness. Experiences of extreme trauma are equally frightening for the
survivor whether the stimulus is war, abuse, severe and sudden injury, or any other

terrorizing and traumatizing intrusion. Survivors of trauma are trauma victims. Their experiences or observations of terror and traumatic events result in symptoms of psychological disruptions manifested by symptoms of avoidance, hyperarousal, intrusive thoughts, fears and nightmares, and confused perceptions of the self (Breslau, 2002; Bride, Robinson, Yegidis, & Figley, 2004; Lantz & Gyamerah, 2002b).

Not all reactions of PTSD stem from experiences of primary trauma. Secondary trauma is the result of experiences in which people observe acts of terror, assist the injured, see death and misery, encounter extreme suffering, and witness inhumane acts of violence. Sometimes referred to as "vicarious trauma" or "compassion trauma," secondary trauma can produce flashbacks, hyperarousal, vigilance, and other symptoms similar to those caused by primary trauma (Bride et al., 2004). Secondary trauma is characterized by behaviors and emotions surrounding knowledge or observation of a traumatizing event. Those charged with helping victims of terror or injury; dealing with death and dying at the scene of injuries; or collecting, transporting, or managing human remains and the personal belongings of the dead are frequently victims of secondary or compassion trauma. Serial traumas are those traumatic events experienced over and over. For example, repeated exposure to child abuse, bombings, and torture are serial traumas. Overwhelming emotions and feelings of helplessness and horror are typically experienced by trauma victims. People experience the same life events and trauma events differently, so a particular trauma event may not be devastating or traumatic for all victims or for all observers (Figley, 1990, 2002; LaRowe, 2004).

The orientation to social work intervention described in this chapter has evolved primarily out of Frankl's (1959) existential work with survivors of the Nazi death camps during and after World War II. Frankl's approach with concentration camp survivors has special significance for social work practice with clients who have experienced trauma and terror.

TRAUMA AND REPRESSION

In Frankl's (1959, 1975) existential understanding of repression and terror, there are meaning potentials to be discovered and acted upon on a conscious level of awareness, even in the terror of a Nazi death camp. People who have been traumatized often use repression to avoid directly experiencing painful memories of trauma and terror (Lantz & Greenlee, 1990a, 1990b). Such repression, however, is a double-edged process. On one hand, it allows the traumatized person to avoid experiencing painful memories of the traumatic experience. But, on the other hand, repression prevents the person from experiencing the meaning potentials that are always embedded in an experience of trauma and terror (Lantz, 1993). The will to find meaning in life renews courage and the need to survive even in the face of very painful events. Frankl's (1959, 1988) ideas about the human will to meaning are especially helpful when one is working with victims of trauma as they try to cope with trauma and terror.

The human spirit provided the strength for Frankl and others like him to survive the concentration camps (Frankl, 1997a; Lantz, 2001; Lantz & Lantz, 1991). Common human experiences of dying, suffering, and feeling guilt transcend any particular culture or worldview. Frankl (1997b) named these three existential conditions of human existence the "tragic triad" (p. 99). Completely realizing these existential conditions in life is not really possible, but the failure to meet one's personal responsibility to do so can be a source of existential guilt. Overcoming existential guilt requires finding meaning in death and in suffering. According to Frankl, finding meaning in life is the primary motivating force of humankind.

Defense mechanisms such as avoidance, repression, denial, and anger reduce the danger of experiencing trauma pain that could be too great to bear. For example, "a person exposed to too much death imagery at too young an age often reacts to such experiences with avoidance, aggression, and a hard shell in an effort to protect the self from the vulnerabilities of love, meaning, and intimacy" (Lantz & Gregoire, 2000a, p. 22). Protecting the self through such defense mechanisms is a central contributing factor to symptoms of PTSD and may become necessary when one experiences trauma events.

The idea that repressed memories of trauma and terror have meaning potentials that have been pulled into the unconscious during repression provides an opportunity to work with the traumatized client (Lantz, 1993; Lantz & Gregoire, 2000b). From this existential point of view, helping the traumatized client to remember experiences of trauma and terror can also be a way of helping him or her to recover those meaning potentials that have been embedded in unconscious memories of trauma. Thus, flashbacks and intrusive memories can be understood as methods the individual uses to initiate a search for the meanings and meaning potentials embedded in memories of terror (Frankl, 1975; Lantz, 1991b; Lantz & Gyamerah, 2002b).

The recovery to consciousness of meanings and meaning potentials that have been embedded in terror can be an extremely painful process for the traumatized individual. On the other hand, such a recovery of meaning awareness can often trigger powerful and dramatic intervention results. Remembering trauma and terror without the recovery of meaning potentials to consciousness is often dangerous and can be extremely damaging to the client (Frankl, 1959; Lantz, 1992b, 1993; Lantz & Gregoire, 2000b; Lantz & Lantz, 2001; Tick, 2005).

EXISTENTIAL HELPING ELEMENTS AND CROSS-CULTURAL FACTORS

The case studies of Mrs. S and Mr. T demonstrate the use of social work intervention from a cross-cultural existential perspective with traumatized clients. The existential helping elements of holding, telling, mastering, and honoring offer a structure for the client-worker relationship in which there is freedom and responsibility as well as opportunity to discover meaning out of crisis and trauma pain. The cross-cultural curative factors of worldview respect, hope, helper attractiveness, control, rites of initiation, cleansing experiences, existential realization, and physical intervention are gateways to understanding another person's worldview.

These eight curative factors are universal to humankind and transcend cultural diversity. Although informed by one's cultural context, cross-cultural curative factors represent common characteristics and are critical to understanding human responses. For example, one's worldview represents understanding of the world as known and experienced, including religious beliefs and survival adaptations as demanded by location and climate. Worldview respect reflects one's sense of being in the world, one's sense of purpose, and explanations for life and death. Hope is another clearly universal human factor. Hope provides strength, faith, and perseverance for the future, for happiness, for good health, and perhaps for life after death. These cross-cultural curative factors facilitate empathy, a critical component in social work intervention and other counseling modalities. Understanding another's worldview and relating to universal curative factors are necessary for effective social work practice. Yet conveying empathy in a diverse world requires one to understand and demonstrate cultural appreciation and sensitivity. Genuine communication of empathy compatible with the reality of another's worldview distinguishes genuine empathy (Chung & Bemak, 2002). Cross-cultural curative factors of control and cleansing experiences are reflected in the following case examples of cross-cultural social work with traumatized clients.

Mrs. S: A Vietnam Era Nurse

Mrs. S served as an army emergency surgery nurse in Vietnam in 1969 and 1970. She worked extremely long hours to save the lives of severely wounded American soldiers. Mrs. S requested social work help in 1985 after surgery and chemotherapy for cancer were unsuccessful and she learned that her prognosis was terminal. She reported, "Since my surgery, I have been having flashbacks where I see dying soldiers whom I worked on in Vietnam."

Mrs. S reported that she had had no difficulty adjusting to civilian life after returning from Vietnam. She reported, "I never talked about Vietnam when I came home because no one wanted to listen." Mrs. S "walled off" her experience in Vietnam.

In this situation, a thirty-three-year-old ex-army nurse who had been exposed to the terrible gore and death of combat in Vietnam was unable to talk about her experiences when she first came home. Fifteen years later, facing death from cancer, she began to get in touch with her past. For Mrs. S, flashbacks served the function of "making me think about Vietnam before I die." Social work intervention with the S family focused upon helping Mrs. S and her family hold and tell her memories of Vietnam, to help her "grieve the young men I lost in Vietnam." The cross-cultural curative factors of cleansing and existential realization emerge here and are interpreted through the knowledge of the reality of lost lives of young soldiers fighting a misunderstood war without a front line in a distant and unfamiliar jungle environment with heavy vegetation and rainfall. Recognition of the sacrifices that Mrs. S made in her tour of duty in Vietnam (cross-cultural curative factor of existential realization) helped the family honor her for the job she did in Vietnam. Commitment to American causes is a strong cultural value that calls for personal sacrifice in extreme situations. Belated recognition of personal sacrifices has been a long-standing concern for Vietnam veterans. The social worker helped the family share Mrs. S's past as a meaningful way of helping the children remember their mother with pride as they faced the struggles of adolescence without a mother (control). Mastering their pain and taking charge of their lives in their mother's absence could only be partially reached as they struggled for control and held onto their hope that somehow modern medicine would extend their mother's life (helper attractiveness).

Mrs. T: Survivor of the Trauma of Sexual Abuse

Mrs. T requested help after she started having "terrifying images of a small and crowded-in space, with creeping bugs and only splashes of light" just before falling asleep. These images triggered anxiety, and Mrs. T had started drinking in order to fall asleep. Mrs. T described the images as having started after her daughter's seventh birthday.

In this clinical situation, Mrs. T started having flashbacks of her own seventh year of life, when she had been repeatedly raped and sodomized by an uncle who told her that he would kill her mother if she told her what he had done to her. The uncle stayed with her family for three months while recovering from a broken ankle.

Mrs. T tearfully recalled having told her mother that her uncle "chased me in the dark and locked me naked in the cupboard under the kitchen sink, where the roaches lived," but her mother had called her a "crazy girl" because she believed her brother more than she did her daughter. Mrs. T remembered her mother saying, "Your uncle couldn't ever run with his poor ankle and would not do such a dirty trick anyway." Mrs. T apparently then repressed these memories until her own seven-year-old daughter began playing house and leaving her dolls amidst the pots and pans under the kitchen sink at home.

Social work intervention with Mrs. T began with the existential element of helping her to hold her memories of terror at the hands of her uncle. As she was empathetically supported in reexperiencing her trauma, she was able to share her experiences and the circumstances of her life at the time (worldview respect). Holding the trauma pain involves catharsis (cleansing) and brings the pain into conscious awareness, where it can be noticed, remembered, and reexperienced. Holding trauma pain requires empathetic availability on the part of the worker as the worker feels the pain, perhaps in small ways, and sometimes as secondary trauma experiences (Lantz & Gregoire, 2000b; Lantz & Gyamerah, 2002b).

Mrs. T talked with her husband to try to understand why her parents had refused to help her as a child. With her husband's and the social worker's support, Mrs. T invited her mother to share what she remembered and asked her why she had ignored her plea for help. Telling about the trauma experience with family members brings the trauma experience into the interactional world and names the trauma. In this phase, the social worker may be confrontational, supportive, or empathetic, but always sensitive to defenses used by the client and other family members to avoid awareness of the trauma experience or the trauma pain. Responsibility for action or inaction is often recognized in this phase of intervention (Lantz & Gyamerah, 2002b).

Mrs. T discovered that her mother had not known what to do, as she loved her brother and doubted that he would ever do "such horrible, dirty things." She convinced herself that her daughter's story was only the result of a seven-year-old child's vivid imagination. Mrs. T's mother admitted that she had not told Mrs. T's father because "your Dad never liked my brother. He always called him a freeloader who couldn't be trusted. Now your Dad's dead, and I can't tell him." The cross-cultural curative factor of rites of initiation is reflected here as the client's mother has a need to confront her deceased husband, an act that would perhaps demand restitution, bring closure, and allow the family to move forward.

Mrs. T was surprised to discover her mother's considerable support for her as well as her anger toward her uncle, who had died several years prior to Mrs. T's discovery of her abuse. Mrs. T found her aged mother to be extremely sorry; she also admitted that she "felt awful for not believing my own child at a time when she needed me most." Her mother was remorseful for having allowed her daughter to suffer alone.

Mrs. and Mr. T reported that perhaps the most helpful part of the counseling experience was the way the social worker helped them to master their trauma and find meaning in Mrs. T's experience of terror and sexual abuse (existential realization). Mastering trauma involves reflection, or in this case, sharing family secrets and rebalancing the family. Here, feelings of anger and aggression are transformed in constructive and assertive actions. New independence and responsibility emerge as denial and avoidance shrink, allowing for new levels of healthy family intimacy (Lantz, 1993).

After reliving her terror, Mrs. T was able to transcend her own pain by helping others and volunteering with a child abuse prevention program that educated children to understand "good touches" and "bad touches" and to report such experiences to parents, teachers, and others in their lives. In this way she was able to honor her trauma pain. Honoring is the final existential helping element, involving conscious awareness of meaning opportunities and opportunities for giving to others. Giving back to the world, to others, is a means of transcending trauma pain (Frankl, 2000; Lantz, 2000c). Mrs. T reported that this volunteer work was a practical way by which she could make her past mean something. She was able to share her experiences from her volunteer work with her husband and to find new meaning in their marriage (existential realization).

Mr. T was able to learn to support his wife during her time of remembering the abuse. Together they talked with her mother to clarify the details of Mrs. T's rape and molestation. Mrs. T was absolved of any feelings of failure on her part to protect herself and felt somewhat relieved that her mother saw her failure to protect her child as her own mistake because she was afraid to confront her brother (cross-cultural factors of cleansing and hope for forgiveness).

EXISTENTIAL APPROACH TO CROSS-CULTURAL SOCIAL WORK WITH TRAUMATIZED CLIENTS

As we review these two clinical illustrations, we note that such a brief clinical review could give the impression that social work intervention with traumatized clients is a short-term approach. This is not the case. In the first case study, intervention lasted from three months before the death of Mrs. S to seven months afterward, nearly ten months in all. The T family was in counseling for almost two years. Social work intervention with traumatized people is most often a somewhat lengthy process. The process of helping begins with establishing the worker-client relationship and structuring intervention through the existential elements of holding, telling, mastering, and honoring.

Establishing the Helping Environment

In social work intervention with a traumatized client, the client and social worker focus upon establishing a helping environment. Developing trust and commitment is a critical part of the helping environment (worldview respect) (Figley, 2002; Lantz, 1993). Traumatized clients may spend a considerable amount of time testing to see whether the social worker will be able to help them manage their memories of trauma and terror in a safe and empathic way. Such testing is largely unconscious. The traumatized client is generally very wise in selecting a social worker. The client can often subconsciously feel whether a given social work professional will be able to work with his or her specific experiences of terror. A social worker should not be expected to be able to work with every traumatized client and should respect a client's desire to work with a different helper, without blaming the client or viewing his or her resistance as pathological. The match between client and social worker is particularly important in situations involving trauma (Lantz, 1992b, 2000c; Lantz & Lantz, 2001)

Holding the Trauma Experience

The existential helping element of holding refers to the process of remembering and reexperiencing the trauma experience. The social worker helps the client remember the specific details of the trauma so that some pain can be released in the process of suffering (cleansing). The client is encouraged to examine the traumatic event or events in detail and to reflect upon how the trauma has disrupted and affected his or her life (hope and existential realization). The client is also encouraged to reflect upon how trauma has disrupted meaning opportunities and awareness of meaning potentials in his or her life. The most common cross-cultural curative factors in this phase of intervention are cleansing and existential realization. Revisiting the trauma experience can help the client to find some potential meaning in the trauma experience. The client is encouraged to tell his or her story of the trauma in a way that often involves sight, sound, taste, smell, and touch as well as his or her reactions to the trauma. The more detail that can be remembered and talked out, the greater the possibility that the client will be able to discover meaning potentials in memories brought into the helping process.

Telling and Recovering Meaning in Trauma and Terror

Existential helping elements of holding and telling are difficult to separate in actual social work practice. Telling facilitates the client's recovery of meaning opportunities that were embedded in the memories of trauma and terror. The traumatized client will not be able to recover fully without finding a way to reframe the experience as a meaning potential (control and existential realization). Frankl (1959) reports that victims of terror can recover most fully when they find a way to make use of the self-transcendent meaning opportunities that evolve out of the traumatic experience. Frankl has consistently pointed out that many victims of the Holocaust were able to realize their human potential fully only after discovering a personally unique way of giving to the world that evolved out of their personal experiences in the concentration camps and their memories of terror. Frankl's ideas about the self-transcendent use of personal experiences of trauma and terror as means of finding a way to give to the world have also been described by Lifton (1973) in his work with A-bomb survivors and Vietnam veterans, and by Lantz (1991a, 1993, 2000c) in his work with the families of Vietnam veterans. Both Mrs. S and Mrs. T were able to discover meaning opportunities for giving to the world that had been embedded in their memories of terror (existential realization).

Memories of terror may also facilitate meaning discovery by helping to explain a specific client symptom or symptom cluster. Often victims of terror develop unusual symptoms that they interpret as meaning that they are crazy. Helping the traumatized client to name a symptom and discover its meaning can often greatly decrease anxiety, improve self-esteem, and help the client realize that he or she is not crazy (control). Hope and control are powerful factors in the healing process. Belief in the worker or therapist is a reflection of helper attractiveness, another cross-cultural curative factor.

Mastering Trauma Pain and Discovering Meaning Potentials

In mastering trauma pain, the social work practitioner helps the client make use of the meaning potentials embedded in trauma and terror that were recovered to consciousness through holding and telling. This is most effective when it occurs through self-transcendent giving to the world. Frankl believes that such giving can occur in a self-transcendent relationship with nature, with an important cause, or with other human beings. Such self-transcendent giving is an effective way to transform survivor's guilt into survivor's responsibility (Frankl, 1959, 1975, 1988).

Lifton (1973) stated Frankl's (1959, 1975) concept of meaning discovery through self-transcendent giving to the world in a different way. In his work with survivors of near-death experiences, Lifton consistently points out that survivors generally have one of two possible responses: they can go numb and repress the experience of near-death and the associated anxiety at the expense of living a full and rich life in the here and now, or they can fully experience death anxiety and let this anxiety evolve into creativity and/or advocacy. Frankl would clearly agree with Lifton's point but would label the responses of creativity and advocacy as self-transcendent giving to the world. In the daily, practical world of social work with traumatized clients, it is the social worker's task to help the client find his or her own ways to transform terror into meaning through creative activities and activities of advocacy or giving. The story of the U family illustrates how this might be done.

The U Family

Mr. U served in Vietnam in 1966 and 1967. When he returned home, he married his high school girlfriend. Mr. and Mrs. U's son, William, Jr., was born in 1970, and Mr. U graduated from college in 1971. He experienced no problems in adjusting to life at home after Vietnam. After being home for fifteen years, he started having flashbacks and intrusive memories about his time in Vietnam. Holding and telling his trauma helped Mr. U remember and tell his wife about killing a Viet Cong soldier who was about the same age as their son and about finding a peasant village in a free-fire zone that was destroyed by American bombing. Through this clinical intervention, Mr. U mastered his trauma experience. Mr. and Mrs. U gained new reason and purpose in life as they found new meaning potentials in his memories as reasons to become better parents to William, Jr. They terminated social work intervention shortly after the existential element of honoring evolved as they became volunteers at a shelter for the homeless in honor of the young soldier Mr. U killed and Mr. U's memory of the village.

In this example, the existential helping elements of holding, telling, mastering, and honoring directed the process of intervention. Cross-cultural curative factors of cleansing, control, and existential realization are venues for understanding the cultural context of this family's life, the social context surrounding the war, and the values of life and societal sanctions against killing youth, in this case, a young soldier. As meaning opportunities were realized, trauma pain was reduced, and self-transcendence, or giving to the world, came about much as described by Frankl.

Honoring and Terminating

Gaining conscious awareness of self-transcendent opportunities to give to the world is an effect of understanding trauma experiences and pain. By giving to others from an empathetic understanding, one's personal trauma pain can protect others from similar pain. It is this giving back of love and caring that overcomes the pain, fear, and powerlessness of trauma. Mastery, control, and power over one's responsibility to create and experience new meaning potentials in life are strong healing factors. Lantz and Gregoire (2000b) caution that holding, telling, mastering, and honoring may seem straightforward and elementary; however, social work intervention structured around elements from an existential approach is not regimented, nor is it prescriptive. Instead, the helping relationship is participatory and flexible, sometimes metaphoric. Outcomes are dependent upon the client's use of freedom and responsibility to find meaning potentials embedded in experiences of terror and trauma. During the process of honoring the trauma, the social worker helps the client find ways to give back to the world, to empathetically understand the pain of others, and to evidence care and giving.

Recognition and celebration of mastery and honoring are appropriate as the helping process approaches closure. Joint assessment and evaluation of outcomes can help the worker and client come to closure. Termination should not occur until the client has had a comfortable period of time to integrate newly discovered meanings into daily life. Premature attempts at termination generally result in a recurrence of symptoms. If there are not remnants of feelings such as anxiety, joyful anticipation, and lingering regret, termination is probably not indicated. In such a situation, the social worker should talk openly about these concerns with the client. An informed and mutual decision about termination may then be reached (Lantz & Lantz, 1991, 1992; Lantz, 1993).

TRAUMAS REALIZED AND UNREALIZED

Thus far in this chapter we have described an existential approach to cross-cultural social work with traumatized clients. Existential helping elements and cross-cultural curative factors have been discussed and presented in case examples of social work with traumatized clients. It is unfortunate that in this new millennium so much effort must go into understanding terror and trauma. Now, decades later, Vietnam veterans continue to give voice to their trauma experiences. The world continues to observe the aftermath of the destruction of the World Trade Center, shootings, bombings, and unprecedented levels of violence in countries like Afghanistan and Iraq. Journalists are being trained to cover and report terror and to attempt to balance daily scenes of terror and destruction (Feinstein, Owen, & Blair, 2002; Simpson, 2004). Social workers are learning more about compassion fatigue and secondary trauma and are part of combat stress teams (Lamberg, 2000; LaRowe, 2004). This is all very different from the level of understanding of trauma experiences and post-traumatic stress disorders that we had during the Vietnam era.

SOLDIERS IN MIDDLE EASTERN WARS

If the lingering symptoms of PTSD from previous wars are any indication, then the lasting impact of the war in Iraq will have enormous dimensions yet unknown. There is deep concern that American veterans of wars in Iraq and Afghanistan are at great risk for PTSD and related psychiatric problems. Frequent and unpredictable blasts, acts of violence, embedded enemies, and the sight of strewn body parts and injured and killed women and children all create severe stress.

In conversations with returned Iraq veterans, we have found the veterans open in discussing but not personalizing violence from the war zone. Returned veterans voice great respect for civilians who welcome them back and offer them jobs. They also discuss symptoms of hyperarousal, vigilance, sleeplessness, and family stressors. In weekly support groups conversation leans toward their fears and the terrors of their experiences. Interestingly, they also feel concern for Iraqi citizens, for youth, and for families who treated them. One veteran's account of trauma is gruesome and inhumane. His account of his most traumatic experience is shared here.

Back from Baghdad

His right knee is stiff with shrapnel still there,
    blasts took his hearing partly out and still threaten his sleep.
A ragged scar on his arm is evidence of defense gone wrong.
Intense, quiet, early thirties, soldier/veteran said his marriage was shaky,
    and his presence scared his child, a boy of only three.
Bagging body parts, searching through rubble for wired explosives;
    civilians, families, children, people in loose clothing, and women with their faces
    covered;
He fought the embedded enemy in a foreign land of sand, a land of heat.
Meeting with other vets and those of us who wanted to know;
    his assignment was a jet fuel tanker truck; he was the driver.
He told of roads made by artillery and others before him.
Convoys had to deliver fuel, food, water, everything.
His were orders to roll on, in a convoy from hell,
    with orders not to ever stop for fear of death or worse;
The convoy rolled on, delivering its important load as charged.
Pulled across the dust filled road, the three-year-old child was tethered to a rope.
Cold and distant, his eyes held grief and guilt, not violence or killing.
He needed no cueing, no words of clarification or reflection;
    it was his duty; he was the driver.

SUMMARY

The full extent of trauma symptoms and trauma services needed are unknown at this time. Cultural values, religion, gender, and age are a few of the variables that affect how experiences of terror and trauma are perceived and how they are managed over a lifetime. Social workers and other professionals can expect to encounter various demands for counseling and assistance for trauma in the coming decades. Veterans Administration facilities are increasingly identifying and treating PTSD of soldiers from military duty in the Middle East. Social work intervention from an existential perspective has been found useful in work with traumatized clients and fits well within social work practice and the context of human diversity and trauma experiences.

6

Native American Clients

AT THE TIME OF FIRST CONTACT BETWEEN NATIVE AMERICANS AND WHITE European explorers, there were approximately 1.2 million Native Americans. About 300 different languages were spoken by different Native American tribes. This population was nearly destroyed by efforts to annihilate or relocate them and to eliminate their culture (Choney, Berryhill-Paapke, & Robbins, 1995; Jackson & Turner, 2004). Increasing numbers of European immigrants brought disease and epidemics to Native People, resulting in thousands of deaths. Others died from starvation and exposure to the elements. The 1838 Trail of Tears relocation march westward to Oklahoma decimated the Cherokee, Choctaw, Creek, Seminole, Chickasaw, and Navajo tribes. Native American population numbers dropped by nearly two-thirds, reaching a low of about 250,000 people at the turn of the twentieth century. By 2000, census data reported about 2.5 million Native Americans (John, 1988; Neal, 2000; Weaver, 1998).

Nagel and Snipp (1993) take the position that none of the four basic sociological processes of racially and culturally heterogeneous societies represents the experiences of the Native Americans. These sociological processes are annihilation, the destruction of a group; assimilation, absorption of a minority group by the dominant culture; amalgamation, production of a "melted" population from the blending of ethnic groups; and accommodation, maintenance of cultural distinctiveness among ethnic groups in a pluralistic culture. Suffering near physical and cultural annihilation and eventual relocation, tribes of indigenous people cling to their few remaining ethnic traditions and spiritual salvation in their struggle for survival.

Although these four common sociological processes can be seen in most groups, Nagel and Snipp (1993) propose that Native Americans' response to ethnic relations is more clearly captured by the process of ethnic reorganization, which "occurs when an ethnic minority undergoes a reorganization of its social structure, redefinition of ethnic group boundaries, or some other change in response to pressures or demands imposed by the dominant culture" (p. 204). In this process, the minority group protects its ethnicity but makes social structure and boundary changes. Not inconsistent with emergent and situational processes, ethnic reorganization occurs over time and in response to shifts in power and oppression as well as social, economic, political, and cultural reorganization. While ethnic reorganization accounts for some changes in Native American culture, Native People have continued to hold onto their ethnic distinctiveness.

There would be even more losses for Native Americans who survived the onslaught of disease, war, relocation, and disenfranchised lifestyles, and who gave up their land and livelihoods of farming and hunting. Hundreds of treaties and agreements imposed more restrictions. Treaties, agreements, and laws define White and Native American relationships, some specific to certain tribes and others more broadly applicable. Evolving in the early 1700s, Indian schools, trade, and treaty negotiations fell under the jurisdiction of the Bureau of Indian Affairs in 1824. By 1887, the General Allotment (Dawes) Act took control of land holdings. Returning some control and providing limited autonomy, the Indian Self-Determination and Education Assistance Act and Indian Child Welfare Act are products of the 1970s (Neal, 2000; O'Brien, 1996). Through all of this, as reservations became a political reality, Native People lost their traditional practices of extracting products from nature and bartering goods in a simple economic system. Forced to send their children to boarding schools or having children placed in foster care or other child welfare arrangements, families became separated and many lost family ties. Poverty, majority-imposed boarding schools, and poorly funded education on reservations are part of the legacy of Native Americans. Problems of alcoholism, mental illness, suicide, and infant mortality bring additional grief (Dubois & Miley, 2005). Moving into the twenty-first century, treaties around land ownership and compensation for seized wealth remain litigious.

Having an early reputation of inattention and poor service delivery, the Bureau of Indian Affairs now has greater participation by Native People due to increased tribal control in accord with amendments to the Indian Self-Determination Act. The new Office of Tribal Justice advanced awareness of tribal sovereignty, whereby Native Nations have power to self-regulate by their own laws and jurisdictions. For some, issues of dual membership in native or majority culture are enhanced by sovereignty. As sovereign entities alongside majority culture, Native Nations have economic rights including the levying of taxes and the operation of casinos. Sovereignty raises concerns around the provision of social services, particularly in view of provisions of the Indian Child Welfare Act that call for tribal or Indian social services and social welfare in child protection and certainly in placement of children in out-of-home care (Cook, 2005; NARA, 1999; Weaver, 1998). Finally, recent national attention has targeted issues of social justice, education, safety, and nurturance of children in communities. During his time in office, President Clinton brought attention to and passed new legislation to address Native American concerns. President Clinton's efforts have brought recognition to tribal colleges and universities as institutions of higher learning.

HISTORICAL TRAUMA

The history of near annihilation of indigenous people in the United States is a series of acts that reduced the Native American population by at least two-thirds. Disease, biological warfare, exposure and starvation in forced relocations, and massacres are part of this history. For those who survived, there would be colonization and separation of families by boarding schools for children, who became lost and suffered physical and sexual abuse at the same time that they were stripped of their culture, religion, and way of life (Weaver, 1999). The legacy of historical trauma— not just individual trauma but trauma for the tribe and community—is one of unresolved grief and loss extending over generations for a population of people. Historical trauma affects all realms of the person—emotional, physical, social, economic, cognitive, political, and spiritual. A wounding of the soul, historical trauma contributes to problems of depression, suicide, substance abuse, and social problems associated with poverty and low self-efficacy (Duran & Duran, 1995). Social work intervention with Native Americans requires that sensitive attention be paid to past experiences of the client and the client's family, group, or community. Asking about what historical events have been part of the client's own experience or the experience of his or her extended family reflects cultural competence and shows respect for the client's worldview.

CROSS-CULTURAL SOCIAL WORK WITH NATIVE AMERICANS

It is remarkably difficult to understand the diversity of Native Americans. Over 350 tribes are recognized by the federal government. The largest clusters of Native Americans are in the southwest, mostly in California, Arizona, New Mexico, and Oklahoma. Only about 40 percent of this minority population live on reservations or in Tribal Jurisdiction Statistical Areas. The majority live throughout cities, towns, and rural areas and have less density in the eastern United States. While indigenous people live throughout North America, only a small proportion live in the far north, where they represent about 15 percent of the Alaskan population (Jackson & Turner, 2004; Neal, 2000).

Cultural competence requires combining knowledge about history, loss, rights, threats to sovereignty, and personal realities in everyday life. For example, when one is speaking with or working with individuals and families, terminology is important, as Native People have preferences for terms of identification. "Indigenous people," "Native Americans," and "First Nations Peoples" are used interchangeably. Nevertheless, honoring individual preference conveys respect. Becoming culturally competent requires gaining new knowledge and skills in addition to gathering information about values, beliefs, diversity, culture, contemporary concerns, and the practices of each client. Trust, family structure, time, religion, and anomic or existential depression in response to present and past traumatic losses are concerns that counselors and social workers need to understand and be ready to explore as necessary when working with Native American individuals, families, groups, organizations, or communities.

Trust

Social workers who are representatives of the dominant American culture should not be surprised if Native American clients do not trust them. Trauma, loss, and grief continue to affect many Native People. Mistrust is deeply embedded in the culture, as most past efforts at "helping" have added to the legacy of loss and displacement. Torrey (1986) points out that in view of the history of loss experienced by indigenous people in the United States, it would probably be a sign of pathology (in other words, massive denial) if the Native American client trusted the white social worker at the outset of intervention. Some of the hurdles that must be overcome in cross-cultural social work practice with Native Americans are language difficulties, different understandings of the amount of physical space that should be maintained between persons, and different understandings of the meaning of eye contact. Recognizing and being knowledgeable of Native People's historical struggle to survive is essential for social work practitioners. Taking time for grief work over historical losses is often a place to begin building trust (Jackson & Turner, 2004; Weaver, 1998).

Social workers outside the Native American culture may be surprised to discover that some Native Americans have different ideas about the meaning of a handshake. In the dominant American culture, a firm handshake generally means that a person is to be trusted. However, among Native Americans, a firm handshake may be viewed as aggressive and disrespectful (Everett, Proctor, & Cartnell, 1983). Many middle-class social workers may also be surprised to learn that many Native Americans consider it a sign of disrespect to question a person in detail about his or her personal life. A white Anglo social worker who is trying to take a good social history may unknowingly be acting in a very disrespectful manner to the Native American client who does not share the worker's positive views about self-disclosure. Direct questioning by a social worker may be experienced as interrogation by the Native American client. Being patient; respecting silence; avoiding linear questioning; and appreciating native values such as sharing, harmony with nature, and supernatural explanations of natural and human experiences are all necessary in culturally competent practice. Openness, some limited storytelling, and sharing of self are means of building trust and opening communication (Jackson & Turner, 2004). While worldviews of circularity and harmony in nature are not easily understood by members of the majority culture, it is imperative that social workers and other helping professionals learn about these important perspectives to being in the world.

Native Americans have a long tradition of respecting both the spoken and unspoken word. It is possible that increased nonverbal skills are a response to an early absence of a common written language and perhaps even contribute to tribal variations in language. Nonverbal language consists of communication through body positions, eye movements, silence, and behavior. Traditions, culture, and customs passed on orally preserve legends and myths of the tribe. Nonverbal communication tends to be important to Native American clients who place great importance upon body language. Following the client's initiative in being silent or making eye contact, social workers need skill and knowledge of communication in a cross-cultural context in order to be culturally competent and self-aware (Jackson & Turner, 2004; Voss, Douville, Soldier, & Twiss, 1999). Congruent verbal and nonverbal communications are important ingredients in effective cross-cultural communication with Native Americans.

Family and Extended Family

Native Americans traditionally value living in an extended family network or tribal arrangements, where concern for each individual is a concern for all. Connected by strong social ties or blood ancestors, clans are often large, with established rules for belonging. Native clans and extended family networks hold deep regard for elder members. Governed by the wisdom of tribal elders, the clan protects its members and prescribes behavior and morality. Elders expect to be cared for in their later years in return for their loyalty and caregiving to extended family members. Whether living in nonnative communities or native reservations, pressures of employment frequently position older adults as caregivers for younger generations, particularly their grandchildren. Grandparent-headed households are among some of the poorest families raising children, and much of the responsibility falls on elderly women, who are sometimes responsible for providing food and clothing (Fuller-Thomson, 2005)

Native American families frequently live biculturally and participate in mainstream education and employment, enjoy both urban and rural lifestyles, and are bilingual. Caught between two different realities, Native Americans live in native and dominant cultures, cope with the political realities and laws of both, and respond to two sets of values and beliefs. Gender roles are different, as providing food and shelter is no longer typical work for men. Males in contemporary families are often unemployed, and as a result, women are becoming breadwinners and assuming more community roles. Roles of elderly males tend to be poorly defined. Along with their wives, many elderly men help in caring for their grandchildren. Children are valued members of tribes and participate in many tribal gatherings and celebrations (Neal, 2000). It is important to note that the role of Native American women has changed not simply due to the feminist movement but in response to cultural evolution. At one time women owned land and household belongings, while men owned weapons and utensils needed for hunting and food preservation. Female elders continue to hold significant roles in many tribes and nations. Some women hold chair or chief positions; for example, Wilma Mankiller became principal chief of the Cherokee Nation in 1985 (Neal, 2000).

Many Native Americans believe that children are born with the power and ability to make important choices and decisions. Due to this worldview, many Native Americans utilize noncoercive parenting styles that encourage the child's self-determination. Human service providers frequently do not understand the value of this Native American concept of noninterference. Unencumbered by expectations about developmental timing, these parenting styles may be misunderstood as negligent by social workers outside the Native American cultural tradition (Everett et al., 1983).

Native Americans often hold a nonmaterialistic view of the world and tend to value other persons based upon their personal characteristics rather than their economic standing. Native Americans generally view sharing positively and tend not to be concerned with the accumulation of material belongings beyond those necessary to maintain life, such as food, clothing, and shelter. It is important for social workers to avoid projecting materialistic values onto Native Americans and then viewing them as dysfunctional because they are not overly concerned with materialistic goals (Attneave, 1982; Jilek, 1982).

Native Americans generally value humility and modesty and view talking about one's accomplishments in the presence of others as ill-mannered (Everett et al., 1983). This may make it a bit difficult for the social worker to identify client strengths during assessment. Practitioners who work with Native American children often push them to be competitive in a way that is not compatible with the Native American tradition of humility.

Time

The Native American client's conceptualization of time is often different from the conceptualization of time held by those in the dominant culture. "Indian time" is more natural and approximate, and fits into the flow of daily living (Everett et al., 1983; Neal, 2000). The white population learns early on to view time in a linear fashion. On the other hand, Native Americans have a spatial view of time, in which events take place at both a location and a certain time. The social worker who gives a Native American client an appointment for a specific time should not be surprised if the client returns for his or her next appointment but feels that the time is not right.

In today's fast-paced world, social workers are encouraged to move quickly, make an immediate diagnosis, develop an initial contract and intervention plan, and begin intervention as rapidly as possible. This action-oriented focus, taught in many schools of social work is generally not compatible with the Native American's respect for nature, belief in the positive aspects of noninterference, or tradition of getting to know persons before working with them. A social worker who is able to develop good working relationships with Native Americans is generally comfortable with a slower process that involves a positive view of silence and the idea that relationship building is not immediate.

Understanding this circular or harmonious orientation to time conveys worldview respect and strengthens the helping relationship. Worldview respect is perhaps the most important cross-cultural curative factor conveying compatibility between the orientations of helper and client.

Religion

There is no single ethnicity or common religion among the nearly 300 legally recognized Native American tribes. Customs, ceremonies, values, languages, and beliefs vary by tribe. In addition to their native heritage, a common thread among Native People is the importance of family and kinship. Extended family roles reach across generations as children care for aging parents, who pass on traditions to their grandchildren. Native elders are revered as wise and trusted leaders whose teachings of connectedness among biological, physical, and spiritual qualities of living things explain nature and provide a worldview (Gesino, 2001; Voss et al., 1999; Yee, 1990).

Religion plays an important part in life for many Native Americans. Most believe in a supreme force and feel a deep reverence for nature. Many believe that emotional problems are caused by spiritual forces or disharmony in nature. For most Native Americans, religion is not just something to be thought about on Sunday; instead, it is involved in all aspects of daily life. Acceptance of things as they are, belief in noninterference, and respect for nature are all elements of most Native American systems of religious beliefs (Jackson & Turner, 2004; Neal, 2000).

Religion and spirituality vary among Native Americans; but harmony with nature and the use of spiritual healers and shamans are characteristic of native beliefs. Ceremonies and rituals are frequently led by shamans with the purpose of maintaining balance among all forms of life and things. Native Americans typically view natural and supernatural worlds as important in life's balance and relationships (Trujillo, 2000).

Religion is closely connected to all eight cross-cultural curative factors. These curative factors have the power to supercede racist or oppressive beliefs and behaviors when incorporated into cross-cultural social work practice methods from an existential perspective. Religious beliefs inform worldviews and are closely connected to hope in life and for life even after death. Ministers, preachers, shamans, charismatic leaders, and others who carry messages of religion and religious beliefs personify helper attractiveness as socially and culturally defined by followers or members of the religion. Without a doubt, religion serves as a means of control, as it defines good and evil and teaches mastery in life through rituals and prayer. Religion prescribes rituals and rites of initiation such as christenings, funerals, bar mitzvahs, healing ceremonies and chants, and other rites of passage in different cultures. The curative factor of physical intervention seems to be less directly tied to religion; however, physical intervention carries sacred and symbolic meaning for many. It is through all these cross-cultural curative factors that individuals define, discover, create, and experience meaning in life. Metaphorically, finding meaning or filling a meaning vacuum creates meaning and purpose in life, or existential realization and motivation for being in the world.

Anomic Depression and the Native American Client

Native American families are consistent recipients of governmental policies designed to break treaties, distance families from their land and natural resources, separate children from families, and disrupt the family's ability to maintain traditions, language, religious beliefs, and cultural patterns. It is not surprising that Native Americans may exhibit signs and symptoms of anomic or existential depression such as social withdrawal, a high rate of suicide or accidental death, and substance abuse. Painful and abrupt losses, relocations, and disruption cause societal or tribal rules to become disengaged and ineffective, thus placing people in states of confusion and meaninglessness. With ethnic and traditional anchors torn away there is increasing vulnerability for depression and suicidal ideation (Jilek, 1974, 1982).

Jilek (1982) further reports that this high rate of anomic depression among Native Americans is quite understandable when we recognize the massive efforts of the dominant culture to disrupt the natural patterns of Native American life. Pressure from the dominant culture has interfered with the traditional Native American sense of harmony with nature and respect for humanity. Jilek suggests that anomic depression among Native Americans may be a logical result of a policy of direct or indirect genocide. States of anomic depression can lead to other dysfunctions including alcoholism and violence, both of which Jilek found in his work with Coast Salish Indian society (Brucker & Perry, 1998; Jackson & Turner, 2004; Jilek, 1981).

SOCIAL WORK INTERVENTION WITH NATIVE AMERICANS

No doubt, Native American clients prefer to work with indigenous social workers. Cultural competence requires social workers to be knowledgeable about individual, group, and within-group diversity of Native Americans. Many prefer to identify themselves by their tribe or nation. Others may be only minimally in touch with their heritage, having long ago moved into urban schools and mainstream careers and culture. Physical characteristics such as hair and skin color are not pronounced for many, particularly those who have ancestors from various races and a mixed ethnic heritage. Some people choose to blend into contemporary multicultural society, while others openly celebrate their ethnic heritage. Social workers must understand and appreciate the unique experiences and qualities of Native People in order to provide either economic or social services.

While not disregarding the biculturalism or urbanization of Native Americans, it is safe to begin where the client may be—that is, to consider the importance of native beliefs, values, and ethnic identity of clients who have Native American heritage. While much of the existing literature about working with Native American clients in cross-cultural counseling comes from the viewpoint of working with those who live on reservations, little has been written about practice principles with more acculturated urban clients of Native American heritage. Not unlike most other groups, Native Americans have great inner-group diversity in education, income, lifestyle, and attitudes toward seeking and accepting medical care.

Two major categories of skills to consider when one is working with Native American clients are communication and commitment skills. First, there are general skills of communication and problem solving that are useful in most helping situations. Communication and problem solving facilitate both empathy and empowerment techniques, which can be genuine and effective. Intervention offered by the social worker from a position of empathic caring and cultural respect has a greater chance of being accepted as useful to the Native American client who follows the Native American cultural pattern of accepting "natural" differences and believes that help is a personal process rather than a technological process (Attneave, 1982; Jilek, 1982).

In the spirit of traditional ways, the client's identity needs time to unfold, and for important realities and worldview to be shared. Social workers should not work too hard at appearing accepting of Native American culture. The Native American client is generally more interested in the worker's willingness to learn about his or her culture than in the worker's display of overly friendly ignorance. For many Native American clients, the social worker who tries too hard will likely appear to be insincere (Attneave, 1982).

Containment skills are extremely important to the helping process. The worker must be able to demonstrate patience, share silences, respect orientation to time, and avoid rushing into direct information gathering (Weaver, 1999). The impatient cross-cultural social worker who presses too hard for either information or action in the initial stage of the helping process will generally earn the client's mistrust and will appear impolite. Being patient, honoring silence, and respecting the principle of noninterference are much more likely to be helpful (Attneave, 1982; Jilek, 1982).

An additional consideration in intervening in the lives of Native American clients is gaining an understanding of worldview and identity. Individual worldviews demonstrate the differences among Native Americans as well as bicultural aspects. A client's worldview is grounded in ethnic beliefs and formal and informal systems; thus, one's worldview is a means for identifying meaning and meaning potentials in daily living. Gaining an understanding of identity from sovereignty and citizenship is equally important. As indigenous people, Native Americans are not just minorities of color or ethnicity. Citizenship is an important aspect in understanding identity and is often a source of great pride. Sovereignty of nations is constitutionally recognized and grants Native Americans the freedom to accept U.S. citizenship or not. Enrollment or membership in a native tribe and membership in a nation provides access to certain support, including health, education, and social benefits.

Attneave (1982) and Jilek (1982) recommend open collaboration and co-therapy with Native American healers if they are available and if the Native American client wishes to utilize such services. They have reported that such a blend of cross-cultural healing strategies is often very useful to the Native American client who has accepted some of the "White ways" while maintaining traditional beliefs. The case of Mr. R demonstrates cross-cultural competence and incorporates cross-cultural curative factors in the process of helping from an existential perspective.

Mr. R: A Native American Client

Mr. R was referred to a social worker because he had become sad and depressed after learning of the suicide of his best childhood friend. Mr. R was referred by an industrial nurse at the factory where he worked. The nurse knew that Mr. R was a Vietnam veteran and referred him to a worker who had experience counseling Vietnam veterans. Mr. R was married, had two children, and had moved to Columbus, Ohio, to obtain employment. He had moved from his reservation in Michigan three years after his return from Vietnam. Mr. R was fairly well adjusted to city life and had given up most of his Native American ways.

Loss of a friend from suicide is a situation that often triggers trauma pain that may emerge as substance abuse or having extended feelings of loneliness or depression. The social worker told Mr. R that he understood that Mr. R had accepted referral from his nurse because he had been suffering from some normal depression after losing a friend. The worker also told Mr. R that reflecting and thinking about it would eventually help. In the initial interview, the social worker did not push for information but told Mr. R that he believed Mr. R would bring up what needed to be told when the time was right. Being cognizant of the importance of the cross-cultural curative factors of hope, cleansing experiences and existential realization, the worker told Mr. R that the worker's job was to listen when Mr. R felt that the time was right to talk. Mr. R remained silent for the rest of the initial interview, as did the worker. Therapeutic silence shared by the client and worker affirmed an understanding of worldview and orientation to time.

Over the next few months, Mr. R told the social worker about going to Vietnam with his best friend from childhood and how they both survived combat and returned home. The worker helped Mr. R hold, tell, master, and honor his trauma pain. Mr. R told how his friend was never the same after they survived Vietnam and that his friend had started drinking after they returned home. Mr. R told about feeling guilty because he had not been able to help his friend and that "I ran out on him when I moved to Ohio." Mr. R felt especially guilty when his friend committed suicide. He didn't understand why "Vietnam hit him so hard but didn't get to me all that much." Holding the trauma experience provided opportunities for Mr. R to reexperience the trauma and for the worker to respond empathically in the process of holding the pain. Telling and naming the pain brings the trauma experience into the relationship, where support can occur.

While Mr. R evidenced growing trust in the social worker, the opportunity to reconnect with familiar healers surfaced as a means of helping Mr. R master his trauma pain, in keeping with his worldview. The worker eventually suggested to Mr. R that some of the answers he was looking for might be found in some of the legends and origin myths of his tribe. The worker suggested that Mr. R make a visit home and talk to some of the elders in his tribe about some of the native traditions and beliefs that he might find to be of help. The curative factor of helper attractiveness emerged as an important source of help in Mr. R's struggle to gain mastery over his painful memories. The holistic form of mind-body-spirit in the Native American approach to health includes physical and spiritual worlds in harmony with the native worldview.

It would be nice to report that Mr. R went home, heard an interesting and helpful myth of native origin, and immediately stopped feeling depressed. Unfortunately, this did not happen. What did happen was that Mr. R slowly began to reconnect with his roots and native culture and eventually decided that his friend had died because he had traded in all his traditional beliefs for "White man's booze." This realization represented mastery of some of the trauma experience. Renewing roots and finding explanations linked to traditional worldview beliefs allowed Mr. R to place boundaries around his loss and to find explanations. In this way, Mr. R was able to experience the cross-cultural curative factor of control in his attempt to master his trauma pain.

Mr. R decided that he would also be vulnerable to continuing problems if he didn't reconnect with his traditions. After seven months, Mr. R reported that he had overcome his depression and no longer would be coming to talk about his feelings of sadness and emptiness. He reported that the worker's listening skills, willingness to go slowly, and encouragement to find meaning in his roots were for him the important aspects of the help that he had received. He said that he had learned that dealing with his depression and denial of his feelings about his friend's suicide were now his responsibility to overcome. Mr. R accepted this responsibility with renewed energy. While not verbalizing the meanings and meaning potentials found in his renewed connections to his past, existential realization was occurring for Mr. R as he found meaning in his existence and likely even greater meaning potentials in experiences before him. Honoring his friend and his experience of trauma pain remains a final step for Mr. R; and if it can happen, it will be at a time and place and in a way that will be congruent for Mr. R and in harmony with his worldview.

The existential helping elements that the worker believes were most helpful to Mr. R were holding, telling, and mastering. Mr. R told the worker that he was happy that the worker respected "my pace and timing" (holding) and that the worker was not pushy and "let me go at my own speed." Mr. R also reported that the worker's ability to listen rather than to tell him what to think was a big help and that this listening helped him feel less depressed (holding and telling). Mr. R also believed that the worker's respect for his culture and encouragement to go back and recollect his roots were of special help (mastering).

The most significant cross-cultural factor of helper attractiveness emerged as Mr. R returned to his tribal origins and to the practices of the tribal elders and shaman. In this case, worker awareness of cross-cultural factors of worldview respect and helper attractiveness helped the worker better understand Mr. R's reality.

SUMMARY

Native American people have survived loss of land and resources and deliberate attempts by the dominant culture to disrupt their language, culture, and values. Native American people come from a variety of different tribal groups and manifest their ideas and beliefs in a heterogeneous way. Nonnative social workers are not generally preferred providers. Some Native People seek only native healers, while others may lack access or may be more bicultural in their worldview. Nevertheless, Native People, like all other people, prefer helpers who have some understanding of their cultural and ethnic heritage.

Trust, helper attractiveness, and a helping relationship are critical to the helping relationship. Cross-cultural social work practice with Native American clients requires that social workers and other professionals be open to a new world of cultural beliefs and practices. Social work intervention from an existential perspective uses elements of holding, telling, mastering, and honoring to structure the helping process, facilitate empathetic availability, and provide awareness and reflection of emotional trauma. This approach is very useful in situations of trauma pain due to physical and spiritual losses, which can cause a sense of meaning or finding meaning potentials in life to be disrupted.

7

African American Clients

THE MOST REGRETTABLE HISTORICAL DEVELOPMENT IN A NATION ESTAB-lished on the premises of freedom and democracy is the history of enslavement of persons of African descent. African Americans have experienced the most victim-ization of any group in both American history and contemporary American culture (Billingsley, 1992; Healey, 2003). Discrimination against and oppression of people of color remain among the most cruel and pathological processes in American so-ciety. The dominant culture minimizes the importance of race, ethnic and cultural heritage of minority populations, and personal identity of individuals outside the majority culture.

Many African Americans have ancestors who were brought to the United States as slaves, while recent immigrants have come for their own reasons. Families have ties in places including the West Indies, the Caribbean, and South America as well as Africa (Brooks, Haskins, & Kehe, 2004; Winbush, 1996). African Americans are not a homogeneous group or population, yet they share the common black experi-ence of encountering extreme prejudice and discrimination because of the color of their skin (Hamilton, 2001; Mwanza, 1990). African Americans are diverse in life-styles, culture, income, ethnicity, education, age, sexuality, religion, and national origin. Equating skin color with national origin ignores the unique qualities of indi-viduals and perpetuates practices of discrimination and white supremacy. Black people share the commonality of race but not the commonality of African descent. Culturally competent counselors and social workers must appreciate the impor-tance of national origin of the clients they serve. Understanding individual world-views in the context of existential psychology and philosophy provides a lens for viewing people's perceptions of their world and their being in the world.

African American social work clients sometimes encounter white workers who seem to deny that racial differences exist, and, understandably, they are frequently concerned that white service providers do not relate to the depth and intensity of pain caused by racism (Boyd-Franklin, 2003). Mr. F, a twenty-three-year-old unem-ployed African American client requesting marital therapy at a community mental health center, expressed such a concern to his worker in one of his initial sessions:

> It's not that I think you will try to be racist. It's just that since you're white, how can
> you understand what it's like to know you can do a job but know that the skin color

you got will screw up your chance? How can you know what it's like to have a six-month-old kid and a wife counting on you to get the job and then seeing that look—the look that tells you the man is not giving any black man any chance at all. If you haven't felt that look, how can you even start to feel what it's like to be me?

Mr. F expresses deep and realistic concern that his white social worker will not be able to understand his experience as a black man. Mr. F is not alone in his concern. Numerous writers in the human service field report that white middle-class helping professionals consistently do not connect with the African American experience and cannot empathize with the oppression, hatred, violence, poverty, or unemployment experienced by African Americans and their families (Boyd-Franklin, 2003; Mwanza, 1990; Winbush, 1996).

According to 2000 census data, African American people in combination with one or more races make up 12.9 percent of the American population; those identifying themselves as black or African American represent 12.3 percent of Americans (U.S. Census Bureau, 2000b). African Americans reside mostly in the South and Northeast and are heavily represented in cities such as Washington, D.C.; Detroit; Baltimore; and Memphis. African Americans are being outnumbered by Hispanic people in the United States. It is projected that by 2010 the African American population will represent 13.1 percent of the U.S. population, and Hispanics 15.5 percent. This change in population is projected to be even greater by 2050, when it is estimated that African Americans will total 14.6 percent and Hispanics will represent 24.4 percent of the nation's population

Marginalization by race, gender, and class places African American and other minority members of color in jeopardy of continuing poverty and oppression (Harley, Jolivette, McCormick, & Tice, 2002). Poverty, female-headed households, and unemployment are experienced far more often by people of color than by white people. While employment and education have increased for minority populations of color, families continue to live in poverty (Harley et al., 2002; Healey, 2003). Research shows that the median income of black middle-class families is about 70 percent less than that of white middle-class families (Oliver & Shapiro, 1996). From 2001 to 2002, white household median income remained about 43 percent greater than black household median income, and white household net worth is about eleven times greater than black household net worth (*Black Enterprise,* 2005; Harris-Lacewell & Albertson, 2005).

African American citizens experience greater unemployment than any other population group in the United States. Recent national surveys report that both the African American middle class and the African American poor rank racial discrimination and unemployment as the most pressing universal problems facing African Americans. African American males average more than twice the unemployment rate of white males, and those who are working are overrepresented in service jobs. African American women fare somewhat better but are less well paid and less frequently promoted than white women (Healey, 2003). Prejudice and discrimination often exclude young black men from employment, hampering inner-city growth and resource development (Healey, 2003). Many of the nation's young men are disenfranchised on social, economic, and family levels by continuing social injustice. The burden belongs to society, to everyone—not just to minority populations.

The experience of minorities of color, particularly African and other black Americans, calls for social justice and relief from suffering and oppression. Competent cross-cultural social work is critical to improving systems and aiding people. White social workers often lack understanding of the processes that are important to serving African American and other black clients. Some of these realities and processes identified in cross-cultural literature are discussed here.

REALITIES AND PROCESSES IMPORTANT IN CROSS-CULTURAL PRACTICE

Afrocentricity

Afrocentricity is defined as "a social science paradigm predicated on the philosophical concepts of contemporary African America and traditional Africa" (Schiele, 1996). This worldview is informed by African American history, culture, African heritage, and traditional African values. Being an African American means celebrating and cherishing traditional languages, references to ethnicity, culture, religions, and beliefs. The Afrocentric paradigm involves assumptions of a worldview of interdependency and connection among elements of the universe. There are interpretations of experiences and meanings that interconnect with spiritual qualities in humans, animals, and objects. Individual feelings, thoughts, and values are important in acquiring new information and experiences through these affective knowledge-building processes (Borum, 2005; Morikawa, 2001; Schiele, 1996). In other words, feelings and emotions are important transports for validity of information from being in the world, and informed by an existential perspective, from experiencing meaning in the realities of daily life. However, just as all white families are both alike and different; black families are alike and different as well.

Recognition and celebration of race and national origin are empowering forces of Afrocentricity. Finding solace in spirituality, traditions, and beliefs external to the self provides support and empowerment. Black Pride movements of the civil rights era gave voice to more internal aspects of the self, including beauty and self-efficacy. Skin color and hair texture, which had previously produced unkind stereotypes, became identifiers of self-worth as a result of oppression by the white majority.

Social movements have helped the black community overcome negative stereotypes and devaluation, enabling personal freedoms to emerge alongside political freedoms (Boyd-Franklin, 2003; Russell, Wilson, & Hall, 1993). Famous charismatic leaders such as Martin Luther King, Jr.; Malcolm X; and Jesse Jackson emerged out of social movements bringing rebirth, celebration, and freedom in both public and personal realms.

Duality

Dubois and Miley (2005) cite the early work of Chestang (1976), which defines cultural duality as living in two worlds—the white dominant world and the black immediate culture. For those who have experienced oppression and discrimination, cultural duality provides a means of coping with daily reality in order to survive in a hostile world. Brown (1981) and Devore (1983) provide an early definition of cultural duality as a coping strategy that many white middle-class social workers fail to understand due to their lack of understanding of the identity conflicts that can arise. Duality is an adaptive technique with roots in slavery. Duality stems from the dominant white culture's questioning of the basic humanity of people of African heritage. During the days of slavery, African people were expected to function in the context of a white culture that discounted their humanity. Duality was developed in this context and helped the African American individual learn to have a public self and a private self for survival in a violent and dangerous white world. This notion of a public self and a private self has helped many black Americans survive in the face of discrimination, hatred, and violence. Viktor Frankl (1959) has pointed out that adaptive methods similar to duality were used by many death camp inmates in an attempt to survive the brutality of the German camps during World War II. Feminist literature reflects similar adaptive practices among women as the women's movement progressed, as women assumed greater public roles in addition to the private roles of wife, mother, and homemaker (Harper, 2000a).

Both Devore (1983) and Brown (1981) warn that white middle-class social workers may classify the process of duality as a maladaptive pattern if they are not aware of the history of ethnic and racial oppression and discrimination in America and racism in present-day American society. They point out that duality is not simply an adaptive strategy of poor individuals of African heritage. Biculturalism or duality is an avenue for a minority group to maintain a sense of ethnicity, a connection to cultural values and norms associated with their heritage, and yet assimilate into the majority culture so as to lessen oppression. Coping in a hostile society in this way allows important aspects of both cultures to be part of the individual's life. Many people utilize dualistic strategies to cope in their public and private lives, between rural and urban lifestyles, and with various combinations of ethnic and religious components in family systems. For minority populations, duality has served as a coping strategy to survive such oppression.

ROLE FLEXIBILITY IN THE AFRICAN AMERICAN FAMILY

Many white middle-class social workers fail to understand the adaptive nature of role flexibility in the African American family. As a result of unemployment, poverty, and racism in the United States, many African families have found it both necessary and advantageous to develop and use a variety of family structural forms that are often misunderstood and sometimes viewed as dysfunctional by white workers with traditional American family backgrounds.

Throughout history, the African American family has consistently demonstrated role flexibility. In many African American families, children help rear their younger siblings and may help to take care of aging grandparents. Mothers and fathers both work when work is available, and both take responsibility for child care. All members of the family help members of the extended family, and every member of the family develops a degree of competence in all the various family roles (Winbush, 2000). Such role flexibility is necessary for African American families to succeed in the face of racism, unemployment, and poverty.

Traditionally taught to be wives, mothers, and caregivers, African American women are among the legions of women who balance multiple roles and understand the challenges of multitasking both at home and at work (Billingsley, 1992; Prince, 1999; Winbush, 2000). While black women succeed in managing multiple roles, their life stories are ones of jeopardy—multiple jeopardy of racism, sexism, and classism (Wright, 2001). The impact of these injustices has produced stigmatization and disenfranchisement for many women.

The stereotype of the white suburban American family is one in which father goes to work, mother takes care of the children and works part-time, and the family's one or two children are encouraged to achieve academic success. Eventually children are to "emancipate," to leave the family and begin their own nuclear family configuration. This image, idealistic to begin with, has all but vanished. In contemporary families, usually both parents work and receive support from school and community programs for preschool and/or after-school child care. As the number of single-parent households has increased, the two-parent family is no longer a reality for many, particularly minorities.

America is evolving into a multicultural nation in which a diverse population struggles to survive the challenges of war, terrorism from foreign shores, and higher costs of living for everyone. Women balance multiple roles as daughters, wives, mothers, and employees. Black women continue to lag behind white women in management positions. Duality of gender and race is a barrier to equality in promotions and earnings (Combs, 2003). Men, particularly black heads of households, strive for more education and better employment, often at the cost of extended absences or long working hours away from home and family. Black males are often denied access to positions of power in corporate America. Other professional and skilled black males frequently experience exclusion and isolation within corporate and professional circles in the midst of contemporary multicultural, technological, and global concerns (Mackie, 1997).

Extended Family Relationships

African American families and communities creatively utilize extended family networks and kinship systems to maximize support for individual and group needs. The context of family is often defined by individual families, some that have lost kinship ties, and others that have extended biological kinship systems. Still other families extend their family or kin systems to include non-kinfolk such as preachers, children raised by the family, caregivers, and biologically unrelated aunts, uncles, cousins, and grandparents. In some poverty-stricken families, absent kinship systems, the community and church have become equally important as extended members of the family system. Churches have long been important to the African American community as well as in the family, regardless of family income (McGoldrick, Giordano, & Pearce, 1996; Winbush, 1996).

Extended African American family systems often share households, food, money, child-care services, emotional nurturance, and financial support. Supporting extended family members is extremely difficult in the face of stress, poverty, unemployment, and racism. Family separation and disorganization are part of the legacy of slavery for families torn from their African communities. Historically, children were a shared concern of communities—hence the familiar African proverb, "It takes a whole village to raise a child." Community lessons concerning the importance of a child to the village continue to be evidenced by community centers and kinship care of African American children. Many children would be lost to foster care and other out-of-home placements in the absence of kinship care (Hudley, Haught, & Miller, 2003; Scannapieco & Jackson, 1996). White social workers may not understand the significance of extended families that often include more than just blood relatives. The strength of the extended family continues to be an important culturally defined adaptive strategy not only for families living on the edge of poverty or at risk of separation, but also for intergenerational meaning in life.

One study of contemporary meaning of motherhood and extended grandmotherhood showed symbolic meanings to include bearing traditions, conveying family history, defining social roles, and caregiving across generations. A sense of elderhood and clan immortality can give spiritual meaning to grandmothering roles in extended family networks (Timberlake & Chipungu, 1992). Although not all grandmothers prove to be equally active in extended networks, grandmothering is familiar and important to many women of different races and nations of origin. Nevertheless, extending family relationships across generations establishes new purpose and meaning in life and conveys traditions and values. Social workers and other helping professionals can benefit from observing and appreciating the resources and strengths that these strong family networks offer families.

The Black Church

The black church is an important institution in African American culture. Emerging in response to spiritual needs before reading and writing were permitted, the church was a safe place, a place away from racism. Celebrations and rituals evolved around births, deaths, marriages, saved souls, and recoveries from illnesses. For hundreds of years, the black church has been a center for the mobilization of support for African American community needs. Spirituality and strong religious orientation in the African American community are important sustaining elements in the struggle to cope with racism, from the days of slavery to the present time (Billingsley, 1992; Cook & Wiley, 2000; Lincoln, 1999). Preachers meet their callings and lead their congregations in search of divine spirituality and freedom (Moore, 2003; Powell, 2000). Providing for spiritual needs as well as food and shelter for some, the church has been a strong influence, as well as a significant force in early community action programs and in the civil rights and black empowerment movements (Mays, 2003; Williams, 1987). Powerful religious and political leaders such as Martin Luther King, Jr.; Malcolm X; and Jesse Jackson demonstrate the religious and political power of the church and of their people. Carrying on the oral tradition of addressing their people, these charismatic leaders helped to bring powerful social change to the nation.

Black churches have served as a central point for socialization and for social support. Having a central role in the lives of many people, the black church has demonstrated the ability to adapt to the changing needs of its members. Representing mostly Protestant denominations, numerous small churches meet for social functions ranging from lunches and brunches, weddings and funerals, to day care and after-school sports activities. Central figures in the church—ministers and their wives, choir members, deacons and deaconesses, Sunday school teachers, and volunteers—are important sources of both spiritual and community leadership. Having many courageous accomplishments, the black church is part of the network of support and a place of acceptance (Boyd-Franklin, 2003; Boyd-Franklin & Lockwood, 1999). While there have been many social and political developments surrounding its significance to the culture, the black church is an entity throughout North America, where its work against systemic discrimination and preservation of the black culture extends throughout the continent (Este, 2004).

From birth to death, spirituality and religion are important forces in the lives of African American families. Spirituality, the expression of emotions, and belief in life after death are part of the world of love, loss, and grieving experienced and expressed through the church. Religious counselors are important resources for parishioners in search of spiritual counseling, particularly in instances of death or of serious illnesses (Moore, 2003). Professionals who are not grounded in religion or do not understand the importance of religion for African American clients do a disservice to their African American clients, and this lack of knowledge may interfere with the helping relationship (Boyd-Franklin, 2003; Boyd-Franklin & Lockwood, 1999).

EXISTENTIAL ELEMENTS AND CROSS-CULTURAL CURATIVE FACTORS: WORKING WITH ELDERLY AFRICAN AMERICAN CLIENTS

Mrs. L: Honoring Her Deceased Husband

Mrs. L, an elderly African American woman brought to the clinic by her two children for depression, reported not being able to sleep, eat, enjoy music, or go back to church since the death of her husband nearly a year earlier. The family expressed surprise that their mother would not see her minister or her church friends and reported that she seemed confused and malnourished. Although Mrs. L's children were focused on their mother's depression, immediate referral was made to assess Mrs. L's physical condition. Given her participation in modern Western society, referral to her primary care physician was simple. This method of physical intervention, a cross-cultural curative factor, was consistent with Mrs. L's worldview and resulted in her family physician prescribing antidepressant medication and nutritional supplements, and encouraging her to continue in counseling. The cross-cultural curative factors of helper attractiveness and physical intervention proved to be very useful, as Mrs. L trusted her physician's advice and returned willingly for counseling.

Mrs. L was seen over a period of two months. She told of her love for her husband and for their two children. Intervention focused on helping Mrs. L to hold, tell, master, and honor the trauma pain she felt at her husband's death. The existential element of holding her trauma pain allowed Mrs. L to revisit her feelings of grief and loss in response to her husband's death.

The worker empathically shared Mrs. L's pain as Mrs. L spoke of seeing her husband for the last time at the church and of her feelings of loss and emptiness. Tearfully, she said, "I just can't go back into that church. If only I had believed how bad he thought his heart was, I would have spent all of my time with him rather than with the choir every weekend and three nights a week." Empathic support helped her master her feelings of guilt about having done what she believed was right at the time, as she had no way of knowing that her husband's heart would fail and that he would die.

In revisiting her trauma, Mrs. L told of how distraught she'd been at the funeral and how she regretted not being able to play her husband's favorite hymn on the church organ just for him on his last visit to their church. "Oh, my dear woman, going back to that church just brings out the demons for me," Mrs. L lamented.

When asked if she thought that she was strong enough to play her husband's favorite hymn for him, Mrs. L said that she had considered taping the music and playing it when she visited his grave. "Why, if my children and church ladies knew I did something like that, they'd think I was possessed!" She seemed surprised when asked not only if she thought she could do that, but if that could be the last secret between her and her departed husband, who had loved her as well as her music and would be honored to know that she, too, could find comfort in the hymn.

Mrs. L found new meaning potentials in sharing her music in this way with her deceased husband, whose spirit she believed was always with her. Consistent with the cross-cultural curative factor of existential realization, she discovered new ways to create and find meaning in remembering her husband.

By the time of termination, Mrs. L had visited the church, taped the hymn, and played it for her deceased husband. She had found a way to return to church and to honor her husband through her talent as an organist. Three months later, Mrs. L was playing for the Wednesday night choir. Mrs. L noted that the choir honored her husband by dedicating their last practice hymn to his memory on each Wednesday night.

RECOGNIZING STRENGTHS OF THE AFRICAN AMERICAN COMMUNITY AND CLIENTS

In the same way that unrecognized prejudice can cause the worker to fail to recognize personal strengths in the African American client, such prejudice can also help the worker to overlook strengths in the client's social network, extended family, and community. The case of Mrs. L demonstrates the strength of her family system and the support that she received from her choir group and church. Interestingly, Mrs. L was so linked to her church community that she felt that this church group might judge her if they knew that she played music at her husband's grave.

Many white middle-class social workers fail to understand the strengths available in the extended family network and African American community that can be mobilized to help the African American client during social work intervention. Such an underassessment of environmental strengths is often manifested by social workers who focus strictly upon internal reflection with the African American client to the exclusion of social action and network intervention (Billingsley, 1992; Lantz, 1993, 2000a; McGoldrick et al., 1996). Effective cross-cultural practitioners do not minimize their own potential for racist attitudes and beliefs and consistently use the process of looking for strengths during assessment as a way to minimize the potential for stereotyping and misunderstanding (Lantz, 2000a).

The process of relationship building between white workers and African American clients can be difficult because of the potential for the worker to give in to biases or stereotypes either consciously or unconsciously. The worker must remember that there are many different lifestyles, family structures, and values within the African American community and make a sincere effort to empathically understand and accept these different lifestyles and community support systems (Hudley et al., 2003; Winbush, 2000). Recognition of differences as well as genuine caring and respect for human sameness in our multicultural society are strengths that helping relationships can be built upon (Boyd-Franklin, 2003; Brooks et al., 2004; Caple & Salcido, 1995).

Mrs. G's Trauma Pain from Rape and Robbery

Mrs. G, a thirty-year-old black woman, requested help at the community mental health center because she was feeling depressed and had begun to suffer anxiety attacks whenever she left home to go to work, run errands, shop, or pick up her son from school. Mrs. G reported that her husband had died of a heart attack two years ago. She told the worker, a white female social worker, that she and her husband had moved to Columbus, Ohio, from their hometown of Atlanta. She has been working at a dry cleaning store to supplement the Social Security benefits she receives for her son. Mrs. G reported that she has felt somewhat depressed since her husband died. Recently, she has started feeling very depressed and fearful after being assaulted, raped, and robbed three blocks from her home. She reported that she had lost touch with her friends after her husband's death and that she has been too embarrassed to return to her family home in Atlanta. She has not maintained contact with her family or her church nor made friends during the six years that she has been working and raising her young teenage son alone in Ohio.

The worker and client agreed that the goals for service at the mental health center would include decreasing Mrs. G's feelings of depression and anxiety, and helping her to get over the "dirty feelings" she reported feeling since the rape, an example of the curative factor of cleansing. Also, finding ways to become involved in the community and make friends is important if she and her son are to feel connected to others.

The social worker used the existential helping elements of holding and telling to help Mrs. G talk about her life and revisit her trauma experiences. Holding her trauma pain as she revisited the rape and robbery, in addition to the earlier death of her husband, was difficult. The social worker provided a holding environment in the sessions through acceptance, empathy, reflection, and client centeredness in the relationship. Holding Mrs. G's trauma pain facilitated revisiting the pain and telling her story as the relationship developed.

Mrs. G told of her efforts to work and to provide for her son. She reported that at times she wanted to give up and commit suicide, but she wouldn't do such a thing because her son needed her so he could follow the path on which his father had put him. In this she was honoring her role as mother and the expectations of her husband. The worker helped Mrs. G to take pride (in other words, find meaning) in how she had refused to let either her husband's death or the rape disrupt her commitment to her son (honoring). Empathetic support from the worker helped Mrs. G recognize her strengths of coping with adversity (mastering) and honoring her commitments to her son and husband. The curative factor of control emerged for Mrs. G.

Having gained a better understanding of Mrs. G's worldview, where independence and self-sufficiency were most significant, the worker was able to emotionally feel Mrs. G's values, norms, and cultural beliefs. The cross-cultural curative factor of worldview respect, empathetically conveyed, helped Mrs. G regain her sense of hope as she told of her losses and victimization. She wanted to take control of her life, a cross-cultural curative factor wherein she believed that if she were better able to manage her life, she would find inner peace and spiritual reward. Yet Mrs. G's strong self-control and self-imposed isolation prevented her from mastering her trauma, an important existential element in the helping process.

The worker gently reflected upon how Mrs. G had refused to ask for help from her family, her old friends, her church, and her community. Mrs. G's tendency to be stubborn and to refuse to ask for help could be both a strength and a weakness as she viewed her world (existential realization) and found new meaning and direction. The worker used encouragement to help Mrs. G begin to reconnect with others and to accept support from her community. Mrs. G's hope for her future was restored as she was able to take pride in having strength and courage in the face of the trauma and pain that she has experienced since her husband's death. Hope is an important cross-cultural curative factor necessary for finding meaning and meaning potentials in an existential sense.

The social worker linked Mrs. G with a minister at a nearby black church. The minister helped her join a church-sponsored support group for women who had experienced trauma from rape, robbery, domestic violence, and the violent deaths of friends or family members. The minister fit Mrs. G's images of a spiritual leader, and she joined the church, where she could experience spiritual renewal (cross-cultural factors of helper attractiveness and cleansing). This minister did an outstanding job of helping Mrs. G to rejoin her church and to make connections with the local black community, where she could feel supported and respected. After eight months of social work intervention, Mrs. G terminated service at the mental health center and reported that the service she had received had "saved my life."

The social worker's repeated demonstrations of respect for Mrs. G's worldview and empathetic conveyance of such respect helped Mrs. G express her feelings of damage and personal violation from her experience of being raped. Telling the trauma and naming her assault in a supportive and empathic helping relationship proved to be a cleansing experience and an important aspect of helping for Mrs. G take control.

SUMMARY

This account of African American experiences is not to be taken as stereotypical or predictive. While all people have a past, present, and future, experiences of opportunity and oppression are very different. Divorce rates, single-parenthood, church and community involvements, and extended family networks are changing for everyone in contemporary and global society. One must ask not whether there is a global world, but "What does a global world mean?" Certainly it is multicultural and has some order of superiority among humankind, as there are always the power holders and the less powerful. But will the hierarchy be based on ethnicity, race, income, technology skills, accumulated wealth, war power, or things yet to be imagined and socially constructed? Regardless of the answer to this question, human needs will continue to need human solutions.

Prejudice, misunderstanding, stereotyping, and unconscious racism can profoundly disrupt the helping relationship between the white social worker and the African American client. The worker's ability and willingness to open him- or herself to multiple realities of the African American community are basic necessities for effective cross-cultural practice. Such openness can help workers to more effectively identify personal, cultural, and environmental strengths of clients and their communities. There is much to learn for all of us—students, professionals, and practitioners in public and private agencies—as we move into this millennium where multiculturalism has taken on new meanings, and boundaries of inclusion are greater than those of exclusion.

8

Vietnam Veteran Clients

THE VIETNAM WAR IS CONSIDERED TO HAVE BEGUN ON AUGUST 5, 1964, AND to have ended on May 7, 1975. Approximately three million American men and women served their country in Southeast Asia in the armed forces during the Vietnam War. Casualties from this war reached 58,000, with another 300,000 wounded and as many as 700,000 requesting help for psychiatric or other readjustment problems. The legacy of this ill-begotten war lives on for many veterans, for their families, and for their children, as new terrors manifest from lingering chemicals. The 250,000 who sought help shortly after the war for symptoms believed to be associated with Agent Orange have been joined by thousands more. An herbicide containing dioxin, Agent Orange is now known to be dangerous to those who are exposed to it, as well as to their offspring (Appy, 2003; Brende & Parson, 1985; Lifton, 1973; Palmer, 2004; Scott, 1992; Tick, 2005). Agent Orange is linked to disabling and life-threatening genetic defects for first-, second-, and perhaps later postwar generations.

TREACHEROUS TERRAIN

The Vietnam War is a poorly understood and undeclared war. Fighting in thick jungles, mud, rain, and rice fields was a new experience for soldiers, who had not been trained for combat in this sodden territory. Soldiers were not morally prepared or trained to kill whole villages or women and children bearing arms. Army recruits, average age nineteen, were promised one-year fighting assignments in Vietnam. For the most part, these soldiers were politically naive and fearful of never returning home as they fought face-to-face and hand-to-hand in battles that had no front line (MacPherson, 2001). The stench of bloated bodies that dotted rice fields and lay partially hidden in minefields and jungle grasses etched memories into postadolescent psyches aged by sights and smells that should never have to be experienced in a lifetime. Directing and taking mortars, spilling blood, bagging body parts—such are the profanities for the mind to hold and for the world to know. Soldiers remember those they killed, those who tried to kill them, and those who died in their arms with words of pain-filled goodbyes. Young soldiers no more, Vietnam veterans returned home to find their heroism uncelebrated and their homecoming unwelcome.

The war that wasn't meant to be took the lives of about three million people.

While political confusion seemed to shroud sanction for fighting this war, television and radio brought live images of combat and suffering to the American population for the first time—so very different from the reports of the American involvement in World Wars I and II. Horrors of war and antiwar protests were brought to the nation and into the lives of soldiers and families as they occurred in real time. Antiwar movements at home were first-rate morale busters for those at war and for many at home. As soldiers returned home, negative attitudes devalued the war as well as those who served and risked their lives. With threats of demonstrations and violence from protestors, some returning soldiers were advised to wear civilian clothing instead of their uniforms (Appy, 2003). The lack of sanction for this war produced feelings of alienation and denial among Americans. Anger, depression, and the feeling that they were not valued by their country destroyed whatever social and political supports many soldiers believed in.

In an ambitious effort to document an oral history of the war, Appy (2003) reports the events of the Vietnam War from the testimonies of 135 war veterans. These veterans tell of waiting for helicopters, foraging for food, searching for booby traps and body parts, feeling numb in the aftermath of being hit by enemy fire, and engaging in face-to-face combat. Some lived with wound infections and contamination from chemical defoliants. There was also the inhumane imprisonment of soldiers and of South Vietnamese civilians accused of political crimes.

The effects of trauma were poorly understood as reports of psychological trauma and depressive reactions flooded in. Many veterans were plagued by repetitive imagery of beatings, close-range killing, blood spurting from new wounds, rape, and sights of whole families being killed. Reports of drug and alcohol abuse added to low national morale and helped to erode social support systems for older teens and young men who had been sent to fight in an unsanctioned war and survive in an unfamiliar jungle. Supports were not in place for soldiers, either in combat or upon their return home, and an economy with high employment left veterans searching for jobs. Economic supports were not in place for postwar assistance. Funding and legislation were needed for debriefing, counseling, education, and employment (Lifton, 1973; MacPherson, 2001; Tick, 2005)

Post-traumatic Stress Disorder

Many veterans still suffer emotional pain caused by their exposure to the horrors of this war and to our country's failure to welcome them back home in a sincere and meaningful way. Unwelcome for having fought a strange war and thought to have committed war atrocities, many were labeled, denied jobs, and discounted for their injuries—even those missing limbs or with other obvious and tragic injuries. Many couldn't speak of their terror and chose to remain silent when they returned home (MacPherson, 2001). For some, home was so unfamiliar that they returned to active duty.

Post-traumatic stress disorder was mostly undefined at the time soldiers came home from the war to their nation and communities. Episodes of flashbacks, depression, substance abuse, anger, emotional numbness, hyperarousal, and other trauma-related symptoms experienced by Vietnam veterans are linked to the war, a catastrophe of the worst sort created by human beings. These symptoms are now understood to be linked to trauma exposures and traumatic experiences suffered in the war.

The definition of post-traumatic stress disorder (PTSD) developed slowly. Dating back to World War I and World War II, the terms "shell shock" and "combat fatigue" were used to describe symptoms now associated with PTSD. Finally in 1976, the *DSM-III* included PTSD-III as a diagnostic category (Scott, 1992). Exposure to a trauma, re-experiencing the trauma, and ways of avoiding traumatic reminders such as numbing and hyperarousal are among the indicators of PTSD (American Psychiatric Association, 1994). Additional important risk factors for PTSD include involvement in a traumatic event and perceptions of a threat to one's life. PTSD can co-occur with other psychiatric disorders and can be chronic or episodic. Confronting the avoidance of memories and feelings associated with the trauma experience is essential. Uncovering these memories is best managed in a helping relationship in order to reduce emotional pain resulting from the experience and terror of the war (Koenen et al., 2003).

A Chopper Ride

Two of them were already dead
and a third was dying
painfully slow.
He did not want to know
the truth about his coming end
and pleaded with his eyes
for me to tell a tale.
So—I held his hand
and talked about
his million dollar wound
all the way back to Qui Nhon
and the 85th
watching him die
listening to my hope-filled lies.

It is difficult to understand why some Vietnam veterans experience problems and others do not. Some veterans report that they have not had emotional problems in reaction to their experiences in Vietnam. Others report serious emotional responses and problems, such as terrifying flashback experiences, powerful intrusive memories, substance abuse, emotional withdrawal, and episodic discontrol. Alcohol and substance abuse are serious problems for some Vietnam veterans, as these chemicals help numb the pain of flashback episodes and intrusive memories of the war. There is cause to believe that domestic violence in the households of some veterans is associated with the veterans' experiences of trauma and violence. These episodes of domestic violence are often related to drug and/or alcohol abuse as well. The relationship between trauma experiences and substance abuse continues to be an area for research (Savarese, Suvak, King, & King, 2001).

Some authorities (Brende & Parson, 1985; MacPherson, 2001) have suggested that the intensity of the veteran's symptoms corresponds to the level of horror experienced in the war, the degree of moral conflict experienced in response to the war, and the degree of personal culpability gained from the experience of war. Of natural catastrophes, accidental catastrophes, and human-induced catastrophes, the last has the capacity to have the greatest impact on those who experience it. Enormous trauma events bring on levels of stress capable of upsetting physical, behavioral, cognitive, and emotional dimensions of humankind.

Fitting with Bell's (1995) assumptions about the severity of human-induced catastrophes, those who experienced Vietnam are likely to experience trauma and PTSD. From a simpler existential perspective, the intensity of the Vietnam veteran's symptoms and problems is believed to correlate to the amount of horror experienced and/or observed during the war and the degree of success the veteran has had in discovering a sense of meaning and purpose in his or her personal experiences in Vietnam (Lantz, 1991b, 1993).

The lives of the men and women who served in Vietnam have taken many diverse paths. Many have found success in a wide range of careers as teachers, lawyers, doctors, dentists, mechanics, technicians, health-care workers, professors, writers, and workers or laborers in all sorts of trades. Some continue to serve in various military reserves and volunteer assignments. It has been debated whether the disabilities and health problems that plague many are PTSD or the result of exposure to Agent Orange. Disabilities and their interventions have been the focus of lawsuits, legislation, and service responsibility of the U.S. Veterans Administration since the end of the war. For veterans, the war is a chapter in the nation's history that lacks resolution and cannot be forgotten.

Now, forty years later and at the point of retirement, many Vietnam veterans continue to bear the pain and carry the stigma of this war. In addition to postwar concerns of psychological problems and counseling needs, physical disabilities and continuing health problems have been part of the legacy of the Vietnam War for American soldiers and for Vietnamese civilians. Half a century after the war, devastation from deadly chemicals is still a problem. The legacy of Agent Orange continues to have the power to inform international interests in ending the use of toxic weapons.

Agent Orange

Herbicides containing dioxins as well as other toxic chemicals coated war-torn areas, forests, fields, and water sources. Broad-leaf defoliants were stored in barrels with color-coded stripes that gave each defoliant its name. Its cloud covering thick jungle forests, Agent Orange's wet blanket was soon pockmarked by dropping leaves. In the wake of the defoliation of the jungle's vegetation, soldiers and civilians passed through, sometimes oblivious to the contaminant and other times held captive in the toxic environment by oncoming enemy forces. This broad-leaf killer destroyed forests and crop growth. Upwards of 33 million acres of forests and occupied land were destroyed. It is estimated that as many as 4.8 million people in Vietnam may have been exposed to the spraying. Of the 1.5 million Americans in the war zone, exposure was high (Palmer, 2004).

The spraying of dioxin, which was fogged by planes between 1961 and 1971, was halted due to concerns that it may cause birth defects. Now nearly half a century later, the extent of Agent Orange's longitudinal effect on the health of those exposed and that of their offspring is unknown. While reaction rates are different among people, numerous disorders caused by exposure to Agent Orange have been identified.

Each year in Vietnam, 35,000 infants are born with birth defects, including misplaced eyes or no eyes at all; missing or limp limbs; organ dysfunction; skin rashes and abnormalities; reproductive tract abnormalities; various cancers; loss of sense such as sight, sound, and touch; and various brain abnormalities (Tick, 2005). Neither the full effects nor the duration of dioxin contamination for humans is understood. Victims of exposure to herbicide are scarcely compensated for their losses. What help and compensation are available now to Vietnamese people are supported by donations from internal and international sources through a fund established by the Vietnam Red Cross Society as recently as 1998. Since 1991 some disability services and compensation have been provided by the Veterans Administration for veterans living on American territory (Palmer, 2004).

Veterans exposed to Agent Orange presented with various symptoms of rashes and sores, cancer, headaches, stomach disorders, numbness in the extremities, and behavioral problems. Some veterans frightened their families with outbursts of rage, episodic loss of memory, violence, and manic behavior. Veterans' accounts of their children's disabilities and genetic defects betray anger, guilt, and regret and tell of numerous defects such as spina bifida, deformed limbs, organ abnormalities, hydrocephaly, cleft palates, and numerous infant deformities, some affecting their grandchildren (Elliott, 2005; MacPherson, 2001).

In the case of Vietnam veterans, volumes of testimonies debate the culpability of chemical companies and government alike. Whether the toxicity of dioxin for human beings was known, whether the dioxin episode was intentional chemical warfare, and who bears responsibility—the government, chemical companies, or ill-formed research studies—are just some of the questions that remain unanswered. War injuries and burdens of genetic defects are personal costs of an unbelievable magnitude. A class action suit on behalf of veterans brought against Dow Chemical was settled out of court in 1984. This settlement of $180 million paid each veteran and his/her family only about $1,000 (Appy, 2003; MacPherson, 2001; Palmer, 2004).

EXISTENTIAL HELPING ELEMENTS AND CROSS-CULTURAL CURATIVE FACTORS IN SOCIAL WORK PRACTICE WITH VETERANS OF THE VIETNAM WAR

A large proportion of American citizens believe that the United States should not have become involved in the Vietnam War. Green (1989), MacPherson (2001), and Tick (2005) have all dramatically documented the disrespect and even hatred that were shown to many Vietnam veterans as they returned home to the United States after facing the challenge of physical survival and watching many of their friends die in extremely violent ways. At times the veterans who survived the war could not survive the message they received from their country that their acts of courage, suffering, and patriotism did not mean anything. Such a message seemed to come from the veterans' government, their communities, and, at times, from family and childhood friends (Lantz & Greenlee, 1990a; O'Brien, 1998). The important meaning potential of the societal ritual of welcoming our young soldiers back home was disrupted by our country's ambivalent feelings about the Vietnam War.

It can be extremely helpful to view social work practice with the Vietnam veteran as a cross-cultural helping process. Many Vietnam veterans experience the same kinds of anomic and existential difficulties as do the other minority culture clients described in this book. Vietnam veterans are not an ethnic, racial, or political minority; however, they are a special population.

Our approach to social work practice with Vietnam veterans is based on a belief in the core importance of helping Vietnam veterans discover and experience a sense of meaning in both their memories of Vietnam and their future lives. This approach takes the view that a failure to discover such a sense of meaning results in what Frankl (1959) has called an existential-meaning vacuum and Krill (1976) has called a problem of anomie. If this vacuum is not filled by a developing sense of meaning and purpose in life, it will be filled instead by symptoms and problems such as anxiety, depression, sexual problems, substance abuse, episodic discontrol, emotional numbness, social withdrawal, and interpersonal isolation. Some Vietnam veterans report flashback experiences and intrusive memories that often rush in to fill or signal the presence of an existential vacuum (Lantz & Gregoire, 2000b).

From a cross-cultural point of view, social work practice with Vietnam veterans should be directed toward facilitating the veteran's personal search for meaning and purpose in life. The social work approach should be directed toward helping the Vietnam veteran overcome both micro and macro disruptions in his or her search for meaning in life. This shrinks the existential vacuum and limits the opportunity for symptom development. Neither the Vietnam veteran nor the social worker can change the amount of horror that the veteran experienced during the war. What can be changed is the veteran's ability to discover and experience meaning and purpose in his or her memories of the war. This kind of meaning recovery can provide considerable relief from emotional pain.

Vietnam Veterans and the Search for Meaning

When Mr. V started seeing a social worker, he reported, "I felt like an immigrant from another country when I first came back from service in Vietnam." Like so many veterans who were returning from the Vietnam War in the late 1960s, Mr. V felt as though he were a stranger in his own country.

The failure of society to say "thank you" frequently disrupted and limited the Vietnam veteran's search for meaning. This societal meaning disruption has made an existential approach to cross-cultural social work a particularly effective method to use with the Vietnam veteran. The following two clinical illustrations demonstrate the potential usefulness of this social work approach with Vietnam veterans.

Mr. W and the Wall

Mr. W and his wife requested social work intervention after the war. He had lost a leg in Vietnam as a result of a mortar attack. The original presenting problem that was very upsetting to his wife was his emotional withdrawal. When Mr. W became upset, he would leave her and the children and be gone for days. Mr. W reported that his avoidance was a way for him to "protect" his wife and his adolescent children. He reported that he did not want to "explode" while he was having intrusive thoughts and flashback experiences.

Although Mr. W believed his intrusive thoughts were "bad and dangerous," the social worker attempted to help him see that they might also have an adaptive function. The social worker attempted to help Mr. W understand that people who experience traumatic events usually undergo a healing process, and that part of this process is a search for meaning in the face of trauma and tragedy. The social worker shared that the intrusive thoughts and flashbacks might be Mr. W's unconscious way of attempting to discover, rediscover, and experience a sense of meaning hidden in his painful memories and intrusive thoughts. The cross-cultural curative factor of control served an adaptive function as Mr. W. struggled with the emotional pain he felt as a result of the horror of the war.

The existential helping process of telling, holding, mastering, and honoring was followed with Mr. W. At first unwilling to talk about his memories on an outpatient basis, he did agree to go into a psychiatric hospital for a short period of time so that he could begin to talk about his memories with the social worker in the safe atmosphere of the hospital setting (control). The hospital represented a refuge that was culturally linked as a place of healing for Mr. W. He felted supported by the cross-cultural curative factor of helper attractiveness as educated and professional doctors, nurses, and therapists made him feel secure and cared for. Telling his memories of war traumas was difficult; and as he began to talk, he reported that he was beginning to develop a feeling of meaning about his experiences in Vietnam (existential realization). He remained in the hospital for six weeks in 1981 and got a good start at openly talking out his memories with both the social worker in individual counseling and with his wife in marital counseling (cleansing). As he shared his experiences of war and of returning from war, his trauma pain emerged from his internal, unconscious world into the interactional world of the helping relationship encounter, where empathic availability could be used to help hold up the trauma experience for deeper reflection and meaning opportunities. Bringing the trauma experience into awareness and into the helping relationship allows the trauma to be named within the helping process (Lantz & Gregoire, 2000a).

The existential helping elements of holding and mastering extended over a period of six years. The social worker worked with the couple in an attempt to help Mr. W continue to share his past and to rediscover meaning and purpose in his past. By the beginning of 1987, Mr. W had told his wife most of his stories. As he revealed his stories and memories and developed a sense of meaning regarding his experience in Vietnam, he experienced a great reduction in flashbacks and intrusive thoughts. These memories diminished in both intensity and frequency. Mr. W eventually stopped feeling afraid that he might "explode" (control). He described everything as "fine," except that his leg still hurt. He could not understand "how a leg you no longer have can still hurt like hell."

Toward the end of his existential helping, Mr. W asked the social worker to go to Washington, D.C., with him to see the Vietnam War Memorial. The social worker had a strong sense that he should honor Mr. W's request (worldview respect) even if it was not a technically correct thing to do in view of therapist-client relationships. The trip was very emotional and powerful for both Mr. W and the social worker. The specific details are not as important as the fact that Mr. W stopped feeling pain in his absent leg once he visited the memorial (cleansing). In some way the trip to the wall helped him to finally discover meaning in the loss of his leg (existential realization). He has suffered no more phantom pain since this trip. The trip to the wall was an opportunity to honor those on the wall.

Mr. X: Guilt and Responsibility

Mr. X began seeing a social worker in a residential facility for substance abuse problems. He was a retired army sergeant major who had served three tours in Vietnam. Mr. X had been admitted to the unit because of serious alcohol abuse. Upon admission, Mr. X did not believe that he was alcoholic but did admit that something was wrong. He had agreed to enter counseling only because his wife had threatened to leave him if he did not seek help. The precipitating factor that led to his admission was an incident during which he had become extremely violent while intoxicated, threatened his wife and family, and physically destroyed the house trailer in which they lived.

Early in the program, Mr. X denied the existence of any major problems in his life, but both his daughter and wife spoke of being afraid of him. His wife reported that he would have recurrent nightmares of his experiences in Vietnam but refused to talk with her about those experiences. He was quick to lose his temper, and his family no longer trusted him. His alcohol consumption had increased, and for the first time in his life, he had received a citation for driving while intoxicated.

The second week, the social worker began to explore the possibility that Mr. X was suffering from PTSD in reaction to his experiences in Vietnam. The social worker confronted Mr. X in group counseling during the presentation of his autobiography. It was here that Mr. X began the telling phase as he told the group that he suffered from recurrent and intrusive recollections of the death of his best friend in Vietnam. Mr. X felt responsible for his friend's death. He talked about the loss of his closest friend and his feelings of guilt for having survived (cleansing).

Mr. X spoke with the group and his social worker about the tremendous shame he felt upon returning to the United States and being called a baby killer. The existential helping element of holding the trauma was difficult for Mr. X as he reexperienced and remembered the pain of combat and the anguish of being with his friend as he died on the battlefield. His method of coping with this loss of meaning and meaning potentials was an attempt to medicate his pain and guilt with alcohol. He stated that he had entered the war with a purpose, "to defend democracy." He left Vietnam not understanding the purpose of the war, and he could no longer make sense of his involvement or of his survival. The social worker's practice with Mr. X focused upon helping him master the trauma that he had experienced in Vietnam (existential realization). Through his suffering and rediscovery of meaning, Mr. X learned the difference between survivor's guilt and survivor's responsibility.

Survivors' guilt is a legacy of the Vietnam war. "Why them?" and "Why not me?" are questions that are asked repeatedly by veterans as they tell their stories. Survivors' responsibility relates to the surviving veterans' concerns about responsibility for their dead friends and guilt for their own survival. In these instances, personal concerns of responsibility overshadow the fact that the war bears the responsibility for death and trauma. Intellectual and emotional absolution of some or all responsibility is important in reducing survivors' guilt. For some, survivor guilt and self-blame delay the ability to hold the trauma pain. Once holding can occur, catharsis brings the anguish into the conscious interactions of the helping relationship, where the emphatic availability of the worker or counselor can help the veteran confront the trauma pain and survivors' guilt he or she has been avoiding.

Honoring, the fourth existential helping element, has helped Mr. X maintain the progress he made. Now, maintaining sobriety, he helps others. He honors his experience of trauma and recovery from PTSD by being available to other Vietnam veterans who have drinking problems. He is very active in the Vietnam veterans' self-help movement.

In this case the cross-cultural curative factors of control, cleansing, and existential realization were used. These factors are culturally congruent, as Mr. X is in charge and has taken control of emotions that he had earlier been afraid to risk sharing with others. Mr. X had been fearful of not seeming to be the stereotypical strong American soldier capable of not showing emotion or losing control. His new awareness of himself in the world brings meaning in life and new opportunities for meaning from his awful experiences (existential realization). His intrusive thoughts and nightmares have greatly lessened in intensity and frequency. In addition, he no longer fears losing control of his temper, and he has reestablished an intimate and meaningful relationship with his wife and family. He has hope for the future, and he no longer drinks.

Near the end of the war, a poem written for Bob, a Vietnam veteran client, by his social worker helped Bob bring repressed meanings into awareness so that he could come to terms with having survived the war (Lantz & Harper, 1991). Bob was shocked by this poem and shared that "going too fast might get me killed," meaning going too fast in counseling could be too painful.

Bob

I saw him crossing the street
trying to avoid me
hauling ass.
Not wanting to explain
why my best efforts had not helped
and why he is back on the street
drinking and shivering in the cold.
Feeling sure I could not understand
his need for distance
from the normal world
who sent him there
to Vietnam
and brought him back
dead inside but still alive
using rot gut wine
to soften the voices
of old dead soldier friends
who call him loud
to join them soon
when he starts to feel alive.

Bob shared his surprise that the therapist understood survivor's guilt (Lantz & Harper, 1991). Survivor's guilt extends far beyond Vietnam veterans—to veterans of other wars, to survivors who have lost loved ones in accidents or natural disasters, and to many others who have experienced the traumatic loss of those they love or respect.

SYMPTOMS EXPERIENCED BY SOME VIETNAM VETERANS

Both Mr. W and Mr. X exhibited a number of problems and symptoms commonly experienced by Vietnam veterans. At times these problems and symptoms present in a clinical cluster that is generally labeled post-traumatic stress disorder (American Psychiatric Association, 1994; Koenen et al., 2003; Scott, 1992). It would be abnormal for Vietnam veterans not to be upset about the way they were treated, both during and after the war. Some of the common problems found when a Vietnam veteran is suffering from post-traumatic stress response are anesthesia, rage, anxiety, depression, substance abuse, intrusive thoughts, and flashback experiences.

Anesthesia

Many Vietnam veterans suffering from PTSD appear cold, distant, detached, and uninvolved. This generally results from the veteran's attempt to repress and suppress painful memories and feelings and to maintain a sense of personal control. Many Vietnam veterans report that they fear these feelings because expression of these feelings is frightening and unpredictable. (Tick, 2005). The veteran's attempt to control and numb these feelings has the negative effect of disrupting meaning awareness. Through the process of suppressing feelings and painful memories, veterans also suppress opportunities to discover and experience meanings hidden in the painful feelings and memories of their experience in Vietnam (Lantz & Greenlee, 1990a; Lantz & Gregoire, 2000a).

Rage

Intense feelings of anger and rage are often experienced by veterans affected by PTSD. Often such feelings are directed toward authority figures such as politicians, helpers, and military officials. Many Vietnam veterans believe they have been treated with profound disrespect by their former commanding officers, by our country, and by their communities. Such feelings of rage sometimes serve as a screening device, in that if the helper and/or authority figure is not frightened away by the veteran's rage, there is a chance that the helper will be able to handle and accept the terror and horror embedded in the veteran's memories of the war (Lantz & Gregoire, 2000a; O'Brien, 1998)

Anxiety

Vietnam veterans with PTSD often act in a hypervigilant way (Lantz, 1991a, 1991b), scanning their environment and avoiding crowded public areas. Both open and confined spaces can be a source of anxiety for many veterans, who sometimes prefer to keep their backs to a solid object, such as a corner or a wall. Such hypervigilant behaviors are often described as pathological by psychotherapists and social workers who have not served in a war, but not by police officers who have experienced personal threat or harm. Hypervigilant behaviors often seem very understandable to social workers and nurses who have personally experienced war.

Depression

Depression is a very common symptom experienced by many Vietnam veterans suffering from PTSD. Classic manifestations of depression such as psychomotor retardation, sleep disturbances, appetite disturbances, concentration problems, and suicidal ideation are frequently experienced by Vietnam veterans. Such symptoms of depression often rush in to fill an existential vacuum when veterans have not been able to discover and experience a sense of meaning in their experiences in Vietnam (Lantz, 1993; Lantz & Greenlee, 1990b).

Intrusive Thoughts and Flashbacks

Traumatic memories of Vietnam often intrude into the consciousness of the veteran, both at night and during the day (O'Brien, 1998). At times such intrusive thoughts are connected with intrusive imagery. Such thoughts and imagery may trigger anxiety, frustration, sadness, and/or rage and are often themselves triggered by stimuli that remind veterans of Vietnam. Loud noises, blood, camouflage clothing (i.e., hunting shirts), airplane noises, helicopter noises, and even rainy weather may all be potent stimuli triggering painful memories and intrusive imagery for the Vietnam veteran. Williams (1983) and Tick (1989, 2005) suggest that such intrusive thoughts and imagery often provide opportunities for veterans to discover and experience a sense of meaning in their experiences in Vietnam, and that the process of helping the veteran to talk out these memories can result in an enhanced level of meaning potential awareness. Such helpful existential reflection will not occur until the veteran trusts that the listener will not run away from his or her horrible memories and emotional pain.

Substance Abuse

Some Vietnam veterans suffering with PTSD escape terrifying memories through the use of alcohol and drugs (Lantz, 1991a, 1991b; O'Brien, 1998). At times drugs and alcohol are used by the veteran to control the emptiness and pain that can fill the existential-meaning vacuum. Although substance abuse does help the Vietnam veteran to control his or her pain initially, this self-medicating strategy also disrupts meaning awareness and promotes depression. The social worker who successfully helps the Vietnam veteran to stop abusing drugs and alcohol must be willing to empathically share the pain that will then emerge (Lantz & Greenlee, 1990a; Lifton, 1973; Lindy, 1988).

Mrs. Y: Army Nurse

Mrs. Y requested help in January 1980, because she had been drinking heavily since becoming engaged. She had been an army nurse stationed in Vietnam for eighteen months in 1969–1970. At that time she was twenty-two years old. Working in emergency surgery in an army surgical hospital, she had toiled extremely long hours to save the lives of severely wounded American soldiers. She reported that she had learned to tolerate the "blood and gore" by "building a wall" and "becoming numb."

Mrs. Y did not volunteer for a second tour of duty. She left the army to return to civilian life and to work as a stepdown surgical nurse in a large midwestern hospital. In this job, she was expected once again to make life-and-death decisions and to function adequately in a crisis situation. She reported that her ability to "go numb" and to "build a wall" again served her well.

Mrs. Y reported that she had lived an organized, systematic, lonely, and emotion-free life until she met Mr. Y in 1979. According to her, Mr. Y "broke down my wall, and I started to feel." Soon she started having flashback experiences where she saw "bloody and broken bodies" just before falling asleep. She also started drinking in order to fall asleep.

In this clinical situation, a twenty-two-year-old Vietnam veteran nurse exposed to the terrible gore and death of Vietnam had learned to handle the terror of the situation by building a wall and going numb. Her "wall of numbness" protected her from the pain of her experiences in Vietnam but also kept her from experiencing a sense of meaning and purpose in the valuable job she had done saving American lives during her time in Vietnam. When she fell in love with Mr. Y, she felt the need to grieve "the young men I lost in Vietnam." Her relationship with Mr. Y forced her to bring down her wall and to reexperience both the pain and meaning she had originally repressed in Vietnam.

The existential helping process was followed in this case. The social worker focused upon facilitating Mrs. Y's recovery of meaning (existential realization) through the process of holding. First, Mrs. Y was encouraged to tell the things she had seen, smelled, feared, and touched in the war. Helping her hold up her experiences for remembering and reexperiencing involved linking her with other veterans who could offer empathy and support in addition to the empathetic availability of the worker (cleansing and control). During conjoint sessions, Mrs. and Mr. Y learned to communicate in a more open and honest way, which represented the cross-cultural curative factor of control for both of them. Viewing their roles as defined by their culture, and interpreting these understandings together, increased their control over their interactions and reduced conflict. At the end of six years—not a brief encounter—Mrs. Y terminated social work intervention one year after the birth of her son, and two years after her last flashback experience. She was finally able to honor her experiences as she honored her image of herself as a nurse who had helped others, who felt their pain, and who now remembers that time in perspective with her worldview and with meaning potentials in her world.

SUMMARY

The experience of living in the world—that is, being in the world—represents a holistic orientation to understanding one's existence in society, in family, and personally. One's worldview encompasses the need to have understanding and trust in the world and is a lens for constructing an image of cultural reality in the world. The ultimate questions in life—"Who am I?" "Where am I?" "What's wrong?" "What's the remedy?"—are answered from one's personal worldview (Walsh & Middleton, 1984).

Worldview respect is the most important cross-cultural factor in gaining cultural competence as a social work practitioner. Anthropologists and experienced cross-cultural social work practitioners consistently point out that nonmedical, verbal, or psychosocial healing does not work unless the healing methods used are compatible with the client's worldview (Frankl, 1973; Jilek, 1982; Lantz, 2004; Lantz & Pegram, 1989).

Cross-cultural social work practice with Vietnam veterans should be directed toward helping them discover a sense of meaning and purpose in both their future and their past. Such a developing sense of purpose and meaning shrinks the symptoms that develop in the existential-meaning vacuum. Existential realization, cleansing experiences, control, and worldview respect are four cross-cultural social work curative factors that are often especially helpful to Vietnam veterans in their personal search for meaning and purpose in life (Lantz, 1990, 1993; Lantz & Greenlee, 1990a). The process of existential helping facilitates the telling of trauma and loss of meaning-making opportunities and provides an opportunity to hold up the trauma pain where it can be empathically supported. Mastering the trauma helps the remembered trauma experience to lose its ability to inflict renewed pain and suffering and helps veterans find ways to honor their experiences of a war whose lack of sanction from the nation tested their sense of hope and worldview respect.

9

Asian American Clients

According to census reports, the number of Asian and Pacific Islander Americans in the United States totaled 10.24 million, or 3.6 percent of the total U.S. population, in 2000. Subgroups represented in this population are Chinese Americans (23.4 percent); Filipino Americans, (18.5 percent); Asian Indian Americans (16.6 percent); Vietnamese Americans (10.7 percent); Korean Americans (10.7 percent); Japanese Americans (7.8 percent); and smaller populations from Hawaii, Guam, Samoa, and other places (12.5 percent). Another 1.7 million people identified themselves as Asian American in combination with another race, resulting in a total maximum population of 11.9 million people, 4.2 percent of the U.S. population. The Asian American population has increased by 72 percent since the 1990 census, a large increase compared with the total population growth of 13 percent in the United States for the same period. Projected to grow by another 8 million people by 2020, Asian and Pacific Islander Americans live mostly in metropolitan areas, with heavy concentrations in Hawaii and California (Schwartz, 2003–2004).

Asian origin refers to native origins from the Far East, Southeast Asia, or the Indian subcontinent. Asia includes 30 percent of the global land mass and about 60 percent of the global population. Attempting to generalize about this large and diverse population is certainly unwise. According to Inouye (cited in Leung & Cheung, 2001), Asian populations consist of at least "twenty-three ethnic groups with thirty-two linguistic groups and more than one hundred dialects" (p. 426). Personal interactions, cultural beliefs and practices, and etiquette are just as diverse as language among Asian people. Religious and philosophical beliefs are influenced by Confucianism, Buddhism, Taoism, and Hinduism. Animism and Shamanism are also religious influences for many (Culture-Sensitive Health Care, 2000; Tan & Dong, 2000).

The literature highlights some of the religious beliefs. For example, Buddhism teaches meditation, transcendence of the self, and acceptance over desire. Taoists teach interconnectedness of body, spirit, and psyche along with nature. Hinduism embraces the ancient traditions of the spiritual worlds of gods and goddesses, reincarnation, and individual responsibility on earth. Adherents of Animism practice rituals and symbolic sacrifices for both good and evil spirits. Shamanism teaches that spirit worlds and human worlds are linked so closely that the balance and counterbalance of all things are critical to human existence as well as that of the universe. This scope of religions produces a rich landscape of beliefs and practices that adds to the mix of cross-cultural diversity in the Asian population.

Asian religions and philosophies teach their adherents to live life in moderation; carry themselves with proper conduct; give gifts of care, love, and recognition; respect authority; and place great value on ancestors and family heritage (Culture-Sensitive Health Care, 2000; Tan & Dong, 2000; Zane, Morton, Chu, & Lin, 2004). Founded on non-Judeo-Christian beliefs, the Asian culture introduced the concepts of yin and yang—the cold and warm, dark and bright—the balance and harmony of all things in the larger cosmos.

Spiritual and cultural beliefs influence perceptions of health, illness, and healing for Asian people. Spiritual healers or shamans are important to personal well-being in the holistic image of mind, body, and spirit. Indigenous healers and ethnomedical practices represent healing and wellness for many, particularly those in isolated regions and others who lack resources or access to medical care. Various beliefs and practices are spread throughout this vastly diverse population. Ethnomedicine involves the use of rituals, herbs, and home remedies. The practices of coining and cupping use the application of hot, oily coins or hot cups to the skin to draw out sources of illness or fever. Home remedies and folk medicine practices in the Asian culture involve traditional rituals of ancestral worship, ceremonies and rubbing practices to remove evil spirits, and a plethora of ointments and tonics made of herbs and various animal excrements and products. While some families continue to rely on traditional remedies for various illnesses, modern and acculturated families tend to seek Western medical care (Borum, 2005; Chung, 1996; Culture-Sensitive Health Care, 2000; Jintrawet & Harrigan, 2003).

Confucianism influences spiritual beliefs and practices. Ceremonies and rituals in respect of ancestors fit in with teachings that subordinate the importance of the self to that of family and family heritage. Ancestral worship honors those who are deceased as well as elderly family members who may remain in their native country. Ancestral worship links Asian beliefs and practices such as beliefs in life after death and reincarnation with religion. One example of an Asian custom unfamiliar to many Western social workers and other helping professionals is the display of offerings of flowers and food on alters in homes and sometimes in family businesses. These offerings are in honor of deceased family members who now watch over the living. Asian cultural groups typically value family honor, dignity, meditation, experience in life, wisdom, and honor. Family hierarchies or levels of membership in families and family enterprises are important structures of authority and subordination (Berg & Jaya, 1993; De Shazer, 1991).

CONSIDERATIONS FOR PRACTICE WITH ASIAN AMERICAN CLIENTS

Asian beliefs and values need to be understood by the social worker if intervention is to be helpful to people of Eastern origin. Providing counseling and delivering other social services to the large and vastly diverse population of Asian Americans call for great appreciation of cultural values and beliefs as well as the cultural and ethnic diversity of this population. Competent practice requires attention to cultural values and individual pride. Explaining the purpose of social services and/or mental health intervention to individuals and their family support systems is a valued service. Two important principles for successful social work practice with Asian American clients are (1) the clinician's understanding of the concept of family in the Asian culture, in which family support is often critical to utilization of care, and (2) the importance of building on strengths of individuals and their family systems rather than approaching intervention from a deficit perspective (Leung & Cheung, 2001). Respecting the values of pride and honor, essential components of the Asian worldview, is critically important to culturally competent practice with Asian Americans.

Asian populations have immigrated for centuries. Many Asian Americans are generations removed from their immigrant ancestors. It is important to take into account when working with Asian American clients that family histories of Asian immigrants may span seven generations or so. The longer a group's history of immigration, the longer it takes for acculturation and assimilation processes to occur. It takes time to adapt to a new culture and to overcome barriers such as language, confusion about nonverbal communication, and different standards of etiquette for meeting, greeting, and leaving people. Eager to maintain their honor and privacy, Asian Americans are often reluctant to seek help for personal, economic, and emotional problems.

Asian Americans tend to underutilize social work, mental health, and counseling services. Asian American clients do request social work and mental health services, but seeking professional help is not usually the first option chosen to relieve stress and emotional pain. When confronted with the manifestation of emotional problems or psychiatric symptoms, Asian American people often feel shamed and are reluctant to seek social services or counseling. Transforming emotional distress into presenting problems of physical distress and seeking help for the physical distress is more acceptable (Hesselbrock & Parks, 2001; Kung, 2003; Sue, 1994; Sue & Sue, 2003). Workers familiar with Asian Americans know that reframing problems positively helps Asian American clients save face and retain a sense of dignity. For many Asian Americans, great emotional distress comes from feeling shame or dishonor instead of guilt, a reaction likely to be atypical of other American clients (Berg & Jaya, 1993).

From a Western perspective, providing services for emotional and psychological problems to Asian populations is further complicated by various ethnic practices and beliefs in the healing powers of herbal remedies, shamans, and various ethnomedical practices. The wholeness of being, or the incorporation of interconnectedness of body, spirit, and psyche along with nature, can be baffling concepts for practitioners who are unfamiliar with the Asian worldview perspective—much less homeopathic and ethnomedical approaches.

Social workers who wish to facilitate an acceptance of service opportunities among Asian American groups must have a basic understanding of the values, beliefs, and practices of various ethnic and cultural groups. Asian American families are like many other families yet unique in their own way. Families of Asian origin are typically patriarchal, show respect for intergenerational members, and have concern for the future lives of family members and the role they will have in the family. Valuing dignity and honor, children learn many lessons through nonverbal and indirect means such as symbolism and modeling by their elders. Social agencies have stronger capacities to serve Asian Americans at the present time than ever before in the history of service delivery. Even as they become increasingly aware of the broad diversity of beliefs and experiences, social workers and other professionals sometimes fail to distinguish individual qualities from the amalgam identified only as Asian American. Enhancing benefits from social and human services for this population requires culturally sensitive approaches to individual experiences as well as culturally competent approaches to intervention.

There are numerous ethnic subgroups represented in the Asian American population. Languages, religions, cultural beliefs, native histories, geographic locations, histories of immigration, and experiences of cultural assimilation vary within each of these groups. Korean Americans, Japanese Americans, Chinese Americans, and Southeast Asian populations are presented here along with considerations for helping and intervening from a cross-cultural perspective. This chapter presents a brief background of each subgroup as well as various beliefs and historical events thought to be useful in informing culturally competent approaches to intervention.

KOREAN AMERICANS

Korean immigrants first arrived in the United States around the turn of the twentieth century. Like many other Asian immigrants, they worked as laborers on sugar cane and pineapple plantations in Hawaii. For the most part young male farmers had left some family behind. Prohibited from marrying white women, many early immigrants lived lonely, isolated lives in anticipation of bringing loved ones to America. Exploited by anti-Asian discrimination, this first wave of laborers was unable to return to their country of origin. Over the next two decades, only about 2,000 Koreans were allowed to immigrate. A small number of Korean brides, students, and political exiles joined this first wave. The second wave began in 1951 after the Korean War, when about 20,000 war brides, war orphans, students, and adopted children arrived on American shores. Physical abuse, suicide, divorce, and domestic violence were experienced by many who came in this wave. The Immigration Act of 1965 brought a third wave of Korean immigrants to the ballooning American labor market. Better educated and economically oriented, this group joined those who had preceded them. Changes in immigration laws again limited additional immigration after 1976. A small number of Koreans joined relatives who had arrived earlier and had gained naturalized citizenship status (Healey, 2003; Kim, 2004; Min, 1988; Sohng & Song, 2004). As a result of immigration and American births, Korean Americans now total 1.1 million (U.S. Census Bureau, 2000b).

An ethnic and racial minority, Korean Americans encountered discrimination and hostility as they worked to make a living through their skills and entrepreneurial abilities. By establishing and operating their own small businesses, many Korean Americans gained independence and economic success. Despite hard work and economic independence, Korean Americans lacked acceptance and struggled with language barriers. In addition to cultural confusion, they experienced exclusion by the cultural majority. Caught in the struggles of minority ghettos and racially mixed neighborhoods, Korean entrepreneurs encountered hostility from White and African-American populations. Constrained to a middle minority role, Korean Americans had to cope with discrimination and racism (Healey, 2003; Sohng & Song, 2004).

Korean Americans tend to seek others of similar ethnicity with compatible interests, professions, or religious associations or who enjoy similar leisure activities (Johnston, 2000; Min, 1988). Koreatown, the large Korean community in California, is replete with storefronts, buying and trading activities, and ethnic foods and accoutrements. Korean homes, schools, stores, and churches fill this highly populated ethnic community that is part of Los Angeles. While representative of Korean culture, Koreatown is atypical of the way in which most Koreans live. Having a relatively recent history of immigration to the United States, Korean immigrants find familiar language, customs, and a welcoming point of entry in Koreatown. Having somewhat insular boundaries, this ethnic enclave is in the midst of multicultural populations in a city that leads the nation in diversity.

Forces behind the successful entrepreneurship found among Korean Americans include values of independence, self-sufficiency, and education. Valuing education as a means to success, Korean families stress learning and often provide after-school tutoring for their children. Students take extra classes in preparation for competitions and for admission to advanced academic programs. The Korean language is vastly different from English and is a barrier for some. First-generation immigrants and those who speak only Korean at home have the greatest difficulty with language. Community groups and church groups often provide help with language skills. Korean families are often involved in church and community and share commonalities and provide mutual support for each other.

Religion is an important factor in Korean families and communities. Many Korean Americans utilize culturally sanctioned ethnomedical cures such as herbal remedies and various rituals. Age-old religious practices carried out by shamans are part of Korea's ancient history and continue to inform health beliefs and practices, particularly for ordinary maladies. Following Shamanism, Buddhist monks spread Buddhism throughout much of China and Korea with the result that Buddhism had become the predominant religion by about 600 AD. It was not until the seventeenth century that Christian missionaries established a new religion that would become the dominant religion. By the 1960s, many Korean immigrants were involved in the Methodist religion, as the church offered resettlement services and social support. Many Koreans attend Korean-speaking congregations. About half of Koreans and 75 percent of Korean Americans are Protestant (Hertig, 2002; PBS, 2005; Kim, 2004).

There are five categories of social relationships outlining duties and obligations of each individual in society that reflect Confucian teachings. These categories are social relations between (1) parents and children, (2) king and subjects, (3) husband and wife, (4) older children and younger children, and (5) friends. Rules defining hierarchies and subordination for both personal and political realms include expectations of proper conduct and decorum. These rules and sanctions partially explain the reserve and demeanor of many Koreans and other Asians populations sometimes referred to as model minorities. This label portrays Asian Americans as having succeeded through hard work and merit but is a superficial compliment said to obscure racial discrimination in both public and private life. Placing emphasis on work and self-sufficiency, labels such as "model minority" really serve to hide oppression and social injustices (PBS, 2005; Locke, 1992; Sohng & Song, 2004).

Traditional Korean culture and Confucian philosophy continue to be strong influences for many. More a philosophy than an organized religion, the Confucian philosophy of life is concerned with life in this world rather than life after death. Confucianism offers many principles for living that are directed toward the development of harmonious social relationships. The philosophy of Confucianism is especially important for understanding the Korean American family, as three of the five social relationship categories involve the family. Confucius emphasized a clear role differentiation between husband and wife, and this principle has led to a system of patriarchy in the general Korean culture. The husband is considered the breadwinner and decision maker in the family and has authority over his wife and children. Although Confucius taught that parents and children should treat each other with benevolence, in the Korean culture this has often been understood to mean that children should demonstrate deep respect and obedience toward their parents. As a result, the traditional Korean family encourages respect and compliance with parental authority throughout a person's life (Min, 1988).

Each Korean American family is in a different stage of transition and assimilation, ranging from the conventional, paternalistic, and authoritarian Korean family to a more Americanized and egalitarian nuclear family. If the Korean American client family is a traditional Korean family, there may be a clash of values between old family values and the more liberal values and attitudes of younger Korean Americans. Such a clash may reduce the Korean American family's opportunities to utilize existing services for family growth and development. The family-centered Korean client may find seeking help outside the family to be extremely difficult and may evidence shame and guilt for publicly discussing personal problems. It is rare for the presenting problem to be the problem of greatest importance for Korean clients. Informal dominant cultural practices are typically approached with a sense of mistrust and unfamiliarity. Trust, respect, and positive regard are all extremely important in building relationships with Korean Americans (Kim & Sung, 2000; Lee & Saul, 1987; Locke, 1992).

Korean American families experience intergenerational conflicts in their assimilation processes. The self-esteem and cultural identity of first-generation immigrants involve ethnic pride and respect for traditional practices. For example, in traditional Korean culture, sons are considered more valuable than daughters, and older children have more authority and power than younger children (Min, 1988). More removed from their cultural roots, second- and third-generation Korean Americans may experience greater isolation, identity confusion, and even rejection of their ethnicity. Younger Korean Americans value authority differently and have adopted American gender roles, according to which spouses are employed, and their work and contributions to the family are valued more equally. Authority, language, and gender roles are stressful for many families. In family-owned businesses, influences of Confucian ideology are seen in family roles, where values of subordination place the husband at the head of the family and as the predominant public relations officer for the business. Women represent "family labor," often without pay, recognition, or economic value (Lee, 2004). Achieving economic independence, continuing assimilation processes, and coping with subordination practices can produce disharmony and sometimes domestic violence among Korean American families. More egalitarian families are less likely to experience violence, but cultural beliefs and practices change slowly (Kim & Sung, 2000).

The Korean concept of *haan* signifies suffering and tragedy associated with life. Intrapsychic processes store painful experiences in the contexts of family, society, and culture. Transforming pain and suffering in order to overcome struggles has four stages: fermenting, reflecting, disentangling, and emptying painful memories (Sohng & Song, 2004). These stages are similar to the four existential helping elements of holding, telling, mastering, and honoring. Sharing one's pain in the safety of the helping relationship facilitates exploration while creating opportunities for new realities. Social workers and other helping professionals facilitate this process through dialogue in which the client's voice becomes directive and the helping professional becomes a partner or "co-participant" (Sohng & Song, 2004).

Working cross-culturally in a co-participant role requires the worker to enable minority clients to tell their stories in narrative, providing an account of their experiences of pain and joy through their own voices, songs, and stories. Empowering and free from cultural bias, narrative processing occurs in dialogue and is egalitarian. Narrative processing provides an opportunity for the client to explore meaning opportunities and find meaning in daily life. Narrative accounts provide a unique opportunity, a new lens from which to peruse another's worldview. In other words, narrative stories help the worker or helping professional better understand the meaning of cross-cultural curative factors in the context of another's worldview. Narratives in the voice of a minority culture client are a lens for the worker to better understand another's culturally informed worldview and the cross-cultural curative factors of hope, helper attractiveness, control, rites of initiation, cleansing experiences, existential realization, and physical intervention.

JAPANESE AMERICANS

The population of Japanese Americans totals nearly 800,000, or about 8 percent of the Asian American population, according to the 2000 census. One of twenty-five categories of groups in the Asian American population, Japanese Americans comprise the sixth-largest group of Asian Americans (Barnes & Bennett, 2002). Escaping unstable economic and social conditions and avoiding Japanese military service, a small number of Japanese immigrants arrived in the United States in 1869. Their numbers grew to about 150 by 1880, when immigration began to increase, and early immigrants often came to work on sugar plantations in Hawaii. Japanese immigrants found employment in occupations that called for hard work, little capital, and a minimal ability to speak English. They worked in agriculture, canneries, fishing and logging camps, and gold and other mineral mines (Healey, 2003; The History of Japanese Immigration, 2000; Kitano, 1988).

By 1908, pressure from labor unions, politicians, and white supremacist organizations brought an informal end to immigration. At the same time, first-generation immigrants, the Issei, were permitted to bring their wives and children, but additional immigration of men was prohibited. Those who were not married turned to their homeland to find wives and were assisted by relatives and friends in Japan or Hawaii. It was common for a bride to be selected through an exchange of photographs. This practice was called finding a "picture bride." Family and kin were closely involved in all steps of marriage, and it was a rare Issei who married without parental approval. Japanese and Japanese Americans viewed Japanese society as one large family in which family norms were reinforced by the ethnic community. In this patriarchal family form, the family's property and power were inherited by the eldest son. Family customs and family celebrations were strongly valued. Truthfulness, simplicity, and principles such as living with few material possessions continue to be important. Living peacefully with a focus on family is also commonly valued. Shintoism was the state religion until World War II, when interest in Christianity grew. Many Japanese accepted Buddhism, but the greatest influence comes from Shinto, the Japanese religion that reveres a number of deities and celebrates nature, land, goodness, and the material world (McDowell & Stewart, 1996).

Having great reverence for culture, their worldview, and life experiences, Issei Japanese Americans taught the next generation about their heritage. The second generation, the Nisei, learned to value family, duty, and loyalty to family and society. Hierarchical family structures placed the male at the head of his family and gave the eldest son responsibility for ancestors. Males were placed higher than females in the hierarchy of the family, and it was important for the wife to respect her husband. Many of the Nisei were eventually able to obtain a good education and to hold onto their Japanese traditions while adapting to the culture of the United States. These early generations experienced racism as well as few social and economic opportunities. The biggest change between the Issei and Nisei generations occurred in marital and family life. The Nisei manifested a belief in choice in the selection of a spouse, romantic love, conjugal bonds over filial bonds, greater equality between the sexes, and greater communication between spouses. Nisei Japanese Americans have achieved high socioeconomic success and have acculturated quickly (Kitano, 1988; Tomaine, 1991).

The most difficult chapter in the history of the Japanese American experience is that of internment, when the Nisei, as well as same first-generation Japanese Americans, were forced to live in concentration camps while America was at war with Japan. Living and working in communities along the Pacific Coast, this concentration of Japanese Americans would be "relocated" shortly after the onset of World War II. Close to 120,000 Japanese were forced from their homes and incarcerated in prison camps behind barbed wires, where guards maintained watch. Internment lasted throughout the war. The newer ways of the Nisei and the third-generation Sansei replaced the traditional social fabric of the Issei. While Japanese Americans were destined to become educated, professional, and successful as a group, the devastation, humiliation, and disenfranchisement of the internment camps can never be forgotten (Fugita & Fernandes, 2004; Tong, 2004).

Imprisonment represents a loss of honor and, for many, the public display of such loss is only further embarrassment. Izumi (2005) notes that Japanese Americans "broke the silence and narrated their historical plight in public" in support of the repeal of Title II, the Emergency Detention Act of the Internal Security Act of 1950. President Richard Nixon signed the repeal of Title II in 1971. This act authorized the government to detain anyone suspected of being a threat to internal security. The 1988 Civil Liberties Act signed into law by President Ronald Reagan made an official apology and restitution of $20,000 to each surviving internee. The first payment was made in 1990 to a 107-year-old camp survivor (PBS, 1999).

Third- and fourth-generation Japanese Americans, the Sansei and Yonsei, are Americanized. Some hold onto the traditions and customs of their ethnic heritage; others do not. Not unlike many other Americans, Japanese Americans value family and avoid displaying their feelings and family problems to those outside the family. For Japanese American families, maintaining privacy from the external world allows them to avoid bringing shame to the family. Arts, education, and economic success are important, as is reflected by their achievement and self-sufficiency. Modesty, restraint, sensitivity, and status in family, caste, class, and gender are powerful influences for many. Age-old traditions in Japan have changed along with political and social changes. After World War II, equal inheritance replaced primogeniture, inheritance to the firstborn (i.e., first-born male). Societal change and acculturation contribute to each generation being more responsible for its own care (Kameoka, 2005).

Social work and other helping interventions with Japanese Americans require a great deal of understanding of their culture, their life experiences, practical and useful assistance, recognition of their heritage, and discussion and exchange of information and solutions for problem solving. As in any other cross-cultural counseling situations, first, counselors and social workers must be aware of their own values and beliefs. Next, it is imperative to have an understanding of the client's cultural background. In working with Japanese Americans, knowing the client and family history of immigration will clarify generational identity. Also, information about internment experiences of the client or of family members is essential. Responses to this devastating event in the history of Japanese Americans range from denial to frustration to intense anger and feelings of disbelief and humiliation.

A common belief among helping professions is that Asian Americans seek counseling reluctantly, if at all. Many traditional beliefs and practices have changed for younger generations. Kamoeoka (2005) finds that influences of *sekentei* reflect decreasing caregiving for elderly ancestors by their younger relatives. *Sekentei* is defined as society and community, and *tei* refers to social appearance or dignity. In other words, many families are providing for elderly relatives in order to avoid public shame and community embarrassment instead of from an absolute sense of duty to protect the family honor. Using caregivers outside the family is frowned upon by many. At the same time, the suicide rate among Japanese elderly is the second highest in the world and is highest for those who live alone. Control of one's existence, and existential realization of one's life are issues that reflect deep cross-cultural beliefs and diversity.

Age-old beliefs such as loyalty to the emperor are unfamiliar to many social workers and counselors who lack a background in Asian history. Nevertheless, competent cross-cultural practice requires attention to the history and location of people in the world, whether in their country of native origin or elsewhere. Without resorting to stereotypes, it seems safe to say that Asian Americans hold great pride and personal dignity. Westerners sometimes interpret such personal pride and dignity as reserved, distant, or even aloof responses by people of Asian heritage. These responses must be understood in the context of cross-cultural influences. At times reserved, politeness calls for the social worker to use indirect or nonverbal cues. Social workers who respond only from their own Western worldviews may discount Asian American worldviews, causing the existential helping process to lose credibility and the social worker to lose attractiveness as a helper. Western solutions to the problems of non-Western clients have the potential to be disjointed and meaningless (Henkin, 1985). Curative factors such as hope, helper attractiveness, control, and avenues for intervention, whether physical or emotional, are culturally informed. In the Asian American experience, these factors are unique to individual and collective Eastern roots.

Dr. U: A Japanese American Woman

Close to her deceased son's birthday, an elderly Japanese American woman with a doctorate degree in the humanities consulted a social worker. Dr. U explained that she had a question to ask. She explained that she had few people to talk with, as she had no living relatives left in either America or Japan.

Shy about telling her personal story, Dr. U accepted encouragement to talk about her son. "You see," she said, "it's been many years since he ran and played in the sunshine, and I'm just an old woman now. I was such a young widow, and he was my only child." As she told of her son, her countenance softened, and warm memories of love and caring came through in the telling of her loss.

Encouraged to explore her feelings of loss, she talked of her son's illnesses—asthma, bronchial pneumonia, and lingering allergies. "We were interred during the war. Yes, the Japanese internment camps killed my son. The cold, the filth, and the vermin in the buildings started his illness. He was only eleven when he died."

Empathic availability helped Dr. U to hold her trauma pain from her loss and to re-experience her anger and feelings of helplessness, as well as her embarrassment at being betrayed by her country. She said that sometimes she dreamed about her son and that the one thing that always came to her in the dream was the stories she told him about what America was like. She asked if visiting the national monuments in Washington, D.C., on her son's birthday would be a good thing to do, or just an old woman's crazy wish.

Dr. U came to counseling upon the recommendation of a friend who knew that she had been experiencing sleeplessness over the past few months. Respect for Dr. U's worldview was conveyed through patience, reserve, and polite explanations of services. Probing and direct questions were not a part of the initial sessions. Respecting Dr. U's wishes for reassurance about the confidentiality and privacy of her visit contributed to the worker's attractiveness as a helper. Putting memories of her family first, Dr. U focused only on her wish to sleep better and thought that talking about her son would help her relax and find restful sleep. The process of intervention focused upon helping Dr. U to tell, hold, master, and honor the trauma pain that had resulted from her experiences in the internment camp and the loss of her only son.

Helping Dr. U hold her trauma pain required the worker to also hold the pain and hold Dr. U so that she could emotionally remember and reexperience her trauma pain. This concept is likely best understood as empathetic availability, the committed presence of the worker to the client (Lantz, 2000b). Providing empathy and support for the client requires that the worker not lose sight of the focus inherent in the existential helping process yet feel the pain in bits and pieces. Holding the trauma pain of the death of her son uncovered Dr. U's self-blame as to whether or not she had done enough. Having suffered in silence for so long, Dr. U responded tearfully to the empathic acceptance and respect for her suffering.

Moving into the second phase of telling, the worker became more direct in confronting the humiliation and anger that the internment camp produced for Dr. U. During her month of sessions with the social worker, Dr. U told of her own suffering in the prison camp and of her futile efforts to obtain good food and medical help for her son, who was sickly. She talked of being with him and comforting him with stories of things to come. She sang about his father, lost at sea, and of grandparents far away in Japan and surely frightened by the war. She tearfully expressed these losses that she had borne alone for forty years. She revealed her fear that she may not have done enough. She remembered when she would fall asleep only to be awakened by her son's raspy breathing—but the night that he died she did not wake up. Getting in touch with her anger about victimization, disenfranchisement, and inability to take her child to a specialist, Dr. U told of the overwhelming helplessness she had felt. Telling was a cleansing experience as trauma pain was revisited and unloaded, and a new sense of direction and responsibility emerged.

Dr. U was able to master her trauma experiences. She felt "whole again" and in touch with her inner strength and worldview (existential realization). She recognized that while she had no control over her son's illness and death, she now has control over her happiness and how she remembers her loved ones.

From the beginning, Dr. U had a desire to honor her son. She came to counseling partially to explain her intention to visit national monuments as a way to honor her son, but she was not in touch with the meaning opportunity counseling could hold for her. Her plans and emotional energy were fragmented. The worker used this opportunity to help Dr. U find a sense of meaning and purpose through the transformation of her trauma experiences. Dr. U found comfort in revisiting how hard she tried to help her son get well. His death was not her fault.

In the case of Dr. U, survivors' guilt emerged from her helplessness to save her son's life. According to Frankl (1959), his experiences as a prisoner in Nazi concentration camps taught him that survivors of great traumas or near-death experiences can transform survivor guilt into survivor responsibility. In this fourth stage, honoring, Dr. U found meaning in life and new meaning opportunities. Her plan to visit national monuments could be the beginning of finding ways to honor her son and to commemorate her own suffering. She exclaimed that she wasn't a "crazy old woman after all!" She would indeed visit all the monuments in the nation's capital and leave the largest wreath that she could carry in the most public spot that she could find in the National Cemetery in memory of her son and of the nation's reparation and apology for the internment camps.

CHINESE AMERICANS

It likely that Chinese people have lived in North America since before the Common Era. Immigration began as Chinese immigrants joined the Gold Rush of the 1800s. Immigration and births now account for 2,734,841 Chinese-Americans living in the United States, the largest Asian-American population reported in the 2000 census (Barnes & Bennett, 2002). Distant shores promised jobs and a better life. Early waves of male immigrants experienced great hardships. Many found jobs in farming, irrigation, railroads, and searching for gold as the frontier pushed westward. Violence and discrimination against the Chinese eventually ensued. As opium smoking spread, Chinese were blamed for having brought this practice with them and corrupting others. Additional immigration was prohibited by the Chinese Exclusion Act in 1882, eased somewhat after World War II, then opened again in the 1960s (Healey, 2003; Hesselbrock & Parks, 2001).

Immigration was difficult, and Chinese men vastly outnumbered women in the United States well into the twentieth century. Industrious Chinese suffered many hardships as a minority with their own race, ethnicity, and language. Chinatowns became tightly structured ethnic enclaves providing safety and exclusion in large cities such as San Francisco and New York. Support networks for jobs, housing, education, and language development connected people. The label of the model minority evolved in the absence of information, as these isolated enclaves provided an economic system for ambitious workers, shelter from sharing daily hardships with mainstream society, and protection for the strong values of family and honor. For example, the stories of trans-Pacific marriages, mail-order brides, and wide age disparities of many couples are mostly untold. Pressures of acculturation along with discrimination placed additional stress on many families. While sparsely reported, domestic violence was endured by many women who sought to avoid bringing shame to the family or risking deportation due to disobedience to their husbands (Yick, 2000).

Like all people, Chinese Americans reflect the ethnic beliefs and practices of their life experiences. Following the philosophy of Confucianism, ethical and moral practices characterize many traditional Chinese families in their relationships at home and at work. Beliefs regarding ancestral spirits, various gods, and eternal life were influenced by Buddhist and Taoist religions, which, although mixed with Christianity to some extent, are still represented in many Chinese celebrations and holidays. Influenced by Confucianism, traditional Chinese families practice family honor and respect for their ancestors, sometimes teaching through moralizing and shaming so that younger generations preserve the family honor. Traditional Chinese families include immediate family members and extended kinship group and clan members. Men hold power in these families and women are relegated to subordinate positions and are expected to obey their husbands and their husbands' parents. Following patriarchal beliefs, a married couple may live with the husband's family. Traditional practices and values are mostly evident among first-generation families and perhaps their children, who strictly follow traditional principles.

In the People's Republic of China, Communism replaced Confucianism from 1949 to 1979. Values of community and achievement gradually replaced values of family and the individual (Fong & Wu, 1996). Long-held values such as hard work and obedience fit easily into the new sociopolitical context for many Chinese. Nevertheless, shifting to valuing the state as supreme was costly to long-held Chinese beliefs and traditions. Immigrants who experienced this believed in production for the general welfare of everyone.

Beginning in the 1920s and 1930s, a sizable second generation of Chinese Americans started small family businesses such as laundries, grocery stores, restaurants, and other small enterprises. Being labor intensive, all family members put in very long hours in family businesses (Wong, 1988). There was no clear demarcation between work and family life for these families. Kinship and hard work were strongly valued, and independent children were viewed as ungrateful.

Carrying the family name and providing for their ancestors are responsibilities of sons for immigrants from this period. Being virtuous, bearing children, and socializing boys and girls are the responsibilities of daughters. Boys are to be nurtured closely by mothers into their teen years, when fathers assume the responsibility to help their sons become men who can honor their duties (Fong & Wu, 1996). Wives and children are more highly valued and hold a higher level of status in the family than they do in traditional Chinese families.

With its population exceeding sustainability, sociopolitical prescriptions began to change in China. In the later 1970s, the single-child policy returned the focus of the family to the child and away from the state. The focus of all family members on the only child elevates the child and places value on the family.

Acculturated fourth- and fifth-generation Chinese American families tend to look like most Americans—adults are employed or work in family-owned businesses. Child care is augmented by day care, preschool, or other babysitting arrangements. Many Chinese Americans live in a major Chinese community, such as Chinatown in New York City or San Francisco. Chinese Americans have experienced many successes; yet, for some, employment in low-wage jobs and poor housing are daily realities.

Healey (2003) notes that structural assimilation has been somewhat more open for the Asian population than other minorities of color. The segregation of African and Hispanic Americans had extremely detrimental impacts on these groups. Healey identified education as a major factor in the success of second and later generations of Chinese Americans in America's social and economic systems. Being enterprising and in the labor market are markers of achievement and success. However, the question is for whom is this Chinese American model intended? Takaki (1993) raises the question of labels such as "success," "model," and "superior" for the

Chinese American minority. Are labels about the age-old values of family, honor, hard work, thrift, and self-sufficiency a warning for other adversity yet to come?

While it is hard to gain an in-depth exploration of any single culture, it is imperative that consideration be given to the social and political cultural experiences of others. For Chinese Americans who hold traditional values, being a client is likely a foreign and unwelcome event. In the twenty-first century, such traditional clients are undoubtedly elderly and likely to have more than one generation of American-born descendants.

The time and place of a person's socialization shape that person's beliefs and values and form his or her worldview. While some components of traditional beliefs and values can be transferred to offspring, the reality of social environments and peer experiences is very different for second-generation offspring in an immigrant family. Knowing whether Chinese American clients have roots in traditional China, in a more progressive China, or in a Chinese American family is essential to understanding their diversity. Cross-cultural curative factors such as control, worldview (including religion and gender roles), and hope for the future and into old age through time-honored practices of dignity and ancestor respect are critical to entering into a helping relationship. The curative factor of helper attractiveness is reflected in greater acceptance of physical healers and potions than of counselors and psychiatrists.

Understanding the extent of Chinese American acculturation is important in understanding the importance of structure and emotional restraints among traditional Chinese, who are best approached formally and logically. The existential perspective calls for the counselor to be empathetically available and to respect the client's worldview. Existential intervention does not require clients to change their frame of reference or call for workers to attempt to force worldview or frame of reference changes. Instead, clients are helped to tell their stories and share their traumas, hold experiences for exploration, master their pain, and honor their experiences in the context of their values, beliefs, cultural experiences, and worldview.

SOUTHEAST ASIAN AMERICANS

Southeast Asia includes Cambodia, Indonesia, the Lao People's Democratic Republic, Malaysia, Myanmar, Philippines, Singapore, Thailand, and Vietnam. In the 1960s, numerous Southeast Asian refugees began to flee their home countries for political and socioeconomic reasons. Having numerous ethnic, racial, religious, and language differences, Southeast Asians are vastly diverse. These people have a long and rich connection to Chinese and Thai influences and to the various religions of the Eastern world. Experiences, history, beliefs, language, and education are remarkably varied. For example, the Hmong come mostly from southern China and northern Vietnam and Laos. They developed their written language as recently as the mid-1900s. Laotians are influenced by Buddhism, speak several tribal languages and dialects, migrated from China before recorded time, and have prosecuted Christians. Khmer influences can be observed in Cambodian art, music, dance, and language, and in the Buddhist religion.

Vietnam is a multilingual country that has struggled for independence. Vietnam was controlled by China, France, and Japan before going to war with the United States. The capital city of Saigon fell in 1975. Communist control by North Vietnam receded as recently as 1991 (Interknowledge Corp., 2005). Vietnamese Americans represent the largest group of Southeast Asian refugees in the United States, now with about 1,123,000 people (Barnes & Bennett, 2002).

Southeast Asian people are survivors of many severe traumas including political repression and governmental harassment. Many have been threatened, beaten, and tormented in reeducation camps. They have witnessed loved ones being killed and have faced death themselves. Numerous losses of loved ones, homeland, status, identity, previous lifestyle, religious beliefs, self-esteem, supporting networks, and affectional ties have resulted in lasting trauma. Guilt as a result of leaving their homeland and family members and friends behind continues to torment some who escaped just to survive. In addition to these losses, many Southeast Asian refugees have also experienced near-death situations due to inadequate food and water on refugee boats and in refugee camps. They have experienced tension and conflicts with other refugees and with authorities. Rapes, persecutions, and witnessing others killed during attempted escapes are not uncommon (Barkan, 1995; Bromley, 1987; Tobin & Freidman, 1983; Zaharlick, 2000).

After experiencing great hardship, emotional distress, and extreme anxiety about their future, many Southeast Asian refugees had high expectations of a better life. They arrived in the United States only to discover further problems brought about by processes of resettlement. These refugees faced not only the stress of adapting to American ways but also basic survival issues such as inadequate housing, financial hardships, and unemployment. Other issues in the resettlement of Southeast Asians include survivors' guilt and a sense of responsibility to rescue family members left behind. Problems of roles and responsibilities emerged as intergenerational conflicts arose in response to acculturation. Age and gender differences as well as social misunderstandings between the refugees and members of the dominant culture contributed to other problems. Dislocation and resettlement have been extremely traumatic experiences for many Southeast Asian refugees (Weiss, 1989; Zaharlick, 2000).

Cumulative traumas of war, flight, persecution, refugee camps, and resettlement contribute to Southeast Asians' vulnerability for mental health problems and psychiatric difficulties. Many resettling Southeast Asian refugees have been reported to be suffering from acute anxiety, major depression, paranoia, insomnia, recurring nightmares, intrusive thoughts, anorexia and weight loss, loss of memory and concentration, headaches, emotional numbing, conscious avoidance of memories of the past, suicidal thoughts, alienation, social disorganization, and social isolation. Constellations of such symptoms are often experienced by Southeast Asian refugees. Some authorities suggest that these cases should not be classified according to their dominant symptom, but as a malady reflective of the problem constellation—trauma syndrome, survivor syndrome, or stress response syndrome (Lantz, 2001; Lantz & Greenlee, 1990a; Lantz & Lantz, 1991).

There have also been reports of sudden death syndrome among Southeast Asian refugees in the United States (Tobin & Freidman, 1983). Sudden death syndrome has been reported among apparently healthy male refugees who went to bed feeling well, only to die suddenly in their sleep with no probable cause of death established by the autopsies. In many of these cases shortness of breath or labored breathing, screams, and tossing in bed immediately preceded death. These sudden deaths may be unconscious suicide triggered by a loss of self-respect and the will to live. Such speculation is based on the fact that many Southeast Asian refugees tend to express their trauma and survivors' guilt in nightmares of spiritual attack, the physiological effects of which are similar to the symptoms preceding death, such as shortness or loss of breath. That is to say, many of those who reported nightmares of spiritual attack are possible survivors of sudden death syndrome. This may explain why sudden death syndrome occurs almost exclusively in male refugees. Southeast Asian men are susceptible to such feelings of guilt, since in their culture it is the man's role to protect his family and homeland (McQuade, 1989). It should be noted that a lack of sensitivity in the host culture to the emotional conflict experienced by resettling refugees can also intensify feelings of loss and guilt. It is not uncommon for Southeast Asian refugees to perceive resettlement problems as a form of punishment for their survival and escape.

In examining the life experiences of Southeast Asian refugees, social work practitioners should look at problematic events before, during, and after resettlement. These could include the horrors of war; brutal persecution under a ruthless regime; physical assaults and threats to life; the loss of one's country, family, and friends; danger and constant fear of capture during escape; anxiety about the future; tension and fear in the internment camps; and the intense cultural confusion experienced in resettlement in the United States. The traumatic experiences of these hazardous events may trigger a disruption in the refugees' most familiar ways of discovering and experiencing meaning, producing a meaning vacuum that is often filled by psychiatric symptoms (Lantz & Gregoire, 2000a; Lantz & Lantz, 2001). For many Southeast Asian refugees, problems in the here and now could precipitate repressed emotional pain about trauma and terror in the past. For example, loss of a job may remind an individual of past losses of family, status, homeland, social supports, and lifestyle. News, newspaper articles, and even movies about wars or the refugee's home country may stimulate the recall of past events that could result in the manifestation of flashback symptoms. Letters from relatives left behind or still in refugee camps and news of family and friends may prompt memories, flashbacks, or feelings of fear, guilt, and shame. Communication barriers and cultural conflicts in the

United States produce misunderstandings, which may in turn, trigger a sense of rejection, social withdrawal, depression, or anxiety attacks (Lantz & Lantz, 1991).

Mr. I: A Cambodian Refugee

Mr. I was referred to a community mental health social worker for clinical services by his sponsoring American host family and by his caseworker at a local resettlement agency. At the time, he was working as a waiter in an Asian restaurant and was attending night school to improve his English. He was referred because he was experiencing anxiety attacks and night terrors. He had expressed thoughts of suicide to both his caseworker and his host family. Mr. I had gone to a different mental health center six months earlier, but stopped going because he felt that the mental health worker at that center did not understand his problems, which had since worsened. Mr. I, who had come to the United States after escaping from Cambodia, had lost his father, mother, wife, and son in a Khmer Rouge work camp prior to his escape and did not know whether his two brothers were alive. Mr. I lived in a refugee camp for three years before coming to the United States.

Mr. I expressed the belief that he had no right to be alive. Since his family had been killed, he too should be dead. He was unable to see his good fortune in surviving, since all the people he loved had not survived. Mr. I said that he had stopped going to the previous mental health center because the worker could not understand "why I am bad and evil." Mr. I reported that he wanted to find a reason to stay alive, but had little hope that such a reason could be found.

Understanding the importance of symbolism and the significance of family in the Vietnamese culture, the worker encouraged Mr. I to tell his story. Using narrative format as the medium, he revisited experiences from his culture that explained his worldview as stories of his life and his pain emerged in his meaning-seeking voyage. As his life unfolded in the telling of his narrative, the worker helped Mr. I reflect on his own words and explore his description of anxiety and depression. Although quite painful at times, holding and telling his pain was therapeutic. Mr. I's life narrative provided a powerful opportunity for empathetic acknowledgment of his pain as well as his strengths.

Mr. I recognized his pain as a response to his war experiences, the loss of his family, and his harrowing experiences as a refugee. Telling his trauma pain through narration was consistent with narrative therapy (Goldenberg & Goldenberg, 2005; White, 1995). Postmodern in its potential for deconstruction as a client confronts meanings and realities in his or her stories, the "essence" of experiences is real and facilitates existential realization in the discovery of meaning and meaning potentials in life. As discussed earlier in chapter 3, approaching treatment from a philosophy of essence allows for creativity and expression of personal strengths (Lantz & Raiz, 2004). The existential perspective places responsibility for change on the client. A man of many strengths, Mr. I's worldview held his Asian and American cultures. The cross-cultural curative factor of hope for the future was particularly important for Mr. I. It follows that intervention can be increasingly helpful as Mr. I gains more functional behaviors and problem-solving capacities.

Holding, telling, and mastering were used to help Mr. I discover and experience a number of meaningful opportunities in his life. Although the mental health worker did not agree with Mr. I that life was meaningless, the worker did agree that Mr. I's continued existence probably depended upon discovering meaningful activities, goals, and tasks that he could do to honor his dead family, ancestors, and friends. Mr. I accepted that his life could have meaning if he found a way to give to the world in honor of his dead family, friends, and ancestors (honoring).

Mr. I continued meeting with the social worker for some time. The worker used holding and telling activities to help Mr. I find a sense of meaning and purpose in life and in his survival despite the tragedy, trauma, and terror he had experienced. He made excellent progress in counseling. After starting to see his social worker, Mr. I became a citizen of the United States, opened his own restaurant, and sponsored numerous other Southeast Asian refugees as they came to the United States. At termination the social worker gave Mr. I the following poem. It reflects how he transformed the tragedies in his life and discovered a sense of meaning and purpose.

He Came from Cambodia

He came from Cambodia
and works sixteen hours a day
seven days a week,
every week
in his Oriental restaurant
that pays his bills
and lets him save enough
to bring another here
from the camp he came through
after escaping the holocaust and the Khmer Rouge.
Each one he brings is a holy prayer
for dead relatives
and ancient ancestors
he has to leave behind.

At the start of social work intervention, Mr. I had no hope that the social worker might help. His previous experiences had confirmed his belief that his worldview could not be understood by a White social work practitioner. Mr. I believed that the mental health workers (both the first and the second) were not capable of relating to his guilt about his family and leaving Cambodia. Mr. I was surprised that the second social work practitioner understood his guilt and had experienced the horror of the Vietnam War. The poem "He Came from Cambodia" enhanced existential reflection, a cross-cultural factor. Written for Mr. I, the poem facilitated existential reflection, hope, and a sense of purity or cleansing. Honoring Mr. I's worldview through existential elements of holding, telling, and mastering served to increase his sense of self-worth and being in the world. Mr. I was most pleased that he could find a way to give to the world in honor of his dead family members and the country he had to leave behind (honoring).

SUMMARY

Asian Americans have generally tried to maintain their social structure and culture with a minimum of visible conflict with the host society. Many have tolerated racism, discrimination, and prejudice from the dominant culture without voicing great protest. The quiet response that Asian Americans have often given to discrimination has been used by the dominant cultural group to minimize the need to provide services to the Asian American client. Social work intervention and other forms of social services are not easily accepted by Asian Americans, as their heritage calls for self-reliance, modesty, and dignity. Allowing outsiders, even professionals, to intervene in personal concerns continues to be an uncomfortable experience.

The influences of age-old principles rooted in Confucian philosophy, Buddhism, Shintoism, and other ethnic religions are unfamiliar to many non-Asian professionals who do not have an understanding of Asian history. Nevertheless, competent cross-cultural practice requires attention to the time and place of people in the world. Asian Americans have great pride and dignity. Counselors and social workers often struggle to communicate understanding when counseling Asian people who are polite, sometimes indirect, and sometimes nonverbal.

The social work profession has been accused of underattention to ethnic minorities, particularly Asians (Kim, 1995). The dominant-culture social work practitioner may have problems accepting that Asian American clients sometimes express emotional and psychosocial problems through somatic complaints (Kung, 2003). Many social work practitioners have difficulty working with Asian American clients because they fail to understand that admitting to an emotional problem may be a "loss of face" (Lee & Saul, 1987; Sue & Sue, 2003). The extent of family structure, self-control, and avoidance of shame is culturally unique to the Asian culture and poorly understood by most social workers. Western social workers do not interpret shame as being associated with not fulfilling social responsibilities. On the other hand, Eastern cultures do not relate feelings of shame to failure and to oneself in debasing terms quite the way many other cultures do.

Fundamental skills needed to work with Asian clients are effective listening, empathy, accepting the client's worldview and view of distress, developing goals that take into account the client's level of acculturation, and understanding the Asian client's environmental situation. It is important to understand the level of discrimination and racism that Asian Americans experience in the United States today. Kim

(1995) calls for professional recognition of the importance of reaching out to Asian Americans, who have historically not received social services. The importance of becoming culturally competent cannot be overstressed, as it is only through increased knowledge and cross-cultural networks that a majority culture social worker can enter into the meaning world of a minority culture client.

10

Migrating and Appalachian Clients

HUMAN MIGRATION IS LIKELY AS OLD AS THE CONTINENTS AND DENOTES movement of people from one location to another, sometimes nearby and sometimes much farther away. Early nomadic tribes moved with their crops in response to seasonal changes, as they lived off their efforts in planting, harvesting, hunting, and fishing. While twenty-first-century animals continue to migrate for survival in response to seasonal changes, humans generally migrate and resettle in response to political, economic, religious, and military pressures.

Although sometimes used interchangeably, the words "migrate," "emigrate," and "immigrate" have distinctively different meanings. People and animals migrate as they move from one place to another for periods of time, sometimes permanently. Only people immigrate or emigrate. The word "immigrate" places emphasis on entering another political entity or moving to a new place or country across political boundaries in hopes of establishing new residence or attaining citizenship. "Emigrate" refers to moving away from one's native place or country and crossing political boundaries in search of residence or citizenship in another place or country. Undoubtedly, voluntary migration is less stressful than having to relocate due to social or economic pressures. People who emigrate from their native country to seek immigrant status in a different country are likely to suffer the greatest stress and trauma, particularly when relocation is in response to war, famine, environmental disasters, or political and religious pressures.

Whether forced out of their native countries or leaving voluntarily in search of new opportunities, ethnic and racial groups encounter challenges of grief, loss, and stress. They experience different values and language, new standards of "normal" behavior, and pressure of acculturation. Having left familiar people and places, immigrants most often experience poverty and economic hardship upon relocation. They frequently are in need of social service assistance for resources such as food, clothing, shelter, and help with resettlement (Fong, 2004; Leon & Dziegielewski, 1999; Potocky-Tripodi, 2002). Additionally, clients may suffer considerable pain, frustration, and anomic depression in reaction to their relocation. Anomie and anomic depression are forms of depression that occur in reaction to a sense of meaninglessness, sometimes called an existential or meaning vacuum (Krill, 1976; Lantz & Gyamerah, 2002b).

CONFUSION OF RESETTLEMENT FOR IMMIGRANT AND MIGRANT CLIENTS

Viktor Frankl named these feelings of meaninglessness, purposelessness, and emptiness in life an existential vacuum. An existential vacuum generally occurs in reaction to a disruption in a person's ability to experience a sense of meaning in life. An existential vacuum is often characterized by feelings of defeat, lowered self-esteem, discouragement, and, at times, moral disorientation (Frankl, 1959; Lantz, 1993, 2002; Lantz & Harper, 1990). This vacuum or "hole" in meaning awareness, if left empty or filled with negatives, has the power to result in feelings of futility and doom that can obscure the future.

A psychiatrist and existential philosopher who experienced the deportation of Jewish people to concentration camps during the Holocaust, Frankl recognized the entirety of human existence. The loss of his family, his deportation, and his eventual confinement in concentration camps contributed to his understanding and naming of the existential vacuum. Frankl identified cultural confusion, sociocultural disintegration, and periods of rapid change as forces that contribute to loss of meaning and a potential meaning vacuum in life. Having meaning in life and looking to the future are essential for human survival, a phenomenon that he recognized among concentration camp survivors (Frankl, 1997b).

Existential frustration and meaning disruption are not simply stressors or problems of adjustment in direct response to relocation. Instead, cross-cultural relocation produces stress in response to changes in fundamental social supports and processes of one's ethnic background, language, values, access to basic resources such as food and shelter, and culturally determined definitions of what is normal and abnormal. Social work literature holds that stress is culturally relative and that "understanding ethnic differences" is essential to understanding individual responses to stressors encountered upon migration (Dubois & Miley, 2005; Fong, 2004; Lum, 2004; Potocky-Tripodi, 2002; Weaver, 1999). Different ethnic minority groups evidence varying responses to changes in daily practices and normative behaviors in experiences of cross-cultural relocation. While many ethnic minority group members experience relocation with relatively minor adjustment difficulties, others experience moderate to severe distress and disruption in their lives. Such negative responses can include somatic distress, emotional distress, suicide, and deep depression. The commonly held view of stress recognizes the pain and distress that are often experienced in cross-cultural relocation but does not address the great vulnerability for meaning disruption and loss of potential to discover meaning. Many who encounter new standards and normative behaviors in a different cultural context experience confusion and loss of meaning in life.

For example, uprooted populations such as Puerto Ricans, Vietnamese, and

Mexican Americans have experienced great stress in response to relocation. Adjustment and assimilation demands following relocation are major stressors for migrating populations. Puerto Ricans have suffered discrimination and devaluation in the United States even though they hold citizenship. Acculturation varies greatly among Mexican Americans, who continue to flow into the southwestern United States, thus keeping alive strong ethnic ties to those left behind. Cultural conflicts, particularly those around values related to the centrality of extended family members, and community bonds produce serious stress and disrupt meaning in life (Gloria, Ruiz, & Castillo, 2004; Mayo, 1997; Sue & Sue, 2003). In the case of relocated Vietnamese, there have been great adjustment problems relating to language, religion, and racial prejudice. Vietnamese have experienced great stress in their cross-cultural resettlement. Having fled their country and encountered hatred upon migration, Vietnamese migrants have experienced serious loss and depression (Barkan, 1995; Zaharlick, 2000). Despite the stress associated with discrimination and exploitation, many immigrants from both of these minority groups have grown to experience acculturation and upward mobility even in the presence of great emotional strain (Healey, 2003; Potocky-Tripodi, 2002).

Although an existential vacuum occurs frequently during times of migration, it can also occur in other situations that disrupt the person's ability to discover, experience, and perceive a sense of meaning and purpose in life. Any situation that disrupts meaning awareness is fertile soil for the occurrence of an anomic existential vacuum (Lantz, 2000b, 2000d; Lantz & Harper, 1990). The following clinical illustrations are typical examples of an existential vacuum experienced by people who are migrating to a new place and a new life.

The M Family from Japan

The M family moved to the Midwest from Japan so Mr. M could remain employed with a Japanese manufacturing company that was opening an assembly plant in the United States. He was one of a group of Japanese managers chosen to plan and open the new plant. Mr. M spoke English, but his wife and three children spoke only Japanese. Approximately three months after their arrival in the United States, Mrs. M twisted and dislocated her eldest son's shoulder and then attempted suicide. Fortunately, her suicide attempt failed, and she was admitted to a psychiatric hospital. In her initial counseling session, she reported to the translator and other staff that she felt empty and alone and that her life had seemed meaningless since she had come to America. She reported that her husband worked twelve hours a day and she was alone in a strange new country without friends, extended family, or support. She had not discovered a place to worship in her traditional manner and did not understand American ways. She said she had attempted to end her life because she felt useless and without hope. Mr. M reported that Mrs. M had never exhibited symptoms of depression in the past and had never before hurt the children.

The N Family from Puerto Rico

Mr. and Mrs. N came to the mental health center because Mrs. N was upset and depressed and had been picking on their two young children. Upon questioning, it became clear that this "picking on" was more clearly described as hitting and slapping. The N family had originally moved from Puerto Rico to New York City and then to the Midwest. Mrs. N reported that her children had been getting on her nerves since the move to the Midwest. Mr. N reported that his wife had never before hit the children. Mrs. N stated that she could find no Spanish-speaking people in the new city and that she wanted to return to New York. She felt uncomfortable at church, as it was an Irish and Italian Catholic church. Mrs. N reported that at times she had received help in New York from a spiritualist, but now she could not find one. She reported feeling empty, as if her life had no meaning or purpose.

The examples of the M and N families reflect the loss of identity and feelings of anomie so often experienced by families who relocate across political or cultural boundaries. Immigration and resettlement of migrants throughout the nation have been and continue to be the heart and soul of our multicultural world. The freedom to move in search of whatever—jobs, space, retirement villas, freedom from political oppression, or to join family members—contributes to the discovery of meaning and meaning opportunities in life.

APPALACHIA: MIGRATION IN AND OUT OF THE MOUNTAINS

Moving the frontier westward, settlers came into the Appalachian Mountains with little more than what their broken-down wagons could hold, often after not finding work in towns and cities along the eastern shores. The influx and influence of immigrants would produce a depository of ethnic and racial diversity that would remake a nation. The Scots-Irish, who arrived in the 1700s, were soon followed by the Germans, Swiss, and English. They were soon joined by Italians, Hungarians, and Greeks. Men of all ethnic backgrounds and races worked on railroads and in coal mines in the Appalachian mountains in the 1800s (Olson, 2004). Understanding the enormous changes of the 1800s along the eastern seaboard, in the South, and in the Appalachian mountains is necessary to understand America.

By the end of the 1800s, as many as 4.6 million Europeans and 900,000 African slaves had entered the United States (Healey, 2003; Park Ethnography Program, 2006). Many settled in the eastern cities, but others pushed the frontier westward, some remaining in Appalachia and others crossing the mountains on their quest for territory and wealth. A depository of diversity, Appalachia would eventually be characterized by storytelling, Celtic music, and folklore; by caricatures of hillbillies and country bumpkins; and by unrelenting poverty misunderstood by the nation as evidence of a lifestyle of uneducated and backwards people.

The politically constructed geographic region of the United States that is known as Appalachia has been called the first and last American frontier (Evans, George-Warren, & Santelli, 2004). Occupied by indigenous people as early as 8000 BC, the region reflects the cultural influence of numerous Native American tribes, particularly the Cherokee, Shawnee, Choctaw, Delaware, Seneca, Mingo, Chickasaw, and Creek. By the 1700s there was a steady flow of European immigrants into the Appalachian Mountains, particularly Scots-Irish, German, and Swiss population groups. African Americans could enter the United States only as chattel (Biggers, 2005). Present almost as long as White settlers, African Americans and Whites worked alongside each other. The Appalachians and the South would be the scenes of fierce Civil War battles, emancipation, and even part of the civil rights movements of the 1960s.

The region proved to hold formidable barriers for wagons and people, including steep terrain and inclement weather. Despite strong resistance and numerous battles between immigrants and indigenous people, the settlers had few choices but to continue in their struggle to establish homesteads and clear land that had been home to the many Native American tribes. Deep valleys, nearly vertical mountainsides, noisy creeks, rushing rivers, rich coal seams, and virgin forests held economic opportunities that would reach into the next millennium and extend far beyond the expectation of early settlers. Lying close to the nation's eastern shores, Appalachia was an American frontier. The mix of Native Americans and immigrants produced bloodshed, intermarriage, illegal whiskey, Civil War heroes, and the brotherhood of coal miners. Generations later, their rich folklore and music continue to reach worlds far beyond the mountain ranges.

The Appalachian Region

Twenty-three million people live in the Appalachian region, a roughly 200,000 square-mile area that covers parts of twelve states and the entirety of West Virginia. The region encompasses 410 counties, and about 42 percent of the population live in rural towns and remote areas (Appalachian Regional Commission, 2006). Extending from Georgia to New York, Appalachia has four distinct subregions. Northern Appalachia reaches from New York into West Virginia and Ohio. This section of Appalachia had its early economic base in steel, coal, and railroad transportation. The Appalachian Highlands include parts of Pennsylvania and Maryland and reaches as far south as South Carolina and Georgia. Associated with stereotypes of mountaineers, the highlands are characterized by folklore, ethnic foods, and country music, particularly string music such as fiddles and dulcimers. Southern Appalachia extends from Virginia through the Carolinas and into Alabama. This area is characterized by the ethnic heritage of the Ozark subculture. Central Appalachia consists of sixty contiguous counties in Virginia, West Virginia, Kentucky, and Tennessee. President Kennedy described this subregion as having poverty and lack of opportunity that made it not so different from third-world countries. Central Appalachia has gained worldwide interest from media stories of mountaineers, miners, and desperately poor families (Harper & Greenlee, 1989). Their covers displaying the hollow faces of Appalachian families and children, magazines in the 1960s marketed stories of poverty, malnutrition, and dangerous work in the extractive industries of coal and timber.

Appalachian Out-Migration in Search of Livelihood

It is estimated that seven million people migrated from Appalachia between 1940 and 1990 (Ergood & Kuhre, 1991; Obermiller & Maloney, 1991). Appalachian migrants began moving to the automotive industrial centers as early as the 1920s, eventually dominating some auto assembly factories in Michigan and Ohio. Since 1980, the speed of Appalachian migration has decreased. The destination of most migration has changed from north to southwest, and to far southern regions of the country (Lantz & Harper, 1989). For example, Cincinnati, Ohio, is known for its large Appalachian community, in which moderately secure families live a little above poverty levels. In-migration has slowed, yet research concerning migrant families in this urban city is still being conducted (Obermiller & Howe, 2000).

According to the Appalachian Regional Commission (2006), net in-migration for the entire region was only 400,000 million people for the period 1995–2000. While 2.1 million people moved in, 1.7 million people moved out. One effect of continuing migration is that the region has a higher-than-average elderly population. The state of West Virginia leads the nation in its proportion of frail elderly. Furthermore, out-migration mostly involves young adults and their families moving away from the region in search of employment and leaving behind a population with a higher-than-ordinary representation of elderly, disabled, and uneducated people.

The continuing pattern of Appalachian migration has resulted in the development of Appalachian urban neighborhoods in sections of cities throughout Ohio as well as in Chicago; Detroit; Pittsburgh; and Gary, Indiana. Often such neighborhoods become crowded low-income ghettoes where Appalachian poverty, inability to access urban resources, and orientation to familiar persons and rural places challenge urban human services, educational systems, and medical professionals. When low-income Appalachian people move to the city, they often discover that they have exchanged rural poverty and unemployment for urban poverty and unemployment (Obermiller & Howe, 2000).

The flight from rural to urban poverty often creates a disruption in meaning awareness for migrating Appalachians. Such a disruption in meaning awareness is a result of poverty, migration, and loss of a supporting kinship network in the life of the Appalachian migrant. Disruptions of meaning awareness and sense of anomie are often followed by a variety of problems and emotional symptoms that Appalachian clients often call "nerves" (Lantz, 1992a; Lantz & Harper, 1989, 1990, 1992).

Appalachia in the New Millennium

Contemporary Appalachia is now much more diversified in industry, agriculture, service industries, retail businesses, tourism, education, and more technological and safer coal mining than it once was. Overall, per capita income is about 20 percent below the national average, still behind but catching up. Broad strategic planning goals through 2010 are to foster civic entrepreneurship, strengthen human capital for global competition, improve regional infrastructure, and continue to develop the region's highway system (Appalachian Regional Commission, 2006). These goals target the need for capacity building and economic sustainability, a vision that is helping to bring Appalachia into mainstream America. Hopefully this can be accomplished without sacrificing the region's multicultural mix of music, language, food, values, and worldview.

Appalachia's history of human and economic exploitation and environmental devastation is chronicled in the work of Harry Caudill (1963), who provides an account of the development of the region as well as its endemic poverty and politics. The purchase by out-of-state coal companies of mineral rights to the homesteads of poor Appalachian families, some of whom were illiterate and unable to understand the economic losses they would incur in selling all but their surface land, resulted in generations of labor and poor safety standards as the companies exported coal and timber from the region and returned little in the way of taxes and nothing in terms of land restoration. Accounts of coal mine wars and battles between coal companies and unions are all part of the history of the region. Perhaps the disservice that Caudill and writers like Jack Weller did to the region was representing the culture as backwards, uneducated, and in need of newcomers to enrich the gene pool of a region where generations of the same family live and reproduce. While calling for assimilation, Caudill presented a dismal picture of the region, depicting an oppressed population as a people without motivation and little to no education. Contributing to stereotypes of isolated mountaineers, Weller's portrayal of fatalistic Appalachian people generally disregards the diversity within the region (Billings, 1999; Caudill, 1963; Weller, 1965).

Social and economic oppression contributes to rural Appalachian poverty stemming from large absentee financial and industrial corporations' control of land and resources. History shows that the Appalachian people have experienced a series of disasters and exploitations, from the pillage of Appalachian forests by outsiders in the 1800s and strip mining in the 1950s and 1960s to the fall of oil prices and resulting unemployment during the 1980s. War and terrorism in the early years of the new millennium brought a global energy crisis, along with renewed interest in mining and a flurry of mining accidents. Live news coverage of the 2006 Sago mine disaster, which cost the lives of twelve coal miners in West Virginia, reached audiences around the world. Despite these hardships, Appalachia is clearly in the midst of economic development, technological changes, and environmental restoration at the present time.

Cross-Cultural Social Work with Appalachian Clients

The ecological approach to social work practice focuses on transactions between people and their environment. Individuals and families living in rural communities, many of whom live off their labor on the land and in forests and coal mines, are in touch with their environment. Small towns and rural areas throughout the region are natural niches for face-to-face transactions, and newcomers are noticed and approached somewhat guardedly. In these communities work is physical; poverty is endemic; and payments from public welfare, unemployment compensation, and disability insurance are common. Social work intervention with Appalachian individuals, families, and communities calls for awareness of people's worldviews and of their histories of migration. Culturally competent practice in the region allows for the application of various approaches to counseling and intervention, including the ecological and existential perspectives.

An understanding and appreciation of the history of Appalachia provide a lens for viewing human needs and shaping helpful intervention. Regional folklore survives as tales of the life and times of mountain families continue to be shared with younger generations. Played on stringed and often handmade instruments, homespun musical verse tells of love, pain, loss, and human endeavors. Arts and crafts highlight the region's beauty. The holdings of local bookstores and libraries document the struggles of early economic ventures in natural resource industries through poetry, stories, and biographies.

While the heritage of ethnic music, literature, dialects, and storytelling in the oral tradition is still celebrated, the region is quite mainstream in modern equipment, upscale housing, fancy automobiles, telecommunications, and media. The U.S. Department of Commerce has funded projects to bring technology infrastructure and training to individuals and communities in remote rural areas, thus reducing the digital divide throughout Appalachia and other rural areas. Low-income, rural, unemployed, and previously technologically illiterate families are experiencing "digital inclusion" (Harper-Dorton & Yoon, 2002). The exchange of people between urban and rural areas has increased dramatically. Lisa Alther (1998), an international author and speaker with roots in Appalachia, tells of coalfields, Confederates, family, denial of her roots, and how her literary work brought her full circle to her roots again. The stories of Alther and other women of growing up and maturing in and from the region are as familiar as any other account of growing up American. Does Appalachia constitute an ethnic group or subculture? No, it's a place where the authors of this book, along with authors like Rick Bragg, can take our shoes off and be at home.

Developing and providing social work services for Appalachian people requires that social work providers have specific knowledge of the very special needs of this diverse group, many of whom hold traditional beliefs and maintain fundamentalist standards. Social workers must have an understanding of the values, beliefs, and lifestyles of clients who live or have lived in the Appalachian region. Developing an empathic and caring approach to social work practice with Appalachian clients requires a basic understanding of the ethos of the region, its history and development, and its socioeconomic problems (Harper, 1996, 2000a; Lantz & Harper, 1989).

Traditional Values of Appalachian People

Appalachian value systems are frequently misunderstood by middle-class non-Appalachian social workers. In order for social workers to be helpful to Appalachian families who live in rural or urban settings and hold traditional Appalachian values, it is critically important that these values be understood. Traditional values include a present orientation with fatalistic views of the future, an emphasis on action versus dialogue, and fierce protection of oneself and kin (Harper, 1996). Traditional Appalachian values and practices have long been handed down through intergenerational processes. Somewhat mediated by social class and world experiences, families living in the Appalachian region are affected by regional ethnic values and practices and often struggle with their identity in response to the culture. Some commonly held values in the region are belief in Protestant fundamentalism, beauty in nature, the importance of place, a sense of self and pride, and family and community.

Protestant fundamentalism. Local and autonomous sects grew in the early years of resettlement in the Appalachian region. These individualistic churches stressed the fundamentals of religious faith and depended only on local resources for leadership and development. Life on the Appalachian mountain frontier was extremely hard and did not encourage the development of an optimistic social gospel in the independent Appalachian churches. In Appalachia, hard work did not bring a sure reward, and Appalachian religion often became fatalistic and stressed rewards in another life. The purpose in such a religion is to reap rewards in eternity, which in the Appalachian tradition means to "accept Jesus as one's personal savior" (Jones, 1983, p. 125). This fatalistic religion was and still is one that fits a realistic people who have endured a history of poverty and hardship (Harper, 1996).

Beauty in nature. Appalachian people demonstrate a deep appreciation for nature and natural beauty and often link their sense of connection with the world around them to religious meaning. Appalachian people have a strong sense of beauty and have developed many art forms that are often called folk art by people who do not come from an Appalachian background (Lantz & Harper, 1989).

Place. The Appalachian's love of place has much to do with the kinship network and the natural rural or mountainous beauty of the Appalachian person's special place in family and home. Seeking meaning through religion and through nature, many generally respect and cherish their native birthplace and the place of their childhood. Many Appalachian people who migrate to urban areas express feelings of discomfort and loss from living in cities where the beauty of nature cannot be seen and where they feel distanced from nature (Harper & Lantz, 1992; Lantz, 1989).

Migration continues to be a two-way adventure as Appalachians maintain second residences in anticipation of return to their native communities upon retirement.

Sense of self and pride. Self-reliance, pride, and individualism are common characteristics of Appalachian people. One could not survive on the Appalachian frontier without a high degree of self-reliance and individualism. Appalachian people have a strong sense of self and a desire not to be indebted to other people. Appalachians sometimes find it hard to seek resources such as welfare aid and community-based medical care. Self-reliance among Appalachian people can be stronger than the desire to get help (Greenlee & Lantz, 1993; Jones & Brunner, 1994). Not inconsistent with self-reliance, many Appalachians are well informed about their well-being and survival in terms of health and nutrition. Appalachian people are humble and realistic in their views of themselves and find it offensive to pretend to be something other than what they are. Bragging and advocating for personal gain are frowned upon, even though there is a strong sense of pride of self, family, and home. Wit, laughter, and regional stories and jokes bring joy to many conversations. A good sense of humor can be a sustaining force during difficult times. Appalachians are quick to laugh at their own behaviors. This same humor, storytelling, and quick wit have contributed to jokes and stereotypes of the region (Biggers, 2005; Billings, 1999; Bragg, 2001; Greenlee & Lantz, 1993).

Family and community. Appalachian people share strong kinship values centered in family traditions. Family loyalty involves a sense of responsibility for each other, cousins, nephews, nieces, uncles, aunts, and even in-laws. Helping family and neighbors is strongly valued even in urban Appalachian ghetto neighborhoods, where people stick together to fight poverty, hunger, and economic deprivation. The importance of family and community supports a strong sense of patriotism. Appalachian people are typically patriotic and voluntarily serve in the armed forces. This love of country is a result of the Appalachian's love of freedom and individualism. Appalachians in military service have long been above draft quotas or expected enlistment; sometimes this is seen as a way out of poverty, and sometimes this is due to a sense of duty. When one visits an Appalachian family in their home, it is not unusual to see photographs of family members in uniform who have died in service to their country. Social workers who have a personal antiwar philosophy can quickly alienate Appalachian clients by making statements that seem unpatriotic or disrespectful to their relatives who have died in military duty.

Mountain Music, Folklore, and Folk Medicine

Appalachian talents have produced illegal moonshine whiskey; banjo strings and country music; colorful folklore involving ghosts, spirits, romance, and life hereafter; recipes fit for the finest restaurants, especially in southern tradition; and a world of literature—poetry and novels. In the oral tradition of the mountains, storytelling became an art. Tales of survival, follies of kinfolk, and metaphoric legends of spirits and salvation entertained listeners. World-famous authors from Appalachia include Pearl Buck, Harriet Arnow, James Still, Jesse Stuart, George Ella Lyons, Louise Pease, Sharyn Crumb, Wilma Dykeman, Homer Hickam, Willa Cather, Thomas Wolfe, and Rick Bragg, to name only a few. Bragg's (2003) account of Private Jessica Lynch's rescue from the Iraqi war and her hospitalization captures the spirit of the young West Virginian soldier and heroine as well as her experiences growing up in Appalachia.

Unlike literature chronicling the life and times of Appalachian people in the struggle for survival, far too many films and television programs depict only stereotypical images of hillbillies that cause the oppressed to laugh at themselves. For example, *The Beverly Hillbillies, Hee-Haw, Green Acres,* and *Li'l Abner* present characters who are country fools, some unable to adapt to "city ways," and others who are either childlike or senile (George-Warren, 2004; Mann, 2003). And then there is *Deliverance,* the infamous film that brings together the stereotypes of ethnic jokes involving trailers, teeth, outdoor toilets, and stupidity. How is it that Appalachian jokes continue to be told in public and in the media? And how is it that Appalachians do not routinely take issue with these ugly, ethnic insults?

In his *Confronting Appalachian Stereotypes,* Billings (1999), provides a scholarly account of the stereotyping of Appalachian culture in plays and in tasteless and gruesome art. He captures American culture's fascination with the image of the hillbilly and the country. Is this sheer ignorance, a pecking order schema? Regardless of the answer, concerns of social justice, oppression, advocacy, and the social work code of ethics require social workers to advocate for justice and respect the dignity of all humankind. Social services are perhaps the most widely available and most numerous services for families and children in Appalachian and other rural areas where professional services and respect for clients make a difference in the quality of everyday life.

DISRUPTION OF SOCIAL FUNCTIONING IN RESPONSE TO MIGRATION

The flight from rural poverty to urban poverty has the power to disrupt self-esteem, a sense of meaning and purpose in life, and general social functioning for the migrating Appalachian family or individual. Even when an Appalachian person does find a job in the city, he or she often loses his or her sense of kinship, place, and beauty. If the person is unable to find a job, the losses in moving to the city are compounded by the fact that he or she is no better off financially. Many migrants end up trading rural poverty for urban poverty. The Appalachian person and the Appalachian family are frequently caught in a socioeconomic double bind. If the Appalachian person does move to the city, there may be a little more economic hope; but there is often an accompanying sense of loss of support, beauty, and the kinship from back home (Lantz & Harper, 1989, 1990; Obermiller & Howe, 2000).

Appalachian individuals and families who do move to the city are seldom welcomed with open arms by city officials, police, educators, or human service professionals (Lantz & Harper, 1989). The ignorance of some urban helping professionals who view relocated Appalachian people as backward, stupid, rednecks, bumpkins, and hillbillies is amazing. It is not unusual for child welfare workers, mental health workers, and educators to model extreme disrespect for Appalachian parents in front of their children, particularly in urban Appalachian settlements. Some Appalachian people endure grinding poverty and yet have the courage to enter foreign urban territory in the hope of improving their economic circumstances.

It is evident that living within the boundaries of a nation does not connote homogeneous lifestyle or expectations. One example of the diversity of American society is evidenced by lifestyles in Appalachia. Personal and human differences within the region give people a very different worldview. It is important for social workers to provide opportunities for relocated clients to discover and experience meaning in their new sociocultural context. The following case illustration demonstrates some of the healing factors that can be helpful in social work practice with Appalachian clients.

Mr. H's Relocation to the City

Mr. H was referred for help by his family doctor on the near west side of Columbus, Ohio. The doctor believed that Mr. H was demonstrating emotional problems by focusing on minor physical problems and concerns. He believed that he was suffering from "nerves." His family doctor reported that Mr. H had been given and had kept thirty-one medical appointments in 1988 and that almost all these appointments were not necessary from a medical standpoint. Mr. H was of Appalachian heritage and had moved from West Virginia to Columbus in search of economic and financial security. He scored a 79 on the Crumbaugh and Maholick Purpose in Life Test at his second social work appointment. A score of less than 92 is considered a good indication that the client is experiencing a disruption in his or her sense of meaning and purpose in life (Crumbaugh & Maholick, 1963; Lantz, 1993).

During the initial stage of social work intervention, Mr. H missed a number of scheduled social work appointments and did not seem motivated to engage in the helping relationship. He reported that he wanted pills for his nerves and did not understand why his family doctor had referred him for counseling.

Mr. H's Relocation

A tall, thin man with sharp features, Mr. H reported that he had a decent factory job that paid well, but that he hated being in the city, "where I got a chance to make it financially." Mr. H said that he stayed at his apartment most of the time and didn't even go to church, as he was not comfortable in the city. He said that he missed a lot of work because of his nerves and had been drinking some to calm himself.

After some resistance and difficulty getting beyond Mr. H's request for something for his nerves, the social worker had him read a children's book called *Come a Tide* (Lyon, 1990). The central character is a young Appalachian woman who describes a flood and her family's problems resulting from the flood. In the story, the family home was flooded, and after the waters went down, the family members discovered that their family treasures had been buried in mud, goo, and slime. The grandmother asserted, "It's time to make friends with a shovel." The entire family started to work. The family members "dug and hauled and scrubbed and crawled" and were eventually able to find their "buried treasures."

When asked to explain the meaning of the story, Mr. H reported that he could now see that his move to the city had "flooded" his life and that "I better start digging to get it back." Mr. H reported that his frayed nerves made sense in that the "stuff that means something to me flooded out when I moved to the city." Mr. H decided that it was the social worker's job to "help me make friends with a shovel" and to "dig out a decent life in the city."

The goal of social work intervention was to help Mr. H either adjust more effectively to life in the city or decide to move back to West Virginia. Mr. H also needed to understand that his nerves were a result of his difficulty in experiencing a sense of meaning and purpose in life in the city and that in order to feel better, he would have to rediscover the meanings, values, and meaning potentials that he could actualize and create in the city.

Cross-Cultural Curative Factors and Mr. H

In working to help Mr. H, the worker did an outstanding job respecting his worldview and using the flood story to help him verbalize important themes in his worldview. The imagery of familiar places and events in the story helped Mr. H hold his sense of loss and recognize his responsibility to "dig out." The existential helping element of holding was met with resistance by Mr. H, as evidenced by his use of alcohol along with his refusal to verbalize his feelings of loss and anomie, or meaninglessness. The worker's commitment to Mr. H and ability to be empathic and available to share his pain and sense of loss provided support. The world portrayed in *To Come a Tide* provided culturally relevant imagery and gave Mr. H the words to describe his pain.

The second element of telling, an important aspect of help with Mr. H, allowed him to experience the cross-cultural curative factor of cleansing. Telling his story of the family and home that he missed, of his confusion in the city, and of his trauma pain of loss and emptiness was a moment of catharsis and an opportunity to discover meaning potentials (existential realization). During social work intervention, the worker provided many opportunities for Mr. H. to ventilate and express sadness about the losses he had experienced by moving to the city (in other words, cleansing). Mr. H named his loss of home and his fears in the city and recognized his responsibility to either go back home or work to adjust to the city.

The third existential helping element, mastery, emerged as the worker linked Mr. H with an Appalachian club at a city settlement house and with a fundamentalist church that was similar to his church back home. The worker also showed Mr. H some good fishing spots near the city where he could engage in one of his favorite activities. These activities provided Mr. H with a sense of control over his situation and hope for the future, both cross-cultural curative factors. It was important for Mr. H that the worker encouraged him to review and renew or replace his values both back home and in the city. Being helped to discover, create, and experience meaning or meaning potentials restored Mr. H's purpose in life. His life in the city began to take on new direction. Existential realization and reexperiencing familiar activities proved to be important. Mr. H came to twenty-three social work appointments over an eight-month period. At termination, Mr. H scored 123 on the Purpose in Life Test, well above the 92–111 range of vulnerability (Crumbaugh & Maholick, 1963). His family doctor reported that he was no longer making unnecessary medical appointments, and Mr. H reported that he was feeling much better and was no longer drinking to help his nerves.

Honoring, the final element in the existential helping process, emerged as Mr. H began to participate in church and fishing activities, much as he had done back home. However, this element was not fully realized during the period that Mr. H continued coming to appointments. As Mr. H acclimates to his urban life, visits family back home, celebrates his new successes, and invites family and friends to visit him, these healing processes will be more complete. Mr. H will have expanded his worldview and realized meaning potentials in his world.

REFLECTIONS ON MEANING AND MIGRATION DEPRESSION

The migration meaning vacuum is described by clients as a sense of emptiness and an inability to find meaning in life after migrating to a new geographic location. In each instance of meaning disruption, the client was separated from his or her usual methods for symbolizing and honoring meaning.

The following case illustration demonstrates many of the cross-cultural curative factors and how they can be used with a family that is experiencing a migration meaning vacuum.

The O Family's Migration Meaning Vacuum

Mr. O was brought to a mental health center emergency unit by the police after they responded to a request for help in a domestic dispute. Mr. O was intoxicated and had hit his wife with his fist. Mrs. O reported that her husband had never hit her or any other family member in the past. Beginning about three months after the family had moved to the city from the mountains of eastern Tennessee, Mr. O began to drink heavily. The family had moved to the Midwest because Mr. O's older sister had found him a factory job there.

After sobering up, Mr. O expressed considerable shame and guilt about his behavior. He said his days had no purpose, that he had problems making friends with the people at his new job, and couldn't even find a church where he felt comfortable. He missed hunting, fishing, and roaming the woods as he had done back home. He reported that in spite of his new job and economic security, he felt hollow and empty.

For some migrating clients, the meaning vacuum is triggered by the client's separation from traditional methods of religious worship. The migration meaning vacuum may result from a client's loss of contact with extended family, friends, kin, and clan. At times such a meaning vacuum is triggered by language difficulties that occur when a migrating person moves into a new culture. For other clients, a meaning vacuum is experienced in response to separation from family and recreational and cultural activities, such as walking in the hills. A migration meaning vacuum is often a reactive or crisis problem, rather than a manifestation of a characterological or long-term personality problem.

A migration meaning vacuum is a type of existential crisis triggered by a contextual event that disrupts one's meaning awareness. Clients can often overcome a reactive migration meaning vacuum when they are helped to rediscover a sense of purpose and meaning in life in their new location and new social situation (Harper & Lantz, 1992; Lantz, 2002; Lantz & Lantz, 1991). The problem generally responds well to existential methods of intervention that make an active attempt to help the family reestablish a sense of meaning and purpose in life (Lantz, 2000c).

The O family reported that the social worker's help in linking them with resources (mastery) and in showing them how to talk with each other in a more effective manner (telling) was extremely helpful. The family members reported that the social worker's questions helped them remember "what we stand for" and "what we are living for" (honoring). The father reported that his relationship with the worker helped him regain his self-respect (mastery). Mrs. O felt the worker tried hard to understand them and treat them with respect (honoring).

SUMMARY

Migrating and Appalachian clients suffer from poverty, class discrimination, and prejudice against their traditional values and norms. Immigrants and migrants move from their native culture or location into unfamiliar and even hostile places. Many Appalachian people have moved to the city to escape rural poverty only to find urban poverty replacing rural poverty. Whether it is the resettlement of a person from an entirely different culture or of an Appalachian migrant, relocation represents trauma in life. Feeling different, being poor, not speaking the language or speaking with an accent, and loss of kinship networks and supports from back home often combine to create many difficult human problems. Relocation often causes anxiety, depression, and a disruption of one's sense of meaning and purpose in life.

An existential vacuum frequently occurs during a period of migration, disrupting the minority culture client's traditional methods of discovering and experiencing meaning. This chapter described the process of such a migration meaning vacuum and offered an existential approach to social work intervention in the context of cross-cultural practice to treat this kind of problem.

11

Women Clients

WOMEN ARE DIVERSE IN MANY WAYS, INCLUDING THEIR WORLDVIEW, RACE, age, culture, experiences, and ethnicity. Understanding the situation of women in their many personal, economic, social, and cultural lives is key to comprehending each woman's worldview. Individual worldviews represent basic beliefs and personal perspectives and answer questions such as "Who am I?" What is my reality?" "What is my life?" and "What does life mean?" Each woman exercises freedom and responsibility in selecting and incorporating particular meanings and knowledge in daily living. Individual worldview is personal and unique and informed by cultural definitions and experiences in the world.

The American woman is perhaps the most diverse symbol of today's culturally pluralist world. She is well educated, economically advantaged, a professional in scientific fields, a nurse, a teacher, a physician, self-employed, a homemaker, a supervisor, worker, a single mother, or a caregiver. She is also poor and illiterate, and has never been employed. She births the nation's children. A bearer of her culture, she knows and socializes others. She knows foods, dress, values, holidays, work, folk medicine, and family roles consistent with her heritage. Despite wide personal differences, women in America share numerous experiences of gender discrimination and oppression in the social and political contexts of their lives (Harper, 1990a, 1990b, 2000a).

Brown (2006), a proponent of feminist therapy, has declared a need for culturally competent practitioners who can acknowledge the political realities of "gender, power, and social location" (p. 16) alongside experiences of power and powerlessness in daily life. The presence or absence of power is both personal and public. Powerlessness and terror have been experienced by many in catastrophes such as the terrorist attacks on the World Trade Center, Hurricane Katrina, and explosions in the Middle East, and on a much smaller scale in tragedies such as the Sago Mine disaster in West Virginia and the Columbine High School shootings. These events have increased feelings of vulnerability for everyone, but particularly for women and children, who have less power to avoid personal harm and overcome forces of violence.

Lower in status than men in nearly every society around the world, women have historically held less power than men. Over 40 percent of the global labor force is female, and women head 30 percent of the world's businesses. Nevertheless, 70 percent of all poor people in the world are women. At the beginning of the twenty-first century, women comprise 75 percent of the workforce in America. Women are paid about seventy-seven cents for each dollar paid to men in the American economy. Worldwide, it is estimated that women make about two-thirds of what men make in the global economy (International Labour Organization, 2004; Rose & Hartmann, 2004). Like their sisters who lack education and position, educated and seemingly powerful women encounter exclusion and barriers to employment, promotion, and career progress. Some women experience multiple jeopardy due to factors such as race, ethnicity, and age. The history of oppression and social injustice has been extremely severe for women with membership in one or more minority groups.

Viewing the oppression of women from a feminist orientation offers perspectives for understanding and modifying personal and social injustices done to women. Feminism is a political ideology that calls for liberation from oppression and is concerned with resisting domination and ending social injustice (Van den Bergh & Cooper, 1986). Approaching the oppression of women from political, social, and cultural spheres, feminist thought addresses the disempowerment and devaluation of women in the world. Feminist philosophy addresses the concerns not only of women, but also of those who are oppressed due to skin color, age, ethnicity, religion, and other minority membership.

FEMINIST PERSPECTIVES

Informed by existentialist philosophers such as Hegel, Husserl, Heidegger, and Sartre, Simone de Beauvoir explained that masculinity is viewed as a positive force in culture while femininity is viewed as a negative force. Historically, the patriarchy has been able to define the cultural, economic, and political statuses of women in society by relegating them to "subject" existence. Beauvoir described gender distinctions in a patriarchal social context as being misdefined and fundamental to reproduction and to identity. She saw the path to women's transcendence over domination and subjugation as requiring creativity and performance through work. Such transcendence, however, becomes a moral journey involving a new sense of being in the world. Overcoming the role of subject and discovering oneself produces a changed sense of marginality (Beauvoir, 1968; Donovan, 1987) Feminist thought has not been static but has shifted as the condition of women continues to change over time in relation to social, political, and geographic contexts.

Three major waves of women's movements reflect the social, political, and economic trends of the times. The first wave began in the nineteenth century and continued into the early twentieth century, when white women gained the right to vote in 1920 in the United States. Women's suffrage called for granting women the right to vote, not total equality. Women marched and held peaceful demonstrations from the turn of the century as they sought voting privileges. Women of color did not count; they were "nonpersons" in the days of women's suffrage. The second wave came out of the social movements of the 1960s and 1970s. The Vietnam War, anti-war movements, student demonstrations, the civil rights movement, and the women's movement were part of the scene. This second wave of feminist thought and action is familiar history to many older women today. Liberal feminism was followed by socialist feminism and radical feminism. The third wave emerged as many formerly radical feminists joined the cultural feminist movement to create a women's culture rather than transform society (Evans, 2002; Payne, 2005). Feminism is not a singular ideology but encompasses a range of viewpoints and multiple women's movements. Liberal, socialist, radical, and cultural forms of feminist theory are major streams of feminist thought that have influenced the opinions and identity of women, social policy, and social work practice with women.

Liberal Feminism

The liberal feminist perspective places importance on gender equality and opportunity for women. Injustices such as denial of opportunities and discrimination in education, employment, and participation in political and economic spheres are examples of gender inequities. Women's work in childbearing, homemaking, and caregiving is not valued as economic enterprise. Liberal feminists identify patriarchal values and traditionally male-dominated institutions as causes of female oppression and seek equal access through legal redress rather than revolutionary restructuring of the social order.

The feminist movement of the 1960s and 1970s gained the label of women's liberation. Working within social systems and processes to change values and increase gender equity is a long, slow process. Far too little attention is paid to different ways in which men and women value and understand internal and external messages. Achieving equality for any disadvantaged group is difficult when power holders are the oppressors. Many women called for equality in the social order of the 1960s and 1970s; however, there was not a united front even among women themselves. Many who remained outside the second wave were traditional women, mothers not in the workforce, and elderly women. Although the civil rights and women's movements coincided in time, early feminists have been criticized for ignoring the voices of women of color (Freeman, 1984; Gilligan, 1982).

Socialist Feminism

Socialist feminism attempts to define gender roles in contemporary society. Socialist feminists identify capitalism and patriarchy as the root causes of female oppression (Abramovitz, 1988). In the socialist feminist theoretical orientation, female oppression stems from both the capitalist class and property system and from male-dominated power relations. Class oppression and gender oppression are

interrelated spheres. The resultant division of labor is based on production (male/
public sphere) and reproduction (female/private sphere) (Eisenstein, 1984; Nes &
Iadicola, 1989).

Socialist feminists define patriarchal social relationships as excluding women
from the public sphere and restricting them to the private sphere. Women contribute unpaid labor in the private sphere, where women's roles are in childbearing,
family nurturance, and food production in support of their families. Women then
remain dependent and powerless because their productive contributions are defined as women's work by employed males, who occupy patriarchally defined social
strata within the socioeconomic class system that dominates the American scene.
Personal and political powers are not within the reach of women, who are disempowered and devalued in this context (Dominelli, 2002; Jaggar, 1983).

Poverty, disempowerment, and traditional gender-role socialization have nega-
tively affected many women and men. Few attempts have been made to understand
the mechanisms by which individuals make sense of oppressive conditions when
they choose not to revolt (Ferraro, 1983). Racial, ethnic, and class differences of oppressed groups of women reduce the distinction between private and public productivity. The socialist feminist movement has been accused of focusing more on
the victimization of middle-class women than on the victimization of other women,
particularly poor women (Abramovitz, 1988). Socialist feminism advocated to overcome oppression by establishing mutual respect between men and women by fos-
tering joint efforts of women and men to eliminate oppression, and by establishing
more androgynous roles in society.

Radical Feminism

Radical feminists call for changing the way equality is created in society.
Changing the balance of power in a patriarchal society requires drastic social up-
heaval, even revolution, in order for male power holders to relinquish some or all of
their control in a gendered society. Dignity, self-determination, and the right to a
different voice are consistent with radical feminists' efforts to bring the agenda for
gender equality into the arena of advocacy, affirmative action, and revolution, if necessary. Radical feminists called for overcoming oppressive societal forces and attitudes surrounding racial, gender, age, and ethnic discrimination (Dominelli, 2002).
The values of the 1960s carry over into social, economic, and connotative meanings
of the cliché "The personal is political."

The progression of feminist theory reflects Western social and political systems.
Radical feminists advocate the creation of a social structure in which all persons are
truly equal. Women around the globe are affected by social and political realities
that shape the social construction of gender roles aside from biological differences.
The socially defined roles of women and men are representative of their gendered
positions within their social order. Nevertheless, the nature of physiology requires

accommodation, as childbearing continues to belong to women. In a radically re-structured world, the duties of child rearing and family caregiving would be equally shared by household partners regardless of gender. Women's contributions to family and home are productive commodities that benefit economic systems, particularly capitalist systems. As radical feminists pushed forward their agenda for women, they were more successful in promoting change to the democratic and capitalist social and economic systems than in reconfiguring gender roles in societal systems (Ghodsee, 2004; Oberhauser, 2005).

Cultural Feminism

It would be elementary to believe that there are clear demarcations in the major streams of feminist thought; nevertheless, cultural feminism is an important dimension in the global landscape of socially constructed gender roles in economies of the new millennium. Joined by some feminists from earlier movements, cultural feminism does not take issue with gender differences but calls for a women's culture where women's production is recognized and their voices are heard. Valuing gender through an economic lens requires equal pay and equal access to work throughout the hierarchy of jobs, not just to waged employment at the bottom rung (Cameron & Gibson-Graham, 2003; Oberhauser, 2005). The kinder and nurturing capacities of women are thought to be important to world order and are recognized as peace-keeping qualities, which, if allowed to be expressed to their fullest capacities, could reduce domestic violence, war, and terrorism (Liss, Hoffner, & Crawford, 2000).

Criticism lodged against cultural feminism includes accusations of antifeminism. Those who call for sexual liberation question whether women's voices can be incorporated into male-dominated societal systems. Many women continue to be greatly disadvantaged by economic and class differences along with socially constructed gender roles that are persistent barriers to equality. Merging of a feminist agenda into existing social, political, and economic systems is more likely to be realized in an advanced technological society where jobs are less gender specific (Echols, 2002; Mumford, 2001).

IMPLICATIONS FOR SOCIAL WORK PRACTICE FROM A FEMINIST PERSPECTIVE

An understanding of the sociopolitical context of women and men in the world as addressed by feminist thought is essential for clinicians and social workers if they are to address experiences of trauma and oppression for which women clients often seek counseling. Gender oppression is experienced by women throughout much of the world, regardless of racial or cultural heritage, but particularly by women who are disadvantaged by class or minority membership. The legacy of the women's movement has many implications for social work practice with women.

Social work is a profession that has long fought against the victimization and oppression of women. Feminist thought has affected human service professionals and become a major force in the social work profession's response to women's oppression. The predominantly female social work profession serves a primarily female clientele in a world where the negotiation of gender in political and economic processes continues to present many challenges. Social work interventions with women take place in generic social work practices as well as more specialized areas of practice, including psychotherapy (Harper, 2000a; Parker, 2003).

Women clients and their families are affected by social, economic, and social class conditions. Given this contextual reality, can there be lasting individual change without accompanying societal change? Requiring a strong orientation to the contextual realities of clients' lives, social work intervention from a feminist perspective is compatible with many approaches to intervention. For example, feminist therapy is compatible with interventions from behavioral, cognitive behavioral, and family systems perspectives (Collins, 2002). Existential and cross-cultural approaches to intervention are compatible as well. Cross-cultural curative factors are believed to be central to feminist practice. For example, the factor of worldview respect allows social workers to understand and appreciate contextual realities in their clients' lives. Other curative factors emerge as women clients seek control over their lives, renew hope for their future, and experience a changing worldview. Women who seek freedom from oppression, violence, and devaluation are typically open to help in discovering and experiencing new meaning and meaning opportunities in life.

Consistent with feminism, social work practice can help establish equal opportunity for American women. The reality-based orientation underpinning much of social work intervention is particularly appropriate for helping women restore a sense of meaning in their lives after experiences of oppression and severe abuse. There are many social work practices that are helpful to women clients; however, most important among these are action for social change, support groups, empowerment in production in the public arena, and protection from victimization and violence.

Social work, not unlike feminist approaches to empowering women, calls for social action and social change. For example, helping women identify gender roles that are characteristic of the socioeconomic situation in which they live provides assistance in reframing role conflict, developing and testing coping strategies, and confronting experiences of labeling and devaluation. Reframing and redefining often allow women to change or ameliorate their experiences (Evans, Kincade, Marbley, & Seem, 2005).

A second practice helpful in social work practice is the development of self-help support groups where women can share experiences and begin to reshape some of the restrictive roles they occupy (Harper, 2000a). Self-help support groups are available for a variety of problems, including substance abuse, eating disorders, marital problems, parenting, breast cancer, and HIV/AIDS (Harper & Shillito, 1991; Lantz & Gregoire, 2000a, 2003)

Social work is known for serving disadvantaged families living in poverty. Assisting women with opportunities to participate in the public or production arena involves activities like training, employment, and education. In addition to meeting basic economic needs, feminist practice focuses on the context of women's lives—experiences of harassment and sexual assault, substance use, feelings of depression, and concerns about appearance and body image. Overcoming dependence and gaining personal power are two ways women can support their quests to redefine their social and personal contexts and to cope with experiences of oppression (Evans et al., 2005).

Finally, a practice function requiring sensitivity on the part of the practitioner is helping survivors of childhood sexual abuse overcome damage from the violation of their personal boundaries. Many survivors of violent abuse have no memory of the abuse itself and lead lives full of hopelessness, despair, and failure. Unaware of the source of their problem, these woman often present with a wide variety of symptoms. Many present with symptoms of alcoholism, drug abuse, general depression, blocked creativity; or eating disorders such as compulsive overeating, bulimia, or anorexia nervosa, as well as low self-esteem and an inability to set personal goals.

Victims of trauma such as sexual assault often utilize repression to avoid directly experiencing the pain of terror again (Harper-Dorton & Herbert, 1999; Herbert & Harper-Dorton, 2002; Lantz & Lantz, 1991, 1992). Protected by repression, the victim avoids exposure to trauma awareness but is also unable to fully experience meaning potentials that are embedded in the trauma. Exploring trauma helps the victim recover lost meaning potentials and have the courage to experience feelings and reach out to help others.

Previously identified empowering principles that can be incorporated in practice with women clients are applicable across many social work practice settings. From their work in the 1980s, Van den Bergh and Cooper (1986) identified five principles of feminist social work practice that seem to stand the test of time in work with women clients from a feminist orientation. First, eliminating false dichotomies enables women to distinguish factors of class, race, gender, and culture in their experiences of oppression. Second, the reconceptualization of power occurs every time a woman takes control, experiences success, and finds meaning and meaning opportunities. Next, valuing process as well as product provides feedback, experiences of goal setting and attainment, and validates abilities and successes. Fourth, naming personal experience provides clarity and identification as well as legitimization. From an existential perspective, renaming is an opportunity to hold experiences of oppression and name the pain and trauma of oppression, as well as to own experiences of success. Finally, "The personal is political" is a metaphor for participating more fully in the public arena. Holding up socially defined gender roles for examination and redefinition is empowering and has the capacity to change worldviews (Harper, 2000a; Van den Bergh & Cooper, 1986).

Mrs. AA: Purchased Commodity

In her wildest imagination, she never envisioned retiring from a nursing career at the beginning of the twenty-first century. Mrs. AA's life trajectory began when she was traded as a commodity at a tender age. When she was fourteen, Mrs. AA was traded for two cows and a pitchfork to a man who was forty years her senior. Isolated by mountains and bridgeless creeks, a ramshackle hut that had once been a chicken coop became her home. Here, without indoor plumbing, she reared her three children and two stepchildren. Handmade bunks, a table, a radio, four straight chairs, and boxes for storage filled the one-room dwelling. She cooked and warmed her shanty on an old, pot-bellied stove. Monthly visits to the country store (two-and-a-half miles of walking behind her husband) were her main contacts outside her shanty home.

Mrs. AA's plight was recognized by a school counselor when this mountain woman joined her only daughter in the freshman class at the local school. Poorly dressed and groomed, she drew attention from other high school students. A somewhat baffled high school counselor sought social work help to obtain resources for Mrs. AA, the forty-year-old freshman student who had almost no formal education or social skills but who had a full range IQ of 140.

The first encounter with Mrs. AA, was painful for the client and the social worker. Mrs. AA kept her head held down and her eyes on her hands. She said, "It is my time to be there for my daughter. I'm afraid for her to walk down the mountain to school. I'm going to get educated, too. I don't know what you can do to help me. Maybe you can tell me." She described herself as feeling "like I am searching for something every day, something I can't have."

In the weeks that followed, stories of her life flowed out as the worker's empathetic availability helped Mrs. AA hold feelings of isolation, devaluation, and trauma from years of living with a violent and much older husband who had traded his livestock for her, a child of fourteen.

Mrs. AA told the worker that she had been afraid the worker would not understand how hard she had worked as a woman and mother to survive on the mountain. The cross-cultural curative factor of helper attractiveness was evident, as the female social worker met Mrs. AA's need for validation from a person of her own gender. The curative factor of worldview respect was extremely helpful to Mrs. AA as she shared her experiences of living in isolation on an Appalachian mountain. The existential helping element of telling allowed her to not only tell of her life but also to name her poverty, victimization, and powerlessness.

Asked what she would do if she could do anything, Mrs. AA replied, "I'd be a nurse." Confronted by the question, "And why can't you be a nurse?" Mrs. AA thoughtfully replied, "I guess I'll just be a nurse one day now" (mastery and hope). Having a new sense of self and direction in life (mastering and existential realization), Mrs. AA defined her goal, however unrealistic it may have seemed at the time.

Mrs. AA kept weekly appointments with her social worker for eighteen months. The social worker arranged for financial support to move the AA family from the mountain and to pay tuition at the local nursing school. Mrs. AA found social supports as she was helped to join various community agencies and a women's auxiliary group at the hospital. She obtained her GED and had impeccable grades as she completed her first year of LPN training. Her cultural experiences in rural living emerged in lapses of personal grooming that sometimes brought threats of dismissal from the LPN program director. Lessons in personal hygiene, hair styling, and makeup proved to be forms of physical intervention, a cross-cultural curative factor, important for Mrs. AA's retention in the program. These contemporary forms of renewal are not so far removed from some of the rituals conducted by shamans in other cultures and at other times in history.

Telling and reflecting about her life helped Mrs. AA connect the meaning of living in the city with her former, isolated existence (existential realization). She told of years of subservience and mistreatment as she reexperienced the trauma pain of violent beatings from her husband during the first twenty years of her marriage. She talked of feeling powerless to change her life because she had felt entrapped by poverty, dependent upon the welfare system, and obligated to follow her husband's wishes. Mrs. AA's worldview demanded that she try to fulfill the role of an obedient wife as a woman should. She named herself "good property," a commodity (cleansing). Power in the family shifted when her elderly husband became frail and dependent upon her. She exercised mastery over years of devaluation as she initiated her education. Her need for affiliation was met through her own productivity in education and in work (control).

During her nursing career, her white uniform was crisp, and her smile quick. Only her timidity in casual conversation and a scar on her cheekbone belied her confidence and served as testimonials to her former life of brutality and oppression. Mrs. AA transcended her life of devaluation and trauma by giving care to countless numbers of elderly patients in a large nursing home (existential realization and honoring). Her acts of kindness—kindnesses that she rarely experienced herself, even during her childhood and early marriage—honored her past experiences. The exception to her life's trajectory of mistreatment was her relationships with her biological children. While mothering was not the focus of her counseling, it became apparent that rearing and nurturing her children are her most treasured experiences.

The irony in Mrs. AA's story is that the inner strength that eventually empowered her to extract herself from isolation, poverty, and physical battering was the same force that enabled her to endure years of abuse and poverty during much of her married life. Mrs. AA's story exemplifies human motivation to find meaning in life by transcending her own hardships and pain to give to others that which she never received. She initiated action to change her life when her daughter turned fourteen, the age she was when her husband purchased her.

In this interesting case, existential helping elements, cross-cultural curative factors, and principles of feminist social work practice identified by Van den Bergh and Cooper (1986) come together. The process of social work intervention followed existential helping elements of holding, telling, mastering, and honoring. From a feminist perspective, Mrs. AA became empowered as she experienced success in living in town, succeeding in nursing training, and working for nearly thirty years as an LPN. She valued these experiences and her children, and eventually saw herself as a role model for her children. Her self-esteem grew as she became economically independent and had her own regular paycheck. New social skills emerged as she made friends in nursing school and found rewarding long-term friendships through her work.

Mrs. BB: Victim of Rape and Abuse

Mrs. BB was referred for social work services by her minister for bad dreams and flashbacks that terrified her and triggered crying spells, sleep problems, and sexual problems. She started experiencing these terrifying memory fragments soon after her oldest daughter turned nine years old. In her flashbacks, Mrs. BB had a recurring image of an older man who was "doing bad things to me." She reported that she had started drinking at night to help herself fall asleep. She also wanted to withdraw from her responsibilities, lacked energy, and was very uncomfortable when her husband initiated sex. She was having trouble going to work and no longer enjoyed her job. Mrs. BB scored 86 on the Purpose in Life test at the end of her first clinical interview. A score of 93 to 111 indicates the subject is vulnerable to the development of an existential vacuum (Crumbaugh & Maholick, 1963). Mrs. BB's low score was a good indication that she was suffering from an existential vacuum along with symptoms of post-traumatic stress disorder. A Purpose in Life test score of 92 or less indicates the presence of an existential vacuum, while a score of 112 or above indicates a sense of purpose and meaning in life.

Mrs. BB had her husband join her in counseling and remained in social work intervention for three years. Empathetic availability on the part of the social worker helped Mrs. BB hold her trauma experience so it could be reexperienced. Telling was a time of remembering and releasing, a catharsis. Emotional support and help in holding the trauma experience allowed Mrs. BB to remember that when she had been nine years old, the man who lived next door to her family started molesting her (cleansing). He molested her repeatedly, had oral sex with her, and took photographs of her victimization. She remembered that the man would kill small animals in front of her to show her what he would do to her parents if she ever told what was happening to her. In fear of what he would do to her parents, she kept the secret. The man also told her that it was her fault he was molesting her because she made him lose control and was evil and "dirty."

Mrs. BB remembered that she had told her parents what had happened to her when she was ten years old, soon after the man moved out of the house next door and left the area. She remembered that her parents had taken her to their family doctor, but that nothing else had happened and "no one did anything."

Mrs. BB, her husband, and her social worker all believed that it was important for her to remember it all and tell people about it. Telling her trauma experience allowed her to name herself as a nine-year-old victim, guilty of nothing. Telling her story with support from her husband and social worker helped her master her trauma. Mrs. BB felt that it was important for her to go to the police and file a complaint nineteen years after she had been molested and abused (cleansing and control). It was important for her to confront her parents (cleansing) about why they never did anything and to learn that her parents did not know what to do at the time. They had received no help from their family doctor, who advised them to ignore it and that she would forget it sooner or later. It was a great help for Mrs. BB when she and her husband had a second wedding ceremony (rite of initiation and cleansing). She reported that she had stopped feeling dirty after Mr. BB "proved he wanted to marry me again even after he knew what had happened to me." The couple's sex life improved dramatically after this second wedding ceremony.

A final element (honoring) for Mrs. BB was her discovery that she was excellent at listening to other women who had been molested or raped. She began volunteering at a local rape crisis center (control and existential realization) and has become a skilled volunteer counselor for other victims of trauma and terror. She also speaks to community groups about rape and assault prevention. Her volunteer work has been a way for Mrs. BB to give something to the world.

At the termination of the helping relationship, Mrs. BB's Purpose in Life test score was 124, and she scored 125 on the Purpose in Life test at her four-year follow-up evaluation. Both scores show that she is experiencing a sense of meaning and purpose in life (Crumbaugh & Maholick, 1963). Mrs. BB reported no problems with depression and no sexual problems. She described herself as "comfortable and happy." She did, however, mention that once a person learns that the world is "dangerous," "she is forever changed" and has a responsibility to "do something to make the world better." Mrs. BB has transformed the experience of being raped as a child into meaning through self-transcendent giving to the world "in honor of my sisters who have also been molested, raped, terrorized, and disempowered."

SUMMARY

Women and men represent the gendered population of the world. Gender is accompanied by personal, political, and social characteristics, including age, race, class, ethnicity, sexual preference, intellectual capacities, developmental disabilities, and disabilities due to accidental and catastrophic events. Defining gender outside the context of ethnic and cultural diversity produces anemic images, plastic beings that lack definition and meaning.

Social constructions of gender define behaviors, roles, expectations, power, and privilege. "These definitions shape images of male or female, not concrete images, but markers that are socially constructed and can be deconstructed by those who are both actors and interpreters of gender behaviors" (Harper, 2000a, p. 76). The societal assignment of definitions of gender is not value free. Women have made great progress in global social and economic environments, but the oppression of women continues to exist. Evans et al. (2005) call for recognition of oppression and integration of diverse worldviews in working with women.

The broad scope of feminist literature makes it impossible to present feminist theory through a single lens. Instead, the flow of theories informing feminist social work practice provides a framework for enhancing meaning and purpose in life. Incorporating a feminist approach to social work practice with women clients is essential to intervention, especially in the face of patriarchal social structures, personal oppression, or severe physical and/or sexual abuse. Feminism and approaches to feminist therapy are compatible with most psychological theories and psychotherapies and are important in intervention from an existential perspective. Social work practice, whether generalist or more specialized, is a natural vehicle for working with women from feminist and existential perspectives. Professional concerns of oppression, social justice, equality, human dignity, and empowerment are applicable in working with women clients.

The challenge to the social worker in working with women clients is to be empowering and to help women experience new ways of making meaning in daily living and discovering new meaning opportunities. Openness to each woman's experiences and potentials is critical to any method of practice. The extent to which action for the empowerment of women and social change for equal opportunity and equal access can restructure social systems is yet unknown. So, too, is the magnitude of change that women's peacekeeping capacities can have on domestic concerns such as domestic violence, sexual abuse, and child abuse. Furthermore, whether or not gender emerges as a determining factor in peacekeeping at international levels, as believed by De la Rey and McKay (2006), is an area for future study. It is possible that participation in peace building from a feminist perspective may make a difference in the experiences of women around the world.

12

Gay, Lesbian, Bisexual, and Transsexual Clients

SEXUAL ORIENTATION IS ONE OF THE MANY ASPECTS OF HUMAN DIVERSITY. Difference in sexual orientation is common to the human species and reflects individual preferences. Sex, gender, and sexual orientation are not necessarily discrete, as men and women can be masculine or feminine in varying dimensions and attracted to men and/or women. Expressions of biologically determined gender are understood by a broad array of socially defined gender role behaviors. Societal definitions of gender roles define masculine and feminine behaviors, statuses, power relations, achievements, and jobs. Gender roles are reflected in family roles of fathers and mothers, and responsibilities associated with procreation. In a predominantly heterosexual world, persons with same-sex orientation are a very diverse minority group—a "rainbow coalition" with differences in race, age, religion, ethnicity, social class, employment, and appearance (Schope & Eliason, 2004). Same-sex orientation is a minority orientation. Societal, religious, and moral prescriptives reflect the majority heterosexual orientation.

Having sexual and affectional relationships is part of meeting physical and emotional needs, regardless of one's sexual orientation. People establish intimate involvement in order to fulfill these basic human needs. While the majority of people are heterosexual, others identify differently. Lesbian and gay persons are women and men who "have a preferential sexual attraction to people of their same sex over a significant period of time" (Masters, Johnson, & Kolodney, 1995).

Same-sex orientation was once considered to be a mental illness and/or an emotional problem by many psychiatrists, psychologists, and social workers in the United States. Removed from the third edition of the *Diagnostic and Statistical Manual of Mental Disorders (DSM-III)*, homosexuality is no longer a label of deviance or mental illness nor a gender identity disorder (American Psychiatric Association, 1982). Transsexual orientation continues to be labeled a gender identity disorder in the *DSM-IV* (American Psychiatric Association, 2000). Gender identity disordered clients express gender confusion. Transsexuals frequently express strong feelings of a mismatch between their emotional and physical states—they may feel psychologically male but constrained in a female body, or vice versa. Transsexuals may cross-dress, experience exclusion and isolation from others, or seek gender reassignment. Individuals with gender identity disorders experience intrapsychic identity struggles that are different from those of men and women whose feelings of confusion and anxiety about sexual orientation stem from fears of stereotyping and oppression. Hostility, prejudice, and hatred continue to be expressed toward gay men and lesbian women despite the significant action taken by the American Psychiatric Association to change diagnostic and classification systems (Brown, 1989; Shernoff, 1984). While attitudes and prejudices have changed for many people, others cling to biases and beliefs that are asynchronous with contemporary attitudes and family systems in the United States and most of the global community.

Definitions of sexual orientation are not always distinct. Some people are attracted to both men and women and choose to maintain bisexual lifestyles. People who chose bisexual relationships are not well understood by straight psychotherapists. Esterberg makes several interesting observations about bisexuality versus monosexuality and issues of choice (American Psychiatric Association, 1994). There are many unanswered questions about boundaries and whether bisexuals are more closely identified with gays and lesbians than with heterosexuals. Confusion about sexual identity, bisexual identity, and changing sexual identities throughout the life cycle are some of the issues concerning sexual identity and orientation.

Following the various human rights movements of the 1960s, gay and lesbian rights have become much more public than they once were. The full range of human diversity existing among people who are alive in the world today is reflected in all choices of sexual orientation. Gay men and lesbian women may be liberal or conservative, religiously oriented or nonreligious. Cultures differ in acceptance and openness toward gender preference and affect individual attitudes toward openness and experiences and beliefs about personal safety. Not all cultures and ethnic groups openly recognize GLBT choices and lifestyles.

Recent population reports of household composition in the United States provide an accounting of same-sex partner households. Based on data from the 2000 census, Simmons and O'Connell (2003) report 594,391 same-sex partner households among 105,480,101 households in the United State. Same-sex partner households have been more recently identified as couple households. Same-sex households are almost equally represented for male couples (51%) and female couples (49%). Simmons and O'Connell also report that same-sex couples are more likely to live in urban areas than in rural areas. Furthermore, large coastal cities, where between 1.3 percent and 2.7 percent of households are same-sex partner households, have a somewhat greater representation of same-sex partners.

It is possible that many men and women have same-sex experiences at sometime in their lives, but the number of those with ongoing same-sex orientation is thought to remain close to 10 percent (Reicherzer, 2005). There is no way at present to know exactly how many gay, lesbian, bisexual, or transsexual persons live in the United States, as many are not willing to share this aspect of their lives with public officials, census workers, or research surveys.

SEXUAL BEHAVIOR AND ORIENTATION

Sexual activity between persons of the same sex has existed in societies throughout the world for most of history. Human sexual behaviors and orientations are associated with socially, religiously, and politically constructed meanings. Sexual orientation spans the human condition of identity on a global scale, as reflected by practices of ancient Greek and Roman men, who frequently engaged in sexual activities with young boys. Masculine prowess was frequently associated with same-sex behaviors in this early period of civilization (Altman, 2002).

Gay rights movements are in different stages in countries around the world. Gay pride parades and demonstrations are held in many countries in support of gay and lesbian rights. Gay pride events are popular in Mexico, despite the historical presence of Roman Catholicism. Celebrations of gay pride in France, Japan, and Thailand incorporate dance, theater, music, and costumes. People fill the streets of Chile in annual events for gay pride (Galliano & Lisotta, 2004). Gay sex is legal in Hong Kong, but not in mainland China or Taiwan. Gay solidarity recently prevailed in Croatia, where gay pride parades had been met with violence in 2002. Drawing attention and participation from Muslims and Jews, gay pride activities in Jerusalem were confronted by great violence at the turn of the twenty-first century. Concerns related to gay and lesbian people throughout Asia are less public and not well understood. The lack of openness surrounding gay rights in Asian culture and Asian literature is discussed by Poon (2004). Given the sparse research, Asian populations and other people of color need to be included in future research relating to gay rights.

Present-day prejudices and discriminatory practices often target those whose sexual identity is different from the societally sanctioned sexual orientation. Although it has gained greater understanding and acceptance, variations in personal sexual orientation continue to be an issue among many. The civil and legal rights of gays and lesbians are a new area for policy development and concern for public debate.

There has been continued growth in global expansion and acceptance of celebrations calling for tolerance. However, prejudice and oppression have not been erased. Gay and lesbian people are often in multiple jeopardy, as many encounter racism, sexism, and ageism as well as homophobia. Some expressions of prejudice come from people who are more alike than different from their targets, as intra-racial and intraethnic acts of discrimination affect many who choose same-sex partners. This is especially true in societies where societal mores support heterosexual orientation and traditional family structures (Bridges, Selvidge, & Matthews, 2003; Poon, 2004). Nevertheless, gay and lesbian lifestyles are becoming much more accepted around the world, especially in the United States.

ROOTS OF HOMOPHOBIA AND SEXUAL ORIENTATION

Homophobia, the fear of homosexuals, involves prejudices and hostilities directed toward people who have same-sex orientation. Homophobic persons sometimes react to GLBT people with hatred, hostility, violence, disgust, or feelings of personal fear or anxiety. Anxieties often relate to concerns of self-identity, erroneous fears concerning the transmission of HIV/AIDS, and fears or guilt associated with societal sanctions and moral or religious beliefs. GLBT people experience oppression and discrimination in social and economic arenas, sometimes from legal and political systems and other times from individual and group homophobia.

Homophobia is deeply ingrained in the American culture. Tully and Nibao (1979) believe that homophobia in the United States has been promoted and prescribed by religious traditions that have evolved out of the Old Testament, and that such homophobic attitudes have been woven into our legal system through legislation that criminalized homosexual acts. The New Testament contains numerous references to marriages, husbands and wives, heterosexual unions, and procreation. The Old and New Testaments are open to interpretation by anyone or any religious denomination.

Laws against homosexual behavior date back at least as far as Roman law. Colonists in early American history punished sodomists with floggings, hangings, and periods of confinement (Robinson, 2003). This history may seem ancient; however, as recently as 2002, sodomy laws continued to be enforceable in fourteen states in addition to Puerto Rico (Robinson, 2005). Legislation against homosexual acts in the United States and the prevailing homophobia in American culture have caused many gay and lesbian persons to fear revealing their sexual orientation. Perhaps for personal safety, many gay men and lesbian women remain covert about their sexual practices. Personal decisions about coming out and openness about sexual orientation are influenced by factors such as fear of hate crimes, discriminatory experiences in the workplace, and exclusion from institutional settings such as the military (Reicherzer, 2005; Tully & Nibao, 1979).

Sexual orientation is a complex phenomenon that cannot be explained by a singular theory. Researchers have applied numerous biological, psychological, social, and behavioral theories in their attempts to explain how people assume one sexual identity over another. Studies of the brain and of hormonal levels and abnormalities (Hyde & DeLamater, 2000) are examples of biological research into homosexuality. A number of psychosocial theories have looked at sexual orientation from differing perspectives. Reflecting the age-old Oedipus complex, psychoanalytic and social learning theories consider same-sex and opposite-sex identification of children and parents. Identity formation involves masculine and feminine components of both males and females, regardless of sexual orientation. Some theories concern events in the sequence of child development and childhood predispositions. While many theories of personality development and sexual orientation have relevance to human development, there really is not a single irrefutable theoretical explanation (Schriver, 2004).

SOCIAL WORK WITH GAY, LESBIAN, BISEXUAL, AND TRANSSEXUAL CLIENTS

GLBT persons are different from heterosexuals in at least two distinct ways. First, they experience more discrimination, stereotyping, and sometimes violence from the mainstream community than do heterosexuals. Second, gay men and lesbian women have greater interest in having intimate and sexual relationships with persons of the same gender than do heterosexual persons. However, these two differences in no way change the important fact that there is tremendous heterogeneity among all people, whether gay or straight. Gay and lesbian people and heterosexuals share the same concerns for physical health, or mental health, and personal well-being. Many have considerable resiliency and coping strengths, as evidenced by the increasingly public nature of gay and lesbian relationships. Same-sex marriages and new research and policies surrounding adoption and same-sex parenting are contemporary issues in the new millennium (Kershaw, 2000; Schriver, 2004).

Selected Cross-Cultural Competencies for Working with GLBT Clients

Counselors and social workers must be informed about all types of minority statuses and learn to individualize each client, provide affirmation, and assist clients with finding or creating affirmative environments. An important cross-cultural difference for many gay and lesbian clients is that their sexual orientation grants them minority status. Unlike ethnic and racial minorities, sexual minority status comes with personal orientation and disclosure. While people of color and specific ethnicities hold the same minority status as their families, in most cases the sexual minority status of GLBT individuals is not shared by their family of origin and perhaps not by their community, particularly when they come from rural areas. GLBT clients who hold multiple minority statuses may be in multiple jeopardy. Therapists need to be prepared to address concerns such as internalized homophobia, religious and extended family concerns, and concerns of gay and lesbian families such as marriage, adoption, artificial insemination by donor, and parenting (Bridges et al., 2003; Israel & Selvidge, 2003; Vanfraussen, Ponjaert-Kristoffersen, & Brewaeys, 2003).

Four important cross-cultural competencies stand out here. First, the primary cross-cultural competency necessary for professional practice with GLBT clients is the practitioner's self-awareness, and acceptance of the sexual orientations of him- or herself and others. Before a social work practitioner attempts to provide services to gay and lesbian clients, the social worker should have already examined and worked through his or her own sexual identity issues, homophobia, and attitudes toward GLBT persons (Israel & Selvidge, 2003). It is not at all unusual for straight social workers to discover while working with a gay or lesbian client that they are having serious negative countertransference problems that disrupt their ability to provide adequate, empathic, and professional services to the client. Beliefs and values surrounding religion, morals, marriage and property laws, survivor rights, and parenting rights, reflect societal oppression and contribute to homophobia (Reicherzer, 2005). Prejudice and anti-gay sentiments contribute to irrational fears of things such as HIV/AIDS, molestation, evil, and God's vengeance. These negative cultural attitudes have the power to create fear, poor self-esteem, and psychic injuries that may inhibit expressions of intimacy and affection. Not being valued by larger society, GLBT clients sometimes internalize homophobic rejection to the extent of self-loathing. Just as GLBT persons are programmed by societal practices and beliefs, so are people who grow up to be social workers and counselors. Self-awareness is critical to cross-culturally competent practice.

Openness, honesty, and acknowledgement of transference or countertransference are conditions necessary for effective helping relationships with GLBT clients. Many gay men and lesbian women believe that openly expressing their sexual identity to society is dangerous and makes them vulnerable to being hurt. As a result, many gay men and lesbian women may be hesitant to reveal their sexual orientation to the heterosexual social worker and may engage in testing behaviors to see whether the social worker can be trusted to be accepting and empathic. We recommend that cross-cultural social work practitioners view such testing behavior as functional and sane, and a client strength. An affirmative social work relationship is critical to helping clients identify the meaning of their experiences as they work to take control of their lives, reshape their worldview, gain coping skills, and discover new meaning opportunities in life (Kocarek & Pelling, 2003; Moses & Hawkins, 1982; O'Dell, 2000). In instances of internalized homophobia, the existential helping process begins by helping clients hold and revisit experiences of oppression in the client-therapist relationship. Empathic availability on the part of the counselor is essential to clients' efforts to reduce fear and terror (hope), tell and name their responses of fear and trauma (cleansing and existential realization), master their sense of self (control), and honor (existential realization) their identity and that of others as they find harmony and new meanings in life (Lantz, 2000c). The existential helping elements of holding, telling, mastering, and honoring identify the trajectory of the helping process and often require months, even years, of therapy as clients discover and accept new meaning potentials in life.

A second important cross-cultural competency with gay and lesbian clients is the ability to understand that they often have problems that have little or nothing to do with their sexual orientation. For example, if a gay or lesbian client requests counseling for depression, the depression may or may not be linked to the client's sexual orientation. It is a mistake and often a manifestation of the helper's homophobia for the social worker to see all of the client's problems as a reaction to his or her sexual orientation or to hatred he or she has experienced from the dominant culture. In other words, GLBT clients seek help for all types of services and problems such as employment counseling, depression, bipolar disorders, phobias and paranoia, schizophrenia, couples and/or marriage counseling, divorce counseling, custody issues of biological children, and workplace discrimination for reasons other than sexual orientation.

Third, competency in understanding personality theory and identity development of the self in relation to others is required of practitioners. The nexus between object relations theory and psychodynamic theory, spirituality, and existential philosophy facilitates understanding of identity formation. Kernberg (1985), a well-known object relations theorist, considers early relations with significant others to be important to ego formation and later to self-esteem. Early attachment to significant others begins the human process of separation/individuation as part of the formation of self and of identity (Bridle, 2000). Object relations theory emphasizes that human relations early in life help form identity of self and others (i.e., intrapsychic dynamics relative to interpersonal relationships and identity).

Personality fusion has been called a problem of separation/individuation by some object-relationship therapists, and a cohesion-independence issue by some existential therapists (Lantz, 1978). Personality fusion consolidates positives and negatives of self and others. All people (gay, lesbian, bisexual, transsexual, or straight) encounter the problem of fusion, or the cohesion-independence issue. In the cohesion-independence issue of human existence, the person is viewed as naturally and normally undergoing a life cycle of two constantly alternating processes: first, being close and cohesive for support and emotional nurturance, and second, being apart and separate for autonomy and independent responsibility. In human growth and development, the person's family, social network, and community provide opportunities for him or her to develop the "real self" through cohesion experiences in which the person learns to be close, and separation experiences in which the person learns to be independent (Lantz, 1978, 1993).

Each individual must learn to be alone and separate as part of the growth of self-esteem and the capacity for self-care. At the same time, each person must also learn to be cohesive and close to other people for the purpose of learning to be intimate and self-transcendent. This human existential issue is neither a lesbian, gay, or straight issue but part of all human experience. Expressions of self are warmly accepted in cases of congruence with expectations by significant others; but incongruent expressions can bring reprimand and rejection. Gay and lesbian persons often learn quite early that coming out and expressing same-sex orientation is, in fact, an act that can place them at risk for discrimination and even violence. As a result, some gay men and lesbian women are not able to find support for the identified or real self within their family of origin, with childhood friends, or within the family of origin's social network. In these instances an individual may be forced to find support for his or her identified self *only* in immediate peer networks or in the gay and lesbian community. Later, the individual may find it difficult to manifest aspects of the real self that do fit the norms or expectations of the gay and lesbian community. The individual may feel afraid to individuate, as doing so may cost him or her the emotional and social support of the gay and lesbian community (Krestan & Bepko, 1980). This issue of cohesion and independence is an existential and developmental problem for all people, not just gay men and lesbian women. Object relations is not a causal theory for sexual orientation, but an approach to understanding intrapsychic dynamics and interpersonal relationships in identity consolidation (Kernberg, 2002). Human development and sexual orientation occur over a range of conditions and choices. Kernberg (2002) notes that bisexual orientation occupies the middle range between heterosexual and same-sex orientation.

Fourth, it is important in cross-cultural social work practice with gay and lesbian clients for the worker to understand that the referral resources the worker usually trusts and utilizes during network intervention with heterosexual clients may not be as helpful with gay and lesbian clients. Homophobic attitudes of individuals in the social worker's referral network may interfere with service delivery. As a result, the practitioner should make every attempt to assess the levels of prejudice shown toward gay and lesbian persons by the referral resources he or she utilizes in his or her daily practice (Lantz & Lenahan, 1976; Moses & Hawkins, 1982). This cross-cultural competency relates to responsibilities that social workers have in areas of social justice and advocacy on behalf of oppressed populations.

Marital Therapy with Gay and Lesbian Couples

In 1975, a time of a different social consciousness more than thirty years ago, the Southwest Mental Health Center in Columbus, Ohio, sponsored a three-day panel discussion workshop. Three gay couples and three lesbian couples who had been together in what they referred to as a marital relationship for over ten years talked to mental health practitioners about healthy gay and lesbian marriages and what marital therapy with gay and lesbian couples should try to accomplish (Lantz, 1975). All six couples reported that they had used traditional marital therapy services at one time or another over the course of their marriage to help them to work out problems. All six couples reported that the social workers they consulted had been straight and that the marital therapy had been helpful. The following themes emerged and reemerged during the three-day workshop (Lantz, 1975):

Toxic messages. All six couples reported that the hatred and disrespect shown to gay and lesbian couples by the dominant straight culture can make them feel bad, evil, crazy, and sick. All six couples believed that the social worker should in some way help couples learn to "cleanse themselves" of the toxic messages they so frequently receive from the dominant culture.

Masked or false face. There was agreement that social workers and other helping professionals should be aware that gays and lesbians learn to hide their true feelings and show a false face to the dominant culture. Gay and lesbian couples often use this skill of masking feelings with each other to avoid conflict and the manifestation of problems. All six couples stated that workers need to help gay and lesbian couples learn that maintaining anonymity is an avoidance skill that can be helpful in dealing with the dominant culture. Nevertheless, a false face or masked identity is often very damaging when used within the gay or lesbian relationship.

Provider homophobia. All six couples believed that the worker should accept responsibility for knowing other professionals and service providers who are not homophobic (Lantz, 1975). Such a responsibility means that helping professionals should check out the level of homophobia of community services and agency representatives.

Homophobic countertransference reactions. All six couples reported that they felt that their own personal social worker had been "slightly homophobic" and at times expressed homophobic attitudes. All six couples believed that what had helped them and their worker to overcome the worker's homophobic countertransference reactions was the worker's openness and willingness to admit that he or she might have some homophobic issues. This openness on the part of the therapist seemed to help all six couples and their worker to work through the problems.

Overly dependent partners. All six couples reported thinking that at times they had become too dependent upon each other and that such dependence and reliance upon the other for emotional support created problems in their ability to manifest the independent side of themselves. All six couples stated that the dominant culture's hostility toward gay men and lesbian women tended to push them to rely only upon each other and to become too dependent. Normal and alternating processes of being close and cohesive, and then being apart and separate, may be clouded by fears of prejudice and homophobic reactions from others outside the gay and lesbian community (Lantz, 1975). This theme relates to the cohesion-independence issue discussed earlier.

Marital Therapy with Ms. K and Ms. S

Ms. K and Ms. S requested marital therapy at a community mental health center. They wanted to improve their relationship and had been referred for marital therapy by a priest at a Roman Catholic church in Columbus, Ohio. The couple had held a marriage ceremony four years earlier and considered themselves to be married.

The couple complained of frequent (but unsuccessful) arguments and a less-than-satisfactory sexual relationship and recognized that they both were wanting to spend more and more time away from each other. Ms. K was in law school, and Ms. S was a teacher, and both stated that they had been having problems for about two years. The couple exhibited a relationship interactional style that involved an overly intellectualizing partner

(Ms. K) and a partner who either withdrew or "acted up" to deal with problems (Ms. S). Both members of the relationship used a number of interactional methods to avoid intimacy.

Ambivalent about their relationship, both partners wanted to "keep it going" but admitted to feeling "smothered" and "controlled." They had some concerns about being in a helping relationship with a male heterosexual social worker but reported that they wanted services from this worker because of his good reputation and his past experience doing marital and relationship therapy with gay and lesbian couples.

The intervention approach used by the social worker with the client couple was experiential and used the time and space of conjoint sessions to help the couple notice and become aware of communication cutoffs that they used to avoid friction. The couple was also helped to notice that by avoiding conflict they were also avoiding intimacy, even after resolving and working through conflict. The social worker was active and direct with the couple in a way that challenged their avoidance and helped them stick with it when they wanted to "cut out" on their problems and conflicts.

In addition to helping this couple openly manifest, talk out, and resolve conflicts, the worker also gave the couple a variety of nonverbal intimacy exercises (i.e., holding hands and using pressure in the hands to express feelings) that they could use to get back in touch with their positive feelings toward each other. These nonverbal exercises stimulated additional concerns that could be talked out during counseling.

Ms. K and Ms. S were seen seventeen times in conjoint relationship therapy over a period of six months. The couple reported good progress and shared that relationship therapy had been of tremendous help. Both Ms. K and Ms. S stated that the social worker's awareness of his own ignorance and lack of knowledge about the gay and lesbian community, coupled with his confidence in his knowledge about relationship therapy, was "refreshing" and gave them hope. They felt encouraged to tell their story and to name their relationship difficulties in the presence of their therapist (helper attractiveness). The couple reported that nonverbal exercises (physical intervention) helped them discover and express feelings (cleansing) and that communication training in conjoint interviews helped them feel more control (mastery). The final factor considered important by this couple was the respect that the worker showed by honoring their sexual orientation and societal experiences (worldview respect).

Now, more than thirty years after this interesting case, requests for marital therapy and/or relationship therapy from GLBT and heterosexual couples are common. Recent years have brought greater openness and acceptance of GLBT relationships and lifestyles as well as the understanding that practitioners must not assume that sexual orientation is the presenting problem for GLBT couples. Responsibility and awareness of acceptance, advocacy, and alleviation of social injustices have emerged in work with clients across the range of sexual orientations (Kocarek & Pelling, 2003).

CONTEMPORARY CONCERNS IN WORKING WITH GLBT CLIENTS

There are several ongoing concerns and trends in the gay and lesbian community. Society has become more tolerant of GLBT lifestyles, and while this tolerance does not eradicate all forms of prejudice or homophobia, certainly there is much more openness about sexual orientation and laws against discrimination based on sexual orientation. Nevertheless, there are concerns such as HIV/AIDS, coming out as a gay or lesbian person, and growing interest in transgender issues, including gender reassignments. Contemporary trends include greater recognition of gay and lesbian marriages, reconstituted families, foster/adoption families, and childbearing by artificial insemination by donor. These concerns and trends are discussed in view of potential service requests for social work service or other professional counseling intervention.

HIV/AIDS

People with human immunodeficiency virus and acquired immune deficiency syndrome are of all ages, races, religions, ethnicities, genders, and sexual orientations. HIV/AIDS is an illness, a transmittable plague affecting millions of people, straight or gay. More than forty million people have HIV/AIDS, including as much as 25 percent of the population of South Africa, one million people in the United States, and two million people in Southeast Asia. At least thirteen million children have been orphaned as a result of their parents' HIV/AIDS infections, and many of them are or will become HIV positive as this global pandemic continues to grow (De Waal, 2004). Safe-sex education, abstinence, and prenatal testing help prevent incidence of new infections. About 40,000 new infections occur each year in the United States, a number that seems to be stable for the time being (Advancing HIV Prevention, 2003). Antiretroviral drugs treat the virus and extend life for individuals and populations in nations that can afford the cost of such intervention. Twenty-five years after its discovery in 1981, HIV/AIDS is a scourge with multiplier effects threatening the global community (Poku & Whiteside, 2006).

The gay community was especially stigmatized in the early days of HIV/AIDS as the disease became associated with homosexuality. Hate crimes, discrimination, and acts of violence targeted gays. Issues surrounding HIV/AIDS continue to fuel homophobia, although HIV/AIDS affects heterosexual people and children worldwide. Gay men, intravenous drug users, bisexuals, and people who have multiple partners are at an increased risk for HIV/AIDS infection. Many in the gay and lesbian community have lifelong partners and live quite responsible and healthy lifestyles. The gay and lesbian community continues to advocate for safe sex and federal funding for research, treatment, and primary prevention programs.

Clients with HIV/AIDS seek medical care and counseling, sometimes to learn more about the virus, perhaps in search of information about safer sex, or perhaps to learn about universal health precautions for protecting others in their family, workplace, and community. Financial resources, medical referrals, and various financial and medication-related needs are frequent service requests. Others seek counseling about their own declining health and impending death. Gay men and women often seek help following the death of an acquaintance or close friend from AIDS. Grief, loss, depression, and existential realization of their own living and dying are concerns brought to counseling. Others may present with deep anger and resentment if their infection came from dirty needles, unsuspected partners, or rape. Competent cross-cultural practice requires knowledge, counseling skills, empathetic availability, acceptance, and affirmation of a valued life in working with clients suffering grief, loss, and anger due to HIV/AIDS.

Coming Out

Prejudice, discrimination, and stereotyping have contributed to the reluctance of GLBT people to reveal their sexual orientations. Beginning the process of coming out requires acceptance of one's sexual orientation or of one's real self. This process is not time limited and often involves personal pain, confusion, fear, eventual tolerance of self, counseling, acceptance of identity, identity consolidation, and pride in identity.

Coming out generally begins with partners, friends, acquaintances, or family members. There is not a particular age or time that fits all people. Acknowledging GLBT orientation in this developmental stage places adolescents at risk for great internal stress and even torment from peers (Beemyn, 2003). The important task for adolescents is forming identity while avoiding role confusion (Erikson, 1963). Adolescent peers play an important role in the resolution of this identity task through their feedback, either positive or negative. Some adolescents may choose to come out, but others may not openly acknowledge their sexual orientation for much of their lives, even well into midlife or old age (Johnson & Jenkins, 2004; Reicherzer, 2005). The process of coming out has the potential to bring both great joy and great despair for gay men and lesbian women.

No longer trying to pass as heterosexual despite the fear of rejection by friends, family, spouse, and even children, requires great courage. For many gay men and lesbian women, the process of coming out involves considerable pain when old friends are no longer willing to remain friends and family members and childhood friends are unwilling to provide acceptance. "Coming out puts you in danger; it lets you find out which friends will stay with you and which ones will treat you like you got the plague" (Anonymous, 1990).

In spite of its potential for great pain and sadness, many gay men and lesbian women view the process of coming out as a liberating, almost lifesaving, activity. To no longer feel ashamed, to feel accepted, and to discover "islands of freedom where you can be yourself" can "take a tremendous load off your shoulders" (Anonymous,

1990). The decision to come out, to accept one's GLBT identity, is a tremendously important life event for gay men and lesbian women. The heterosexual social worker should not attempt to work with this clinical situation without professional knowledge and cross-cultural competencies to work with people of different colors, ethnicities, marital status, and religions, as well as the elderly and those affected by disabilities in the gay and lesbian community. Furthermore, good consultation and supervision from a qualified and experienced gay or lesbian practitioner are essential (cross-cultural factor of helper-attractiveness).

Transgender and Gender Reassignment

Biological and psychological factors surround the "third sex," or transsexual persons (Cooper, 2002). Gender is assigned at birth generally upon declaration of the nature of the newborn's observed genitalia. Gender identity is then followed by behaviors associated with male and female roles—boys wear blue, and girls wear pink; boys are more aggressive, and girls are more submissive; boys get teddy bears and trucks, and girls get dolls and beads. Once defined, biological identity becomes an identifier that follows one through life and determines one's legal and social statuses, which bathroom one will use, which health risks one must worry about, and whether one will be the bride or groom when married. Identity is further characterized in relationships with personal, familial, and social boundaries. If one does not feel comfortable in his or her gender role—that is, if the assigned gender does not fit—gender confusion and transgender identity may occur. Resolution through gender transformation or reassignment is a major physiological and psychological undertaking. Gender confusion and requests to change identity, including surgical gender reassignment, are classified as gender identity disorders in the *DSM-IV* (American Psychiatric Association, 2000).

Transgender people may feel as though they are confined by dress or physiology to a gender with which they do not identify. Transsexual or transgender people are perhaps the least visible and most underserved sexual minority population. Often the target of hostility and marginalization, transgender people may choose to remain silent and continue to pass as whatever gender was assigned at birth. Others choose to be open about their gender identity and to be known by male or female names depending upon their appearance and how and when they choose to be recognized by friends, family, colleagues, partners, and strangers. Still others choose gender reassignment and undergo counseling, hormonal therapy, and invasive surgery. Gender reassignment is becoming the choice of more and more transsexual people and requires personal commitment to expensive and intrusive hormonal and surgical intervention as well as long-term counseling for the client and his or her partner (Koetting, 2004).

In addition to biological and psychological factors, social and political issues surround sexuality. Social, political, and legal concerns related to privacy, equality,

and conceptualization of gender surround gender confusion and transgender identity. These social, political, and legal concerns must be considered seriously by state
and local governments now and in the future (Cooper, 2002).

The case of Mr. Y is a good example of a worker's ability to be nonjudgmental,
empathically available, and informed. The client, a young gay man, was afraid to
come out to his family and to the small conservative community where he lived. His
fears were indeed real and reflected rational self-preservation in view of homophobia in the rural community in which he lived. However, he was experiencing increasing depression and anxiety concerning his identity.

Mr. Y's Coming Out

Mr. Y, age twenty-one, presented with the request for help, as he was afraid to live in
the small rural community where his family had always lived. Helped to hold his feelings
of fear and trauma pain, he was able to share that he was afraid he was gay and wanted to
change so that no one would ever know. He had thought of "being a girl" so he could be
with another man in a "normal way." While somewhat confused, the desire to change represented the curative factor of hope for Mr. Y. Living an open gay lifestyle was just outside
his worldview. The therapist's empathic availability helped this young man hold his fear
of his own identity as well as his fear of potential violence from others in his community.
He told of being alone and of his religious and conservative family life; yet he was able to
name his attraction to men. He told of avoiding dates his family and friends arranged for
him and of his fantasies about other males and asked if he was really "queer."

Through guided imagery, Mr. Y was able to imagine going to another state, visiting
a gay bar, and just being "real." He asked to replay the imagery several times. Mr. Y said,
"I feel like I can do this for real" (existential realization). He began to master his fears
and his sexual orientation. Mr. Y agreed to see a counselor in another city where he could
be more open about his own sexual orientation.

Mr. Y's initial request to "change" was fueled by his own homophobic fears and
real concern for his safety. Unable to name or express himself as a gay person, he was
in great trauma pain. He was able to express his need to come out only after holding up his trauma of oppression and fear of homophobic violence (worldview respect). As he revisited his experiences in the presence of the worker's empathic availability, he was able to name his sexual orientation as gay.

So, how did this case end? After about a year, Mr. Y made a second appointment
with the first worker so that he could report his progress and talk about his new life.
With the help of his second counselor, an experienced practitioner in a gay and lesbian community, Mr. Y had moved from his rural hometown and relocated to a large
midwestern city. After months in counseling, he joined a gay community and now
has a partner who respects his wishes to maintain his silence out of respect for his

aging parents. Mr. Y found a way to honor his own identity while respecting the strong religious and conservative values of his parents. He reports being happy and feeling "whole" for the first time in his life (cleansing and control).

Gay and Lesbian Families with Children

Gay and lesbian families with children are a recognized family structure of the twenty-first century. More and more children are being parented by gay or lesbian couples. Gay and lesbian activism has helped inform public policies and attitudes and has brought legal changes to the institutions of matrimony and adoption. Gay and lesbian marriages are increasingly gaining legal status and recognition in some states. Spousal and partner benefits are being granted for same-sex couples in some workplaces. Societal transition from the family structure of heterosexual parents and their biological children has evolved slowly, even more slowly than the acceptance of single-parenthood.

Perhaps the first stage in the evolution of new family structures in the mid-1900s came with the creation of new types of families as some single mothers with children from previous relationships became the heads of their households while others remarried, creating stepfamilies. Some created families with their lesbian partners. Whether she is divorced or has never been married, the sexual orientation of a woman with biological children is seldom a concern outside her family. As societal attitudes have changed, so have family and parenting styles. Parenting by gay and lesbian individuals and families is gaining acceptance. Children enter gay and lesbian families sometimes when a parent is granted full custody, sometimes only on weekends as visitation permits, and sometimes as a foster or adoptive child. Single-parent adoption of children has been permitted in most states for many years. More recently, two-parent adoptions by same-sex couples are now recognized in as many as twenty-five states (Curtis, 2005). Some lesbian couples are choosing to have children by artificial insemination by donor and to create families with a biological mother and a social mother (Vanfraussen et al., 2003). Constellations of gay and lesbian parents and their biological and adopted children are growing.

Early research has focused on the stability of relationships and social support networks surrounding lesbian families. There were concerns about the mental health of parents and psychological development of their children, as well as social stigma, molestation, and gay and lesbian identity of children. However, research concerning children from gay and lesbian families is relatively recent and is not broadly representative. Most early research focused on lesbian mothers, as parenting by gay men gained recognition somewhat later. Many studies lack randomization and representation of class and skin color and have small sample sizes. There are validity challenges around states of biological parenthood versus other kinds of parenthood (Flaks, 1995; Golombok, Perry, Burston, Murray, Mooney-Somers, & Golding, 2003).

Studies generally find that children in same-sex families are well adjusted, have positive parent-child relationships, evidence the same gender-typed behaviors as children in heterosexual families, and are thought to be equally influenced by their peers as are children in typical heterosexual families (Erera & Fredkisen, 1999; Kershaw, 2000; Leung, Erich, & Kanenberg, 2005; Perry, Burston, Murray, Mooney-Somers, Stevens, & Golding, 2003). After extensive literature reviews and investigation, Flaks (1995) concludes that there are no significant differences between children raised by gay and lesbian adults and those raised in heterosexual families. Children in two-parent gay and lesbian families are found to be as well adjusted as other children despite the considerable prejudice and heterosexism that gay and lesbian families must cope with (Kershaw, 2000). Recognizing gaps in studies of various parent-and-child populations, a recent study of gay and lesbian families that had adopted special-needs children reports similar findings in terms of child well-being. It is possible that same-sex couples may actually be doing a better job of parenting special-needs children, including older children who have experienced multiple placements (Leung et al., 2005).

Rich opportunities for future study are increasing as children continue to be parented in a variety of family forms and lifestyles. Interdisciplinary research opportunities abound in more than just traditional areas of interest. For example, how children raised in gay and lesbian families parent their children, utilize counseling, lead communities, and relate to global concerns of peace and well-being are potential areas of future study. There are many opportunities for social workers to develop culturally competent knowledge and skills to work with gay and lesbian families and to explore their own feelings concerning parenting.

SUMMARY

Social workers have a professional responsibility to reduce social injustice and oppression and to advocate for justice. While homophobia and discrimination against GLBT people have eased somewhat, it would be naive to believe that oppression has ended and that gender orientation is no longer an issue.

Van den Bergh and Crisp (2004) and Kocarek and Pelling (2003) identify attitudes, knowledge, and skills as areas necessary for competent social work practice with sexual minorities. First, social workers and counselors attitudes toward GLBT clients need to be identified and named. Self-awareness is critical to working with others, particularly in counseling GLBT clients. Remnants of homophobia from childhood can arise. It is not uncommon for issues of transference and countertransference to arise when one is counseling clients concerning sexual orientation. Supervision and personal counseling help many counselors grow professionally. Personal values and moral judgments all need to be considered so that clients with different sexual orientations are treated in a nonjudgmental and open manner. Second, knowledge is critical to gaining competence and current information. Social workers must have knowledge about GLBT people, including theoretical approaches to personality development, social functioning, and the political and legal ramifications of minority membership. Third, skill development includes competencies assessment and counseling as well as abilities to discern internalized homophobia, identify and/or help develop personal support systems, and utilize appropriate referral sources for GLBT clients as needed. Also, culturally competent counselors will attend to upgrading personal knowledge and skills, utilize qualified supervision, perhaps seek personal counseling concerning issues such as transference or homophobic reactions, and participate in ongoing continuing education and professional development, for example, by reading professional journals and keeping abreast of current research (Van den Bergh & Crisp, 2004).

From an existential perspective, the helping elements of holding, telling, mastering, and honoring provide a structure for clients to explore their painful emotions and traumas from experiences in their lives and take control of such experiences for the future. In addition to individual growth and recovery, social injustices and acts of oppression call for advocacy on numerous levels. The social work profession's commitment to practice from an ecological perspective recognizes transactions and dynamic interactions between people and at the interface of people and the environment. Not unlike many other minority groups, GLBT people are affected by their social environments. Social work with various-sized social systems is appropriate when one is working with clients, particularly in situations of social injustice and oppression.

Social workers and other helping professionals need to anticipate emerging concerns as social and political changes around the needs of gay and lesbian individuals, couples, and families unfold. Emerging concerns calling for attention from the social work profession include legalities of marriage and property, custody and inheritance for children, bereavement in instances of partner or spousal death, and same-sex partner/spousal benefits. Ongoing challenges of inclusivity and affirmation of GLBT persons call for advocacy and sensitivity to promote safe and nurturing environments (Neeley, 2005).

Although this chapter has not attempted to definitively explain either development or identity of sexual orientation, it is hoped that the reader will have enough information to explore those approaches that fit most closely with his or her professional perspective and worldview. Working with people who live their lives from a minority perspective provides a rich opportunity to understand another piece of the human condition from a different perspective and to empathetically be part of that experience.

13

Elderly Clients

OLDER PEOPLE IN THE WORLD

Human longevity of the twenty-first century is unprecedented in the history of humankind. Modern medicine, scientific advances, and healthier lifestyles are forces that are reshaping the physical processes of growing old and extending life expectancies throughout the world. People are living longer, healthier, more productive lives than ever before. Having aged gracefully with good health and active interests, older adults enjoy a variety of activities, including sports, travel, and community and cultural activities. As they have fun in their golden years, the well elderly with busy social lives are not seeking social services.

Opportunities abound for philosophers, scientists, and other helping professionals to gain a new understanding of living with meaning and purpose throughout the life span. The identifiers of "older" and "aging" are socially constructed terms informed by cultural values, religion, and social and geographic customs. Some societies call for elder respect, some identify caregivers, and some revere older individuals as wise elders to be followed. There are societies that identify retirement, loss of utility, frailty, and death and dying as stages of older adulthood. The present understanding of aging seems to be tainted by transference from those who regard the elderly as ill or frail. From such a perspective, old age is associated with the end of life and human mortality.

Understanding the existence of older people as they live in the world potentially holds great wisdom for diverse cultures. Each society's elderly population is part of the diversity of the world (Frankl, 1988). Older persons age sixty-five or older represent more of the world's population than ever before. The number of older persons is projected to rise from an estimated 7.1 percent of the total population in 2002 to an estimated 16.5 percent in 2050 (U.S. Census Bureau, 2004b). For the moment, a cross-sectional bit of the world's elderly encapsulates a global sense of experience from significant events in modern history. One such example is World War II veterans around the world, who share a similar configuration of experiences and form a quilt of international memory. Their collective memory is a synthesis of globally historical moments viewed through ethnically and culturally informed lenses common to individual experiences of being in the world and confronted by significant emotional traumas of war.

The world's elderly share commonalities of biological processes of aging and represent a worldwide collective memory. Some experience similar anxieties that stem from existential uncertainties of life. These uncertainties trigger a sense of meaninglessness, confusion, anxiety, and depression. Older persons can be at risk of victimization, poverty, loneliness, and discrimination in youth-oriented societies where they are not valued and are sometimes even forgotten. While aging is a normal process, old age is sometimes accompanied by loss of predictability and direction in life. On the other hand, many well elderly enjoy meaningful and rewarding lives as they experience dignity and new meaning opportunities.

Some elderly people feel frustration and confusion in their purpose and meaning in life in response to changing roles and occasional feelings of disenfranchisement. Informed by cultural, religious, and societal values, a person's worldview provides a lifelong orientation to interpreting meaning in life. Living without purpose or meaning places one in a state of existential frustration, a meaning vacuum (Frankl, 1984). Experiencing life without meaning is a particularly vulnerable state for elderly people, who may fill their meaning vacuum with self-pity, depression, and withdrawal from their external world. "The loss of relationship with the outer world is existentially important in the process of aging, along with a stronger dependence on the inner world" (Langle, 2001, p. 211). Langle cautions that the task of letting go eventually takes place in old age, even for those who have had long and exciting careers. Fast-paced modern lifestyles leave little room to prepare for letting go and finding inner peace. The abilities to let go and to continue on in old age with integrity and dignity are achievements to strive for, according to Erikson (1963).

According to Fry (2000), religiosity, spirituality, and personal meaning in life become increasingly important as one ages. Existential approaches to personal and psychological well-being of older people place great credence on these realms of human existence. Increasing human longevity in the twenty-first century presents opportunities and challenges for us to gain a broader understanding of living in the world for a long time.

Social workers generally practice from a psychosocial approach in their work with older clients. Meeting social needs may require great effort in securing social, health, and mental health services; economic resources; advocacy for human rights and needs; and protection from social injustice. Social workers and other professionals who work with older clients should not view aging populations as homogeneous either in terms of human diversity or in their capacities to contribute to the social and economic well-being of humankind. While resources and protection are important, these services often obviate attention to the importance of meaning and new meaning opportunities in the older person's life.

In the United States, the elderly population differs by age, class, race, ethnicity, sexual orientation, religion, political preference, wellness, and lifestyle. Older persons' perspectives and approaches to meaning in life vary according to birthplace, life experiences, and the degree to which cultural assimilation or accommodation has occurred. Elderly individuals who immigrated to America from China, Japan, Greece, South America, Poland, Ireland, Italy, Germany, Vietnam and other places have multicultural self-images informed by all their life experiences.

THE CHANGING DEMOGRAPHY OF AGING POPULATIONS

The global population reached six billion in 1999, according to U.S. Census Bureau estimates. Census data report that one of every fourteen people was over the age of sixty-five in 2002; at that time, this age group represented 7.1 percent of the global population (U.S. Census Bureau, 2004a). The aging population is projected to triple by 2050, when people over age sixty-five will represent 16.5 percent of the world's population. This rapid increase in the percentage of the elderly is a result of longer life expectancies and declining birth mortality rates. The proportion of women of childbearing age is expected to decline from 26 percent to 23 percent by 2050. Aging is a global phenomenon in which the achievement of longevity represents enormous success for humanity and has the potential to change the social order of the world.

The anticipated burst in the growth of the number of elderly people is expected to occur in 2011, when the baby boomers become sixty-five, through 2030 (Curl, Larkin, & Simons, 2005). Growing old in America is an increasingly important matter. Like the rest of the world, Americans are living longer and having babies less often. In 1990, one of eight Americans was age sixty-five or older. By the year 2050, those over age sixty-five will represent one of five Americans (20.7%), about 86.7 million people. Black elderly are expected to increase from 8.1 percent of the African American population in 1995 to 8.8 percent in 2030. The proportion of Hispanic elderly in America is projected to rise sharply from 4.5 percent to 11.2 percent over the same time period (Shapiro, 2004).

Overall life expectancy in the United States reached 77.6 years in 2003, with life expectancies for white females at 80.5 years and 75.4 years for white males (National Center for Health Statistics, 2005). Men are living longer than ever before and are closing the gap between their life expectancy and that of women.

Sixty-five is generally considered to be the age of retirement and the age at which one becomes eligible for Social Security benefits (slightly older for those born after 1940), as well as the beginning of older adulthood. For some, old age and retirement are accompanied by fixed incomes, including Social Security and pension benefits. Newman and Newman (2003) consider older persons in late adulthood to be those between ages sixty and seventy-four, and they identify very old age as beginning at age seventy-five. A widely accepted classification of older adults defines ages sixty-five to seventy-four as the "young old," ages seventy-five to eighty-four as "old-old," and eighty-five and above as "oldest-old" (Hooyman & Kiyak, 2005).

Higher poverty rates have been shown to correlate positively with increased age, a fact of life for some minority elderly individuals. Old age frequently brings loss of income as well as death of one's spouse and ill health, which create even greater personal and economic losses (Winbush, 2000). African American women are the poorest group in the United States, as factors of race and gender placed them in sub-servient and low-wage jobs for much of their lives. According to census data, about 10.8 percent of all White households were below the poverty level in 2004, as op-posed to 24.7 percent of all Black households. Census data show that 9.8 percent of all people over age sixty-five are living at or below the poverty level established by the Office of Budget Management for 2004 (DeNavas-Walt, Proctor, & Lee, 2005). Not all elderly people are poor. Recent data report that about 49.2 percent of elderly have annual incomes of $35,000 or above, and 29.8 percent have incomes of $50,000 and above (Experience Corps, 2005). This diversity in economic well-being requires a wide range of accommodations to meet the needs of all elderly people, the wealthy as well as the poor. Social work serves many; however, many also work with finan-cial planners, bankers, and family to manage estates and lifetime care.

Aging and Diversity

Within the diverse population of elderly people, some are poor, dependent, and disadvantaged, while others are productive and self-sufficient. The debate of en-titlement versus productivity is a continuing and value-laden concern that is influ-enced somewhat by demands from the social, political, and economic changes awaiting America's elderly population in the coming years. Costs for the growing elderly population present new challenges and opportunities as pension incomes, Social Security benefits, and health-care benefits take on new definitions and are af-fected by social welfare policies. Regardless of diversity or worldview, people in this age group are living younger longer and are a potentially strong political force in ongoing issues of entitlement versus productivity. Social and economic changes that are on course for aging America may well produce the greatest social move-ment of the twenty-first century (Brown, 2003; Moody, 2002).

There are great similarities among all people experiencing the process of aging, as well as culturally defined differences. Each ethnic minority group has socially constructed definitions of aging, being old, being valued or devalued, and defining roles for their elderly family members. Some of these culturally defined differences are evidenced among minority groups in American culture. African American, Native American, and Asian American communities are three groups that define roles and the caregiving of elderly somewhat differently in the amalgam of American society.

African American elderly people enjoy respect from friends and relatives for their experiences in life and are often close to their religious and family networks. Despite the jeopardies of being old, black, poor, and often in need of medical care, the African American elderly maintain social involvement with friends, families, and "fictive kin," or those who are not biologically listed but are considered to be family members (Chatters, Taylor, & Jackson, 1986; Timberlake & Chipungu, 1992). Extended family duties include grandparenting roles for older family members. African American elderly keep a kinship network that includes persons from early affectionate relationships, often from early struggles to overcome oppression. Spirituality and church involvement are important sources of support. Church funerals are an important part of the end of life for the elderly and their families (Fried & Mehrotra, 1998; Moore, 2003).

Among Native American elderly people, "the essence of Indian elderhood is grandparenting" (Green, 1995, p. 234). Older women perform many parenting duties for their grandchildren, freeing young mothers to be economically productive. This intergenerational caregiving is a means of teaching culture, values, respect, and communication. Informal caregiving extends across generations as a part of everyday living. Meaning in life is realized through intergenerational communities and purpose in family living. Rituals and customs surrounding death and dying vary among tribes. Old age and the end of life are part of the natural order, yet death is feared and sometimes associated with surreal images, particularly for Navajos. Lakotas spend time grieving, view and touch their deceased relative, and believe in joyful afterlife reunions (Fried & Mehrotra, 1998).

Strong ethnic ties are important to Chinese elderly people, who look forward to the prestige that comes with old age and logically follows the authority and respect gained through lifelong family solidarity (Allison & Geiger, 1993). Practices of patrilineal authority, respect for elders, and religious practices celebrating ancient legends and ancestors contribute to respect for the elderly in Chinese communities (Locke, 1992; Wong, 1988). Retirement and disengagement are culturally prescribed roles in Chinese families. The elderly often live in familiar ethnic communities but apart from their children, who often move to suburban or more upscale areas. Green (1995) notes that immigrant Chinese parents find their familiar ethnic community much more supportive than suburban living. Elderly family members are revered well into old age. Cultural influences affect how symptoms of dementia and Alzheimer's disease are normalized and treated as a part of old age (Yeo, 1996). Researchers continue to investigate whether dementias vary across ethnic groups or whether interpretation and response are critical variables that mask prevalence in some societies (Larson & Imai, 1996).

In Japanese and Japanese American families, the eldest son, charged with the responsibility of caring for his parents, can expect more support from his brothers than from his sisters, who have in-laws with the same expectations. A surprise sixtieth-birthday celebration is often a rite of passage from middle age to a time of less responsibility for Japanese adults. Different generations of Japanese Americans are influenced by different religions. Buddhist rituals and beliefs that call for acceptance of death are not subscribed to by third-generation Christian Japanese Americans. It is not uncommon for third-generation Japanese Americans to be ambivalent about traditional beliefs related to death and dying, such as allowing time for the spirit to leave the deceased (Berk, 2004; Fried & Mehrotra, 1998).

Vietnamese Americans face problems of adjustment, particularly as they age and experience isolation due to strong ethnic ties that may be less important to their sons and daughters, whose American preferences formed quickly. Disempowerment and loss of ancestral roots are very painful for aging Vietnamese. Extended kinship systems are broad and include both living and deceased members. Elderly family members are valued in the patrilineal system of Vietnamese families, where the grandfather serves as head of the nuclear family until his death. Traditional Vietnamese culture defines women's roles as secondary to those of fathers, husbands, and sons. The eldest son is expected to care for his mother in the event of her widowhood in old age (Tran, 1988).

The experiences of African American and Hispanic elderly people in the United States share some similarities. While African slaves were torn from their roots and forced into slavery in a nation far from their homeland, many Hispanics immigrated in search of whatever work they could find. Some elderly people in minority populations of color experience early deterioration due to lifetimes of hard physical work. Among aging Mexican Americans, there are those who have economic hardships from years of low-wage seasonal work, lack of benefits, ineligibility for Social Security, and citizenship status (Fried & Mehrotra, 1998). Low wages and menial labor provide little cushion for retirement. Religious beliefs and faith are important in the lives of older Hispanic Americans; however, persons of lower socioeconomic status are less likely to be involved in formal religion (Berk, 2004). Minority elderly people in the United States in the twenty-first century are diverse in health, income, education and employment backgrounds, and are living longer, healthier lives than ever before.

Minority and majority populations of elderly people risk potential loss of meaning in their lives. Living alone and moving into care facilities are isolating activities that can result in depression and loss of meaning. Anglo American elderly people struggle to fulfill culturally established expectations of independence and self-sufficiency in retirement. Far too often the elderly experience great disappointment and lose their potential for discovering meaning as they encounter isolation, poverty, and loneliness away from family and friends. This population of dependent elderly people is the portion of the older adult population requiring the most care and resources.

MYTHS ASSOCIATED WITH THE PROCESS OF AGING AND OLDER PEOPLE

Ageism is the negative perception of aging and older people. Ageism reflects fears associated with aging. Discrimination against mature and older adults is not just a problem after retirement for people above age sixty-five. The Age Discrimination in Employment Act protects workers age forty and above from discrimination in the workplace. The range of prohibited actions includes age discrimination in advertising, hiring, firing, compensation, and retaliation in instances of charges of or protests against discrimination or oppression due to age (Hooyman & Kiyak, 2005). Employment and retirement are only part of the social context of aging and are likely to be affected by physiological and cognitive changes that occur along the life cycle. People live, work, and age differently. Unfortunately, ageist attitudes cloud perceptions of individual differences in the aging process.

Myths surrounding the needs of the elderly evolve from an accumulation of life experiences and fears of the unknown. The fact that more people will be living longer presents a bittersweet realization for young and old alike. There are numerous myths about growing old and being elderly, some of which are discussed here.

Aging is mostly the same for all people, as all older people have the same needs. This myth denies the vast diversity of the increasing number of people above age sixty-five. Racial, ethnic, educational, and life experiences of the people in this group differ widely. Stereotypical characterizations of the elderly as disengaged, senile, set in their ways, and useless are becoming a thing of the past. The new elderly in the first decade of the twenty-first century have greater longevity and better health, and many continue to work well into their seventies and even beyond (Naleppa & Reid, 2003).

Retirement begins at age sixty-five for most people. Retirement is a socially constructed phase of aging linked to retirement benefits and Social Security systems in the United States and parts of Europe. Lifestyle and attitudinal changes are accompanying the rapid increase in America's aging population, particularly for people in late adulthood (i.e., ages sixty to seventy-five). These "third age" Americans are playing an ever-more important role in the workforce (Brown, 2003; Experience Corps, 2005). Some older adults continue to work in their present jobs, while others retire with benefits and find different employment. Women tend to have their own retirement pensions, education, and specialized employable skills and are productive longer. Nevertheless, research shows that while additional income is important, older people identify being valued and useful in terms of overall quality of life as primarily important (Ruchlin & Morris, 1991).

Elderly people who have adequate income and retirement benefits now will not experience inequality in years to come. In view of widespread concerns about Social Security shortfalls, some believe that people will be working longer in an effort to sustain their economic independence (McGuiness, 1989). This prediction is coming true for several reasons, only one of which is income. Self-esteem, active interests, a lack of role clarification for valued contributions to society after retirement, and a refusal to recognize approaching old age are just some of the reasons why older people continue to work. Health care, nursing home care, and housing are expensive, and some elderly people are not able to afford them. Some families assist their elderly relatives by providing these basic commodities even in situations where it is an economic hardship to do so.

Physical, cognitive, and psychological functioning decline sharply and make older adults dependent earlier. Schulz and Salthouse (cited in Cohen, Sandel, Thomas, & Barton, 2004) report that about 88 percent of persons older than sixty-five are in reasonably good health. Ninety percent of those who are age eighty-five or older need little assistance in their immediate surroundings, and only 25 to 30 percent of those eighty-five or older experience any of the dementias associated with old age. Good physical and mental health are key factors to living independently in old age. Only about 5 percent of older adults live in convalescent care or nursing homes (Jarvik, 1990; Kart & Kinney, 2001).

Sexual dysfunction, depression, and isolation accompany aging. In reality, some older people maintain old friendships and make new ones. People continue to function sexually throughout the life span in the absence of illness and anxiety about performance. People with inactive and disengaged lifestyles are at risk of even greater inactivity and poorer relationships in older age, including sexual relationships (Kart & Kinney, 2001). People who are sexually active throughout younger and middle adulthood are likely to maintain sexual interest and activity well into older adulthood.

Elderly people in particular ethnic groups are likely to be supported by inter-generational kinship systems. As extended family ties decline due to things like lack of mobility, family breakup, and family problems; younger generations are becoming much less likely to support their older relatives. Research shows varying degrees of support of older family members in terms of income and need (Cantor, Brennan, & Sainz, 1994; Curl et al., 2005). In other words, economic security provided by intergenerational systems is declining.

These and other myths about the elderly are prevalent and contribute to some people's disregard for the quality of life of older adults. Despite such myths, it is clearly apparent that the graying of America represents a growing and potentially powerful political group. More older people are responding to policy issues concerning the welfare of the nation's aging population. The commercial buying power of older adults calls for fewer advertisements for cosmetics and fashion using young and beautiful people; fewer bland observer or dependent roles for older actors in movies and television; and fewer ageist slurs about arthritis, wrinkles, and graying hair. The buying power of the growing proportion of elderly is a powerful economic force in the overall economy.

THEORETICAL APPROACHES TO AGING

Erikson (1963) defined the positive psychological stage of old age as achieving integrity while avoiding despair. Integrity involves living with dignity, accepting life, and being able to integrate life's successes and failures positively. Despair is quite the opposite pole, where unhappiness, past failures, and regrets cloud the value of life and living. A life well lived is like a cup that is filled versus a cup that is half empty. From an existential perspective, emotional pain is associated with life stages such as children leaving home, chronic illness, retirement, and moving toward grandparenthood. The task of the therapist is to help older clients work through existential pain and remember and celebrate meanings from the past and discover new meanings in the future (Lantz & Raiz, 2004).

Many early approaches to aging and lifestyle changes focus more on the individual than on transactions in the social environment. Early role theory associated age with the roles people carry out, including roles for middle age and old age and role losses in preparation for the end of life. Activity theory (Maddox, 1963), disengagement theory (Havighurst & Albrecht, 1953), development theory (Sheehy, 1982), and continuity theory (Atchley, 1972) are some of the early approaches that have frequently been used to explain the phenomenon of aging. Some believe that the most serious flaw in both continuity and disengagement theory is the omission of meaning. These theories have been described as occurring in a "phenomenological and ethnomethodological desert" (Clark, Pelham, & Clark, 1988).

Activity theory suggests that successful aging involves keeping active, extending the middle-age years and activities, and remaining socially and emotionally involved well into old age (Maddox, 1963). In other words, it is likely there is a direct correlation between high activity levels and success in aging. Some active people with multiple roles continue to participate in these activities into old age, but others seem to gain little satisfaction from such activities. Older people are not always able to value participating in many activities or get beyond persistent poverty or ill health. Activity theory pays little regard to the impact of the social environment on the process of aging. Rather than quantity of activities, quality is a much greater predictor of successful aging and well-being (Ritchie, Ritchie, & Dietz, 2001).

Disengagement theory assumes that over time the relationship between an elderly individual and society is one of mutual withdrawal. From this approach, disengagement is universal and intrinsic to human nature. Disengagement theory is not a theory of human development or senescence. In this functional approach to aging, the older person disengages or withdraws at a natural pace. As one's external involvement decreases, inner reflection and engagement are thought to occur. As the older person's capacities decline, so does his or her involvement. Many social workers no longer view disengagement theory with great enthusiasm. Generally people remain active in everyday life rather than voluntarily withdrawing as they grow older (Clark et al., 1988). Berk (2004) raises the concern that disengagement may be more a result of a lack of social stimuli and support than of any basic need to withdraw. Disengagement suggests a void of meaning and purpose.

Continuity theory assumes that activities continue throughout life and that adults maintain their social involvement well into retirement (Atchley, 1972). The relationship between the aging person and society is protected as familiar roles are kept or redefined to accommodate diminished activity while maintaining stability of self (Atchley, 1989). Habits, personality, and lifestyles remain constant throughout life and afford familiar strategies for adaptation to aging without loss of self-esteem (Lantz & Lantz, 1989). Continuity theory explains situations of declining health or disability as individual problems and illnesses rather than as voluntary disengagement.

Development theory recognizes life-span development and asserts that individuals acquire new roles, activities, and interests as they pass developmental milestones. The normal physiological processes of aging bring changes to skeletal and soft tissues of the body. As senescence or natural aging progresses, physical abilities and strengths decline. In the absence of illness, physical abilities are usually adequate to sustain activities and self-care. A study by Guttman (1984) confirms that some retirees find dignity in maintaining their professional skills and interests well into old age.

One recent approach taking into account interactions and balances between older adults and social systems is social exchange theory. Shifts in roles and opportunities occur between older adults and society, older adults and economic systems, and older adults and people in their immediate social environment. Social exchange theory takes into account the cost-benefit return of individual contributions to society versus the costs associated with supporting them (Maramaldi & Naleppa, 2003). Not being a simple cost-benefit economic construct the quality of everyday life in an aging and ever-more progressive society does not lend itself well to productivity measures. Reciprocity—give and take—continues to take place in transgenerational interactions and transactions as one ages and support needs and opportunities for support become different.

The social constructionist approach to aging considers individual interactions and transactions in everyday life to be actions that create and define meaning and purpose in individual lives. This post-positivist approach recognizes meaning in individual living in a social world, a recognition not unlike the existential perspective advocated by Frankl (1988), Krill (1979), and Lantz (2004). Social constructionists call for gathering information about the aging process through uncovering meanings in life narratives through ethnographic and qualitative research methodology. Narratives from older adults carry meanings far beyond sheer quantitative data relating to age, income, frailty, and wellness. Hooymen and Kiyak (2005) observe that aging and ways to care for the aged are socially constructed concepts, some of which should be addressed by social welfare policies. However, as population changes begin to reflect a much broader representation of old and very old adults, social welfare policies are likely to need restructuring.

Social constructivism supports critical theory and allows for a feminist perspective as older adults participate in developing models for creating new knowledge and understanding the nuances of aging in contemporary society (Hooyman & Kiyak, 2005; Moody, 2002). Understanding aging from the perspective of aging persons themselves is significant, but taking into account the importance of gender and power is critical as well. Feminist theorists recognize the importance of gender, power imbalances, and definitions of health, wellness, family, and the societal roles of women. Given the preponderance of elderly women versus elderly men, paying attention to the feminist perspective is important in linking information, practice, and meaning in aging.

LIVING LONGER AND LIVING BETTER

Social and economic needs of the past have defined retirement as a form of entitlement. Just as being forced into early retirement has created existential frustration and loss of meaning for some older adults, so may being forced into productivity during their retirement years create similar frustrations for today's young and middle-aged adults. Such extended productivity may contribute to frustration or meaning vacuums for adults looking forward to leaving their jobs and preparing for retirement. Extended work requirements could take away options to retire and relax in the golden years. Loss of autonomy at the end of the life cycle is particularly overwhelming for those who have maintained self-direction throughout their lifetimes.

Caregiving

Improved nutrition and health care have increased life expectancies. Healthy lifestyle changes are reducing and delaying the debilitating aspects of aging. Nevertheless, at one point or another along the trajectory of advancing age, older adults may experience chronic illnesses, widowhood, physical frailty, or deterioration in psychological functioning. The burden of caregiving falls most heavily upon female family members (Riemenschneider & Harper, 1990). Caregivers who suffer the most are those who have few societal supports and limited financial resources to use in purchasing other types of care, including respite for themselves. The costs of caregiving may include financial losses, depression, anger, role overload, intergenerational struggles, family disruption, and loss of employment (Berk, 2004; Cohen et al., 2004). While many caregivers experience intrinsic rewards from their caregiving, this additional burden is not rewarding for everyone.

It is important for social workers and other helping professionals to recognize that family caregivers may be overburdened. Advocacy is needed to create more alternative care services such as day treatment programs, community-supported nursing homes, assisted living facilities, and affordable or subsidized institutional care for dependent elderly people who are in need of total care. Home teams and adaptive equipment enable the elderly to remain in their own homes longer and can make living at home possible for elderly individuals who need support to maintain independence. More staff-supported units are needed for elderly couples who wish to remain together but are unable to live without skilled care. The aging process should be a protected, meaningful voyage that allows all people to maintain their dignity (Lantz & Lantz, 1989).

Dealing with Loss

Many well elderly people age naturally and experience little loss of health or mobility. They make successful adjustments to social, psychological, and economic changes as they occur throughout the life cycle. The well-being of the elderly is contingent not only upon physical strength but also linkage to social supports such as financial, medical, and recreational systems. Emotional and psychological well-being are crucial to coping with loss. Loss associated with aging is a series of normal but painful episodes that occur throughout the life span. Deaths of loved ones, illness, injuries, divorce, physical and/or mental deterioration, and failed hopes can disrupt meaning in ordinary daily routines. Identifying potentially meaningful adaptations and seeking ways to fill emerging or existing meaning vacuums can restore a sense of meaning and purpose in life for the elderly.

Preventing Elder Abuse

Elder abuse is not generally a crime committed by strangers. Family members, friends, spouses, and caregivers are typically the perpetrators of elder abuse, which may involve nutritional, physical, and emotional abuses. The burden of caregiving is only one of the causes of elder abuse. Societal mores, values, and regard for older adults are important variables in the configuration of elder care and abuse. Family relationships and issues of respect and dignity are important variables that relate to how elderly family members are treated and cared for.

Social workers and other professionals who discover potential or actual abuse of elderly clients are confronted with issues of autonomy and self-determination. Linzer (2004) discusses the value conflict of autonomy versus beneficence, a serious ethical dilemma in situations of competent older adults who are believed or reported to be at risk of abuse. Even older adults who report their own abuse may choose to remain in the abusive living situation. Maintaining follow-up and contact are some alternatives in situations of client autonomy and demands for confidentiality.

In some situations the elderly person desires change, while some may not be competent and need protection from formal services. Other situations may require police involvement. Some situations of elder abuse can be resolved with family counseling and assistance such as respite care to relieve stressed caregivers. According to Wolf (2000), at least one in six elderly people is at risk of abuse. This estimation of elder abuse may be much lower than actual incidence rates. Connected to social, cultural, and personal family values and lifestyles, elder abuse is a problem that must not be ignored.

Caring for Dependent Elderly Persons at the End of the Life Cycle

Caring for the dependent elderly in a growing population of elderly people is a major national concern that is ill provided for in our market economy. At least three-fourths of dependent elderly people live outside institutional care systems. However, these people are often physically disabled and generally have more than one critical or chronic disorder. Health-care costs are consuming personal wealth and creating health-care crises in the United States as well as many other parts of the world.

Social work is often the profession at the interface of the dependent elderly person, extended family, and health-care system. The social worker may serve many network intervention functions in situations of illnesses such as heart disease, mental illness, diabetes, cancer, and other serious disorders. Social service network intervention occurs when resources are pooled to facilitate care, including medical, hospital, and nursing home services; home health care; hospice care; and grief counseling for the patient and for family members. Medical science has equipped practitioners to provide the level of care needed by most dependent elderly; ironically, society's valuing of the dependent elderly has not kept pace with technological progress.

Dementia and Alzheimer's Disease

While depression is a serious affliction for some elderly people, perhaps the most dreaded disorders of old age are dementia and Alzheimer's disease. Dementia may be caused by a range of disorders, including vascular or arteriosclerotic disorders, Alzheimer's disease, Parkinson's and Huntington's Chorea disorders, head trauma, alcohol abuse, and AIDS. Some indications of dementia are lower alertness; sleep disturbances; memory loss; thinking and perception impairment; speech difficulties, including inability to recall words; disorientation; and delusions (Cavanaugh & Blanchard-Fields, 2002). Symptoms of vascular dementia may appear in late adulthood and progress very slowly but may never become totally disabling.

Alzheimer's disease is perhaps the least understood of all the dementias. Alzheimer's disease affects about 5 percent of people ages sixty through seventy-four and becomes much more prevalent in old age, affecting as many as 50 percent of people over age eighty-five (Hooyman & Kiyak, 2005; National Institute on Aging, 2006). Perhaps linked to genetics, brain deterioration occurs in Alzheimer's disease as neurofibrillary tangles and neuritic plaques form in brain tissue (Cavanaugh & Blanchard-Fields, 2002). The early stages of Alzheimer's disease look like much the rest of the dementias. However, progression and end stages of the disease are extremely debilitating, requiring total care of patients, who are no longer functional, continent, or cognizant.

Caregiving for people suffering from dementia can extend over decades, at great expense to families and to nations. Social work and other helping and medical professions are primary providers of services, including individual and family counseling, provision of assistive equipment, assisted living, and convalescent care facilities. Sensitive awareness of a patient's ethnicity, worldview, and life experiences is critical to involving the patient in quality care to the extent of his or her abilities as long as possible. Demands for assisted living and for skilled caregiving are increasing as people live longer and as the onset of debilitating disorders occur somewhat later and last well into old age.

Confronting Stereotypes

Elderly people are often viewed as being frail, unproductive, and poor. These stereotypes are reactions to the lack of value given to elderly persons in America and to fear of old age. The diversity of aging populations requires that cross-culturally competent practitioners gain awareness of their own biases and values. Social work and other helping professions can maximize the assessment of strengths and prevent discriminatory practices by working with aging clients from a wellness model of human nature.

A Case of Alzheimer's Disease: Mr. and Mrs. J's Experience

Referred by his physician, Mr. J, a seventy-four-year-old African American male, had recently been diagnosed as having Alzheimer's disease. On his intake day, he had somehow driven the family car to the clinic. While having forgotten his last name, he was pleased that he had left his wife at home and joked that "she will be mad at me."

Mr. J was pleasant and seemed to have no understanding of why his physician was worried about him. He commented, "I know the man on your door, but I can't seem to remember his name. Do you know the man on the door?" The stranger in question that particular holiday season was Santa Claus.

Mr. J, a retired coal miner, was becoming a problem for his wife, his only caretaker. The couple was childless, but they did have friends who visited regularly. Mr. J could no longer be trusted to light his pipe, do small chores around the house, go outdoors without supervision, or completely dress himself without assistance. Several community resources assisted with transportation and meal preparation. Volunteers and friends provided respite for Mrs. J, who shouldered the burden of caregiving for her husband.

Existential reflection and realization experiences provided some benefit to Mr. J, both as an outpatient client and eventually as a nursing home patient. These experiences involved conversations about nature, the weather, birds, objects in view, and sometimes people who came to his memory. Mr. J found meaning and pleasure in conversation and the sounds of laughter. For him, meaning could only be immediately experienced, as he had little recall of either remote or recent events in his life. He enjoyed social exchanges, made eye contact, and liked to be joined in watching cartoons on television. Mr. J welcomed his friends into his life, forgetting their names but not the feeling of their relationships. Finally, even when he became unaware of his surroundings and was unable to recognize his wife, Mr. J was still always less agitated during her daily visits.

Mr. J's physical and mental states deteriorated rapidly, and he was admitted to a convalescent care facility for medication management of Alzheimer's disease and circulation problems associated with diabetes. Mr. J died six months after entering the care facility, a little less than ten months after he failed to recognize "the man on the door."

Mrs. J: Grief and Widowhood

After her husband's death, Mrs. J experienced crying episodes, weight loss, sleeplessness, and periods of severe fatigue. She worried about being alone, as her house felt empty, and she didn't want to "face life alone." Upon being asked by the social worker how long she and Mr. J had been in love, Mrs. J replied, "Forever, since we were just young 'uns." Mrs. J wanted to be reassured that "forever" lasts beyond a lifetime and that she would always have Mr. J's love. Mrs. J had experienced considerable loss as reality slipped away from Mr. J, but she held onto meaning from her recollection of their many years together.

Existential treatment elements were used with Mrs. J. She was helped to hold her loss and grief in the presence of the worker's empathetic availability. Sometimes exhausted from weeping, Mrs. J. relived the trauma of her husband's death. She told her memories of their life together and brought pictures to her treatment appointments. As she mastered her grief and regained composure, she shared that her husband would have wanted her to help others like him.

A few months after her husband's death, Mrs. J began to volunteer to help Alzheimer's patients and their families. She found meaning and purpose in life by giving to others some of the kindnesses that had been given to her during her time of despair. She found a way to honor her husband as she helped others cope with Alzheimer's disease, a thief of personhood. Dedicating her work with other victims of the disease to the memory of her husband emerged as a meaning opportunity that allowed her to discover new meaning and purpose in life (existential realization).

Mrs. J and the Curative Factors

For Mrs. J, the worker's willingness to join her emotionally in her deep despair was the most important curative factor. Mrs. J believed that the worker "joined my world" (empathetic availability). Such empathy is the deepest way to demonstrate worldview respect. Consistent with cross-cultural curative factors, catharsis or cleansing experiences occurred as a result of the worker's active empathy. Mrs. J was helped to process and manage her grief through her volunteer work in memory of her husband. Her involvement helped her experience existential realization in life and new meaning opportunities. Social work treatment was effective in helping Mrs. J cope with her husband's progressive illness and reduce the existential vacuum from which she suffered in response to her loss. As Mrs. J redefined herself and her role in helping others, the social worker's job was finished.

Mrs. V: Old-Old

Mrs. V is the first author's mother. Mother of two, widowed at age fifty, and retired from her nursing career at age seventy, she is looking forward to her ninety-first birthday. A resident in a convalescent care facility since age eighty-eight, she suffers from late onset of vascular dementia or perhaps Alzheimer's disease. Her wit, humor, and chatter provide interesting avenues to understanding the prism of her mind as she travels in and out of time zones in past and current memory. She says, "Of course I get confused—I have too many memories to keep straight."

Having finished lunch on a day when she was less aware than usual, Mother rolled the remaining cookie crumbs into a tight little ball, placed the cookie crumb ball on the table, and said, "Think I'll feed my dog that cookie." Ready to do the job for her, I asked where her dog had gone. "Oh, under the table, of course." She chuckled.

Mother watched as I dropped the cookie crumb under the table. I thought about where my mother's mind had taken her. I said, "You know, you take such good care of your dog."

Mother sat up straight in her wheelchair as she adamantly stated, "I'm very proud of how well I take care of my dog—and of my bird. Do you remember how I drove my bird to the vet to have his leg put back together after he flew into the ceiling fan?"

Then we talked. As her daughter, I remembered that summer more than twenty years ago and the bird with the tiny splint. The presence of an empathetic listener brought a flood of narrative from that long-ago time as Mother talked about how the bird escaped from his cage, and how tenderly the pet clinic treated the tiny creature. As she explored memories from long ago, the dog under the table became just another lost memory. Reminiscing brings pleasure and inner peace for Mother even when her memories are viewed retrospectively through a lens somewhere deep in her aging brain.

Reflections on a life well lived represent inner peace and mastery of the experience. For Mrs. V, the existential treatment elements of holding and telling the experience in the time zone of her mind brought satisfaction and existential realization for the moment. The lesson to be learned from the narrative of Mrs. V is that communication with elderly individuals suffering from confusion and loss of memory at the end of life requires special sensitivity on the part of social workers, nurses, physicians, and other caregivers. Discounting conversation from another time, correcting misinformation, and realigning conversations in the here and now are all insensitive and useless. There are many rewarding opportunities for practitioners who can follow the path of the aging human brain and enter the place and time of being in the world for the moment. Narratives such as this reflect existential realization and quality of life and reflect accomplishment of Erikson's

(1963) eighth stage as psychological integrity continues even for dependent and frail elderly.

SUMMARY

Gaining competence in cross-cultural social work practice with the elderly demands a deep awareness of professional values and biases. The helping relationship between the worker and the elderly client can be disrupted by several forces. First, worker bias and prejudice toward the elderly can impede the worker's ability to be an effective cross-cultural social work practitioner. Second, social values that American society holds regarding the elderly affect the design of the caregiving system and reflect the priorities and biases of the population at large. Third, advocating for the needs of older adults requires young adults and professionals to confront their own mortality and look for meaning throughout the full life cycle. Finally, the debate of entitlement versus productivity, rather than quality of retirement, is a result of economic concerns rather than the belief that life is meaningful as long as the human spirit is present (Frankl, 1988).

To view old age as a malady negates the integrity of the human spirit (Keith, 1982). Being old in different cultures involves different culturally prescribed ways of making and discovering meaning. Aging cannot be isolated from the cultural context in which it occurs if the processes of aging are to be understood cross-culturally. Ethnic and cultural beliefs and practices need to be explored at both group and individual levels so that individual meaning potentials can be better understood. An old person continues to be who he or she has always been in the multicultural schema of the world, and his or her worldview reflects experiences of living in the world. Nevertheless, role transitions can result in meaning disruption and loss of meaning in life, as daily practices and familiar routines change in response to advancing age (Lantz, 1993).

In their research on multiethnic elderly populations, Cantor et al. (1994) remind their readers of the importance of addressing issues of "status and differences when working with minorities of culture, rather than merely relying on ethnic differences in norms and values as such" (p. 126). Each culture prescribes age-appropriate social roles and generally provides transitional experiences from one role to another, hopefully from one life stage to another.

When elderly clients experience a meaning vacuum as they become unable to create or discover meaning in their world, they may fill this vacuum with confusion or depression and may even lose the will to live. Their ability to create and discover meaning may be encumbered by illness, frailty, the onset of Alzheimer's disease, or the deaths of elderly friends or family members. A cross-cultural approach to helping must identify the defiant capability within the human spirit to overcome the limitations of the body, psyche, and environment (Frankl, 1967; Popielski, 1990).

This strength can surpass undue hardship even in situations where the end of the human life cycle seems inevitable (Frankl, 1959). Self-transcendence can be attained as the human spirit's potential for fulfillment is met throughout all stages of life (Frankl, 1959; Harper, 1990a). It is the social worker's responsibility to facilitate reflection and to recover meaning awareness and enhance meaning-making capacities, even to the extent of transcendence over fear and loss associated with nearing the end of life (Lantz & Lantz, 1989).

References

Abramovitz, M. (1988). *Regulating the lives of women.* Boston: South End Press.

Ackerman, N. W. (1966). *Treating the troubled family.* New York: Basic Books.

Advancing HIV prevention: New strategies for a changing epidemic—United States, 2003. (2003). *Morbidity & Mortality Weekly Report, 52*(15), 329–332.

Allison, M. T., & Geiger, C. W. (1993). The nature of leisure activities among the Chinese-American elderly. *Leisure Sciences, 15,* 309–319.

Alther, L. (1998). Border states. In J. Dyer (Ed.), *Bloodroot* (pp. 22–30). Lexington: University Press of Kentucky.

Altman, D. (2002). Globalization and the international gay/lesbian movement. In D. Richardson & S. Seidman (Eds.), *Handbook of lesbian and gay studies* (pp. 416–425). Thousand Oaks, CA: Sage.

Altman, N., & Davies, J. M. (2002). Out of the blue. *Psychoanalytic Dialogues, 12*(3), 359–360.

American Psychiatric Association. (1982). *Desk reference to the diagnostic criteria from DSM-III.* Washington, DC: American Psychiatric Association.

American Psychiatric Association. (2000). *Diagnostic criteria from DSM-IV-TR.* Washington, DC: American Psychiatric Association.

American Psychiatric Association. (1994). *Diagnostic and statistical manual of mental disorders* (4th ed.). Washington, DC: American Psychiatric Association.

Andreou, C. (1992). *Inner and outer reality in children and adolescents: Intercultural therapy.* Oxford: Blackwell Scientific.

Anonymous. (1990). *Reflections on a lesbian's experience in therapy with a male, heterosexual therapist.* Unpublished manuscript.

Appalachian Regional Commission. (2006). *The Appalachian region.* Retrieved March 10, 2006, from http://www.arc.gov

Appy, C. G. (2003). *Patriots: The Vietnam War remembered from all sides.* New York: Viking.

Atchley, R. (1972). *The social forces in later life.* Belmont, CA: Wadsworth.

Atchley, R. (1989). A continuity theory of normal aging. *The Gerontologist, 29*(2), 183–190.

Attneave, C. (1982). American Indian and Alaska Native families: Emigrants in their own homeland. In J. K. McGoldrick, J. Pearce, & J. Gordana (Eds.), *Ethnicity and family therapy* (pp. 55–83). New York: Guilford.

Barkan, E. R. (1995). Out of the carnage and into the crucible: Southwest Asian refugees journey from old worlds to a new one. *Journal of American Ethnic History, 14*(4), 53–58.

Barker, R. (1999). *The social work dictionary* (3rd ed.). Washington, DC: NASW Press.

Barker, R. (2003). *The social work dictionary* (5th ed.). Washington, DC: NASW Press.

Barnes, J. S., & Bennett, C. E. (2002). *The Asian population: 2000.* Retrieved September 2, 2005, from http://www.census.gov/prod/2002pubs/c2kbr0116.pdf

Bass, S., Kutza, E., & Torres-Gil, F. (1990). *Diversity in aging.* Glenview, IL: Scott, Foresman.

Beauvoir, S. de. (1968). *The second sex.* New York: Modern Library.

Becerra, R. (1988). The Mexican American family. In C. Mindel, R. Habenstein, & R. Wright (Eds.), *Ethnic families in America* (pp. 141–159). New York: Elsevier.

Beemyn, B. (2003). Serving the needs of transgender college students. *Journal of Gay and Lesbian Issues in Education, 1*(1), 33–50.

Bell, J. L. (1995). Traumatic event debriefing: Service delivery designs and the role of social work. *Social Work, 40*(1), 36–43.

Berg, I., & Jaya, A. (1993). Different and same: Family therapy with Asian American families. *Journal of Marital and Family Therapy, 19*(1), 31–38.

Berk, L. E. (2004). *Development through the lifespan* (3rd ed.). Boston: Allyn and Bacon.

Bemstein, R. (2004). *Hispanic and Asian Americans increasing faster than overall population.* Retrieved July 25, 2005, from http://www.census.gov/Press.Release/www/releases/archives/race/0018.html

Biggers, J. (2005). *The United States of Appalachia: How southern mountaineers brought independence, culture, and enlightenment to America.* Emeryville, CA: Shoemaker & Hoard.

Billings, D. B. (1999). Introduction. In D. B. Billings, G. Norman, & K. Ledford (Eds.), *Confronting Appalachian stereotypes: Backtalk from an American region* (pp. 3–20). Lexington: University Press of Kentucky.

Billingsley, A. (1969). Family functioning in the low-income Black community. *Social Casework, 50*(10), 563–572.

Billingsley, A. (1992). *Climbing Jacob's ladder: The enduring legacy of African American families.* New York: Simon and Schuster.

Binswanger, L. (1963). *Being-in-the-world.* New York: Basic Books.

Black Enterprise. (2005). Earnings gain, wealth loss. *Black Issues in Higher Education, 21*(13), 33.

Borum, V. (2005). An Afrocentric approach in working with African American families. In E. P. Congress & M. J. Gonzales (Eds.), *Multicultural perspectives in working with families* (pp. 242–266). New York: Springer.

Boyd-Franklin, N. (2003). *Black families in therapy.* New York: Guilford.

Boyd-Franklin, N., & Lockwood, T. W. (1999). Spirituality and religion: Implications for psychotherapy with African American clients and families. In F. Walsh (Ed.), *Spiritual resources in family therapy* (pp. 90–103). New York: Guilford Press.

Bragg, R. (2001). *Ava's man* (1st ed.). New York: Alfred A. Knopf.

Bragg, R. (2003). *I am a soldier, too: The Jessica Lynch story* (1st ed.). New York: Alfred A. Knopf.

Brende, J., & Parson, E. (1985). *Vietnam veterans: The road to recovery.* New York: New American Library.

Breslau, N. (2002). Epidemiologic studies of trauma, posttraumatic stress disorder, and other psychiatric disorders. *Canadian Journal of Psychiatry, 47*(10), 923–930.

Bride, B. E., Robinson, M. M., Yegidis, B., & Figley, C. R. (2004). Development and validation of the secondary traumatic stress scale. *Research on Social Work Practice, 14*(1), 27–35.

Bridges, S. K., Selvidge, M. M. D., & Matthews, C. R. (2003). Lesbian women of color: Therapeutic issues and challenges. *Journal of Multicultural Counseling and Development, 31*(2), 113–130.

Bridle, S. (2000). The seeds of the self. *Enlightenment Magazine.* Retrieved February 15, 2006, from http://www.wie.org/j17/kern.asp?pf=1

Bromley, M. (1987). New beginnings for Cambodian refugees—or further disruptions. *Social Work, 32*(3), 236–239.

Brooks, L. J., Haskins, D. G., & Kehe, J. V. (2004). Counseling and psychotherapy with African American clients. In T. B. Smith (Ed.), *Practicing multiculturalism* (pp. 145–166). Boston: Pearson.

Brown, A. (1981). Duality: The need to consider this characteristic when treating Black families. *The Family, 8,* 88–89.

Brown, L. (1989). Lesbians, gay men and their families: Common clinical issues. *Journal of Gay and Lesbian Psychotherapy, 1*(1), 65–77.

Brown, L. S. (2006). Still subversive after all these years: The relevance of feminist therapy in the age of evidence-based practice. *Psychology of Women Quarterly, 30*(1), 15–24.

Brown, P. M. A. (1990). The wisdom of family therapists. *Clinical Social Work Journal, 18*(3), 293–308.

Brown, S. K. (2003). *Staying ahead of the curve 2003: The AARP working in retirement study.* Retrieved May 1, 2006, from http://research.aarp.org

Brucker, P. S., & Perry, B. J. (1998). American Indians: Presenting concerns and considerations for family therapists. *American Journal of Family Therapy, 26*(4), 307–319.

Burgos-Ocasio, H. (1996). Understanding the Hispanic community. In M. C. Julia (Ed.), *Multicultural awareness in the health care profession* (pp. 111–130). Needham Heights, MA: Allyn and Bacon.

Burgos-Ocasio, H. (2000). Hispanic women. In M. C. Julia (Ed.), *Constructing gender: Multicultural perspectives in working with women* (pp. 109–137). Belmont, CA: Brooks/Cole.

Cameron, J., & Gibson-Graham, J. K. (2003). Feminising the economy: Metaphors, strategies, politics. *Gender, Place and Culture, 10*(2), 145–157.

Canclini, N. G. (1992). The hybrid: A conversation with Margarita Zires, Raymundo Mier, and Mabel Piccini. *Boundary, 2*(20), 77–92.

Cantor, M. H., Brennan, M., & Sainz, A. (1994). The importance of ethnicity in the social support systems of older New Yorkers: A longitudinal perspective (1970 to 1990). *Journal of Gerontological Social Work, 22*(1), 95–128.

Caple, F. S., & Salcido, R. M. (1995). Engaging effectively with culturally diverse families and children. *Social Work in Education, 17*(3), 159–171.

Caudill, H. (1963). *Night comes to the Cumberlands.* Boston: Little Brown.

Cavanaugh, J. C., & Blanchard-Fields, F. (2002). *Adult development and aging* (4th ed.). Belmont, CA: Wadsworth.

Chatters, L. M., Taylor, R. J., & Jackson, J. S. (1986). Aged Blacks' choices for an informal helper network. *Journal of Gerontology, 41*(1), 94–100.

Chau, K. L. (1990). A model for teaching cross-cultural practice in social work. *Journal of Social Work Education, 26*(2), 124–134.

Chestang, L. (1976). Environmental influences on social functioning: The Black experience. In P. J. Cafferty & L. Chestang (Eds.), *The diverse society: Implications for social policy* (pp. 59–74). Washington, DC: National Association of Social Workers.

Choney, S. K., Berryhill-Paapke, E., & Robbins, R. R. (1995). The acculturation of American Indians: Developing frameworks for research and practice. In J. G. Ponterotto, J. M. Casas, L. A. Suzuki, & C. M. Alexander (Eds.), *Handbook of multicultural counseling* (pp. 73–91). Thousand Oaks, CA: Sage.

Chung, C. Y., & Bemak, F. (2002). The relationship of culture and empathy in cross-cultural counseling. *Journal of Counseling and Development, 80*(2), 154–160.

Chung, E. (1996). Asian Americans. In M. C. Julia (Ed.), *Multicultural awareness in the health care profession* (pp. 77–110). Needham Heights, MA: Allyn and Bacon.

Clark, W., Pelham, A., & Clark, M. (1988). *Old and poor.* Lexinton, KY: Heath.

Cofer, J. O. (1990). *Silent dancing: A partial remembrance of a Puerto Rican childhood.* Houston, TX: Arte Publico Press.

Cohen, H. L., Sandel, M. H., Thomas, C. L., & Barton, T. R. (2004). Using focus groups as an educational methodology: Deconstructing stereotypes and social work practice misconceptions concerning aging and older adults. *Educational Gerontology, 30*(4), 329–346.

Cohn, D. (2005, June 9). Hispanic growth surge fueled by births in U.S. *Washington Post,* p. A1.

Collins, K. A. (2002). An examination of feminist psychotherapy in North America during the 1980s. *Guidance and Counseling, 7*(4), 105–111.

Colon, E. (2001). A multidiversity perspective on Latinos. In G. A. Appleby, E. Colon, & J. Hamilton (Eds.), *Diversity, oppression and social functioning* (pp. 92–108). Boston: Allyn and Bacon.

Combs, G. M. (2003). The duality of race and gender for managerial African American women: Implications of informal social networks on career advancement. *Human Resource Development Review, 2*(4), 385–405.

Cook, D. A., & Wiley, C. Y. (2000). Psychotherapy with members of African American churches and spiritual traditions. In P. S. Richards & A. E. Bergin (Eds.), *Handbook of psychotherapy and religious diversity* (pp. 369–396). Washington, DC: American Psychological Association.

Cook, R. (2005). *Indian nations tribal sovereignty.* Retrieved July 15, 2005, from http://www.americanindiansource.com/sovereignty.html

Cooper, D. (2002). Imagining the place of the state: When governance and social power meet. In D. Richardson & S. Seidmen (Eds.), *Handbook of lesbian and gay studies* (pp. 231–252). Thousand Oaks, CA: Sage.

Corbin, J., & Strauss, A. (1990). Grounded theory method: Procedures, canons, and evaluative criteria. *Qualitative Sociology, 13*(1), 3–19.

Crumbaugh, J., & Maholick, L. (1963). *Purpose in life test.* Murfreesboro, TN: Psychometric Affiliates.

Culture-Sensitive Health Care: Asian. (2000). *What language does your patient hurt in? A practical guide to culturally competent care.* Amherst, MA: Diversity Resources.

Curl, A. L., Larkin, H., & Simons, K. (2005). Special section: Innovations in gerontological social work education factors affecting willingness of social work students to accept jobs in aging. *Journal of Social Work Education, 41*(3), 393–406.

Curtis, C. (2005, April 14). *Indiana court clears gay couple to adopt.* Retrieved February 27, 2006, 2006, from http://news.yahoo.com/s/po/20060414/co_po/indianacourtclearsgay coupletoadopt

De la Rey, C., & McKay, S. (2006). Peacebuilding as a gendered process. *Journal of Social Issues, 1*(62), 14–153.

DeNavas-Walt, C., Proctor, B. D., & Lee, C. H. (2005). *Income, poverty, and health insurance coverage in the United States: 2004* (No. Current Population Reports, P60-229). Washington, DC: U.S. Census Bureau, U.S. Government Printing Office.

De Shazer, S. (1991). *Putting difference to work.* New York: Norton.

Devore, W. (1983). Ethnic reality: The life model and work with Black families. *Social Casework, 64*(9), 525–531.

De Waal, A. (2004). Everything you ever wanted to know. *Index on Censorship, 33*(1), 27–37.

Dominelli, L. (2002). *Feminist social work theory and practice.* Basingstoke, Hampshire: Palgrave.

Donovan, J. (1987). *Feminist theory.* New York: Ungar Publishing.

Dubois, B. L., & Miley, K. K. (2005). *Social work: An empowering profession* (5th ed.). Boston: Allyn and Bacon.

Duran, E., & Duran, B. (1995). *Native American post-colonial psychology.* Albany, NY: SUNY Press.

Echols, A. (2002). *Shaky ground: The sixties and its aftershocks:* New York: Columbia University Press.

Edwards, D. (1996). *Shamanism—general overview—frequently asked questions.* Retrieved July 10, 2005, from http://www.faqs.org/faqs/shamanism/overview

Eisenstein, Z. (1984). *Feminism and sexual equality.* New York: Monthly Review Press.

Eliade, M. (1964). *Shamanism.* London: Routledge and Kegan Paul.

Elliott, L. (2005). *Agent Purple and Agent Orange.* Retrieved December 3, 2005, from http://www.cbc.ca/news/background/agentorange

Erera, P. I., & Fredkisen, K. (1999). Lesbian stepfamilies: A unique family structure. *Families in Society: The Journal of Contemporary Human Services, 80*(13), 263–269.

Ergood, B., & Kuhre, B. (1991). Demographic characteristics of the region. In B. Ergood & B. Kuhre (Eds.), *Appalachia: Social context, past and present* (3rd ed., pp. 65–98). Dubuque, IA: Kendall/Hunt.

Erikson, E. H. (1963). *Childhood and society* (2nd ed., rev. and enl.). New York: Norton.

Este, D. C. (2004). The Black church as a social welfare institution: Union United Church and the development of Montreal's Black community, 1907–1940. *Journal of Black Studies, 35*(1), 3–22.

Evans, K. M., Kincade, E. A., Marbley, A. F., & Seem, S. R. (2005). Feminism and feminist therapy: Lessons from the past and hopes for the future. *Journal of Counseling and Development, 83*(3), 269–277.

Evans, M.-L., George-Warren, H., & Santelli, R. (2004). *The Appalachians: America's first and last frontier* (1st ed.). New York: Random House.

Evans, S. M. (2002). Re-viewing the second wave. *Feminist Studies, 28*(2), 259–267.

Everett, F., Proctor, N., & Cartnell, B. (1983). Providing psychological services to American Indian children and families. *Professional Psychology, 14*(5), 588–603.

Experience Corps. (2005). *Fact sheet on aging in America.* Retrieved April 15, 2006, from http://www.experiencecorps.org

Fabry, J. (1979). The noetic unconscious. *International Forum for Logotherapy, 2*(1), 8–12.

Fabry, J. (1994). *The pursuit of meaning.* Abilene, TX: Institute of Logotherapy Press.

Feinstein, A., Owen, J., & Blair, N. (2002). A hazardous profession: War, journalists, and psychopathology. *American Journal of Psychiatry, 159*(9), 1570–1575.

Ferraro, K. (1983). Rationalizing violence. *Victimology: An International Journal, 8,* 203–212.

Figley, C. (1990). *Helping traumatized families.* San Francisco: Jossey-Bass.

Figley, C. R. (2002). *Treating compassion fatigue.* New York: Brunner-Routledge.

Flaks, D. K. (1995). Research issues. In A. Sullivan (Ed.), *Issues in gay and lesbian adoption* (pp. 21–38). Washington, DC: Child Welfare League of America.

Fong, R. (2004). *Culturally competent practice with immigrant and refugee children and families.* New York: Guilford Press.

Fong, R., & Wu, D. Y. (1996). Socialization issues for Chinese American children and families. *Social Work in Education, 18*(2), 71–82.

Frankl, V. (1959). *Man's search for meaning.* New York: Simon and Schuster.

Frankl, V. (1967). *Psychotherapy and existentialism.* New York: Simon and Schuster.

Frankl, V. (1969). *The will to meaning.* New York: New American Library.

Frankl, V. (1973). *The doctor and the soul.* New York: Vintage Books.

Frankl, V. (1975). *The unconscious God.* New York: Simon and Schuster.

Frankl, V. (1984). *Man's search for meaning.* New York: Washington Square Press/Pocket Books.

Frankl, V. (1988). *The will to meaning: Foundations and applications of logotherapy.* New York: New American Library.

Frankl, V. (1997b). *Man's search for ultimate meaning.* New York: Insight Books.

Frankl, V. (1997a). *Viktor Frankl—recollections: An autobiography.* New York: Insight Books.

Frankl, V. (2000). *Recollections: An autobiography.* New York: Perseus.

Freeman, J. (1984). *Women: A feminist perspective.* Palo Alto, CA: Mafield.

Frie, R. (2003). *On the nature of therapeutic interaction.* San Francisco: Existential-Humanistic Institute. Retrieved August 25, 2006, from http://www.ehinstitute.org/articles/?method=display&ArticleID=1007

Fried, S. B., & Mehrotra, C. M. (1998). *Aging and diversity: An active learning experience.* Bristol, PA: Taylor & Francis.

Fry, P. S. (2000). Religious involvement, spirituality and personal meaning for life: Existential predictors of psychological wellbeing in community-residing and institutional care elders. *Aging & Mental Health, 4*(4), 375–387.

Fugita, S. S., & Fernandes, M. (2004). *Altered lives, enduring community: Japanese Americans remember their World War II incarceration.* Seattle: University of Washington Press.

Fuller-Thomson, E. (2005). American Indian/Alaskan Native grandparents raising grandchildren: Findings from the census 2000 supplementary survey. *Social Work, 50*(2), 131–139.

Galliano, J., & Lissotta, C. (2004). Worldwide pride. *The Advocate, 917,* 81–86.

George-Warren, H. (2004). A hillbilly timeline. In M.-L. Evans, H. George-Warren, R. Santelli, & T. Robertson (Eds.), *The Appalachians: America's first and last frontier* (pp. 109–112). New York: Random House.

Gesino, J. P. (2001). Native Americans: Oppression and social work practice. In E. C. G. A. Appleby & J. Hamilton (Eds.), *Diversity, oppression, and social functioning* (pp. 109–130). Boston: Allyn and Bacon.

Ghodsee, K. (2004). Feminism-by-design: Emerging capitalisms, cultural feminism, and women's nongovernmental organization in postsocialist Eastern Europe. *Signs: Journal of Women in Culture and Society, 29*(31), 727–753.

Gilligan, C. (1982). *In a different voice: Psychological theory and women's development.* Cambridge, MA: Harvard University Press.

Gjerde, P. F. (2004). Culture, power, and experience: Toward a person centered cultural psychology. *Human Development, 47*(3), 138–157.

Gloria, A. M., Ruiz, E. L., & Castillo, E. M. (2004). Counseling and psychotherapy with Latino and Latina clients. In T. B. Smith (Ed.), *Practicing multiculturalism* (pp. 167–189). Boston: Pearson.

Goldenberg, I., & Goldenberg, H. (2005). Family therapy. In R. J. Corsini & D. Wedding (Eds.), *Current psychotherapies* (7th ed., pp. 372–404). Belmont, CA: Brooks/Cole.

Golombok, S., Perry, B. J., Burston, A., Murray, C., Mooney-Somers, J., & Golding, J. (2003). Children with lesbian parents: A community study. *Developmental Psychology, 39*(1), 20–33.

Gordon, M. (1964). *Assimilation in American life.* New York: Oxford University Press.

Green, R. (1989). *Homecoming: When the soldiers came home from Vietnam.* New York: Putnam.

Green, R. (1995). *Cultural awareness in the human services.* Boston: Allyn and Bacon.

Greenlee, R., & Lantz, J. (1993). Family coping strategies and the rural Appalachian working poor. *Contemporary Family Therapy, 15*(2), 121–137.

Grieco, E. M., & Cassidy, R. C. (2001). *Overview of race and Hispanic origin* (No. C2KBR/01-1). Washington, DC: U.S. Department of Commerce, Economics and Statistics Administration, Bureau of the Census.

Grove, D., & Haley, J. (1991). *Conservations on therapy.* New York: Norton.

Guttman, D. (1984). Logophilosophy for Israel's retirees in the helping professions. *International Forum for Logotherapy, 7*(1), 18–25.

Guzman, B. (2001). *The Hispanic population* (No. C2KBR/01-3). Washington, DC: U.S. Census Bureau: U.S. Department of Commerce, Economics and Statistics Administration.

Hamilton, J. (2001). Racism: People of color. In G. A. Appleby, E. Colon, & J. Hamilton (Eds.), *Diversity, oppression, and social functioning* (pp. 53–69). Boston: Allyn and Bacon.

Hancock, B. (1998). *Trent focus for research and development in primary health care: An intro-duction to qualitative research.* Retrieved June 30, 2005, from http://www.trentfocus .org.uk/Resources/Qualitative%20Research.pdf

Hanmer, J., & Statham, D. (1989). *Women and social work.* Chicago: Lyceum Books.

Hanscom, K. L. (2001). Treating survivors of war trauma and torture. *American Psychologist, 56*(11), 1032–1039.

Harley, D. A., Jolivette, K., McCormick, K., & Tice, K. (2002). Race, class, and gender: A constel-lation of positionalities with implications for counseling. *Journal of Multicultural Counsel-ing and Development, 30*(4), 216–238.

Harper, K. V. (1990a). Meaning and midlife tragedy: A logotherapy approach. *International Forum for Logotherapy, 13*(2), 76–78.

Harper, K. V. (1990b). Power and gender issues in academic administration. *Affilia, 5*(1), 81–93.

Harper, K. V. (1996). Culturally relevant health care service delivery for Appalachia. In M. C. Julia (Ed.), *Multicultural awareness in the health care professions* (pp. 42–59). Boston: Allyn and Bacon.

Harper, K. V. (2000a). Appalachian women's ways of living within and beyond their cultural heri-tage. In M. C. Julia (Ed.), *Constructing gender: Multicultural perspectives in working with women* (pp. 69–87). Belmont, CA: Wadsworth.

Harper, K. V. (2000b). Seamen's aid society. In A. M. H. Zophy & F. M. Kavenik (Eds.), *Handbook of American women's history* (2nd ed., p. 502). Thousand Oaks, CA: Sage.

Harper, K. V., & Greenlee, R. W. (1989). Photo essay: Promise and poverty in Appalachian heart-land. *Human Services in the Rural Environment, 13*(2), 42–47.

Harper, K. V., & Lantz, J. (1992). Treating cultural confusion in the relocated rural child. *Social Work in Education, 14*(3), 177–183.

Harper, K. V., & Shillito, L. (1991). Groupwork with bulimic adolescent females in suburbia. *Social Work with Groups, 14*(1), 43–56.

Harper-Dorton, K. V., & Herbert, M. (1999). *Working with families and children.* Chicago: Lyceum Books.

Harper-Dorton, K. V., & Yoon, D. P. (2002). Information technology in rural nonprofit agencies: Local concerns and global potentials. *New Technology in the Human Services, 14*(3/4), 24–33.

Harris-Lacewell, & Albertson, B. (2005). Good times? Understanding African American misperceptions of racial economic fortunes. *Journal of Black Studies, 35*(5), 650–683.

Havighurst, R., & Albrecht, R. (1953). *Older people.* New York: Longmans and Green.

Hayes-Bautista, D. E., & Chapa, J. (1987). Latino terminology: Conceptual bases for standardized terminology. *American Journal of Public Health, 77*(1), 61–68.

Healey, J. F. (2003). *Race, ethnicity, gender, and class* (3rd ed.). Thousand Oaks, CA: Pine Forge Press.

Heidegger, M. (1962). *Being and time.* New York: Harper and Row.

Henkin, W. A. (1985). Toward counseling the Japanese in America: A cross-cultural primer. *Journal of Counseling and Development, 63*(8), 500–503.

Herbert, M., & Harper-Dorton, K. V. (2002). *Working with families, adolescents, and children* (3rd ed.). Oxford: Blackwell Publishers.

Hertig, Y. L. (2002). *Cultural tug of war: The Korean immigrant family and church in transition.* Nashville, TN: Abingdon.

Hesselbrock, M. N., & Parks, C. (2001). Asian Americans: Ethnocentrism and discrimination. In G. A. Appleby, E. Colon, & J. Hamilton (Eds.), *Diversity, oppression and social functioning* (pp. 131–144). Boston: Allyn and Bacon.

The history of Japanese immigration. (2000). *The Brown Quarterly.* Retrieved November 3, 2005, from http://www.brownvboard.org/brwnqurt/03-04/03-4a.htm

Holmes, R. (1991). Alcoholics anonymous as group therapy. *International Forum for Logotherapy, 14*(1), 36–41

Hooyman, N. R., & Kiyak, H. A. (2005). *Social gerontology.* New York: Pearson.

Hudley, E. V. P., Haught, W., & Miller, P. S. (2003). *Raise up a child.* Chicago: Lyceum Books.

Hyde, J. S., & DeLamater, J. D. (2000). *Understanding human sexuality* (7th ed.). Boston: McGraw-Hill.

Interknowledge Corp. (2005). *Vietnam.* Retrieved September 5, 2005, from http://www.geographia.com/vietnam

International Labour Organization. (2004). *Facts on women at work.* Retrieved February 2, 2006, from http://www.ilo.org/communication

Israel, T., & Selvidge, M. M. D. (2003). Contributions of multicultural counseling to counselor competence with lesbian, gay, and bisexual clients. *Journal of Multicultural Counseling and Development, 31*(2), 84–98.

Izumi, M. (2005). Prohibiting American concentration camps: Repeal of the Emergency Detention Act and the Public Historical Memory of the Japanese American Internment. *Pacific Historical Review, 74*(2), 165–193.

Jackson, A. P., & Turner, S. (2004). Counseling and psychotherapy with Native American clients. In T. B. Smith (Ed.), *Practicing multiculturalism* (pp. 215–233). Boston: Pearson Education.

Jaggar, A. (1983). *Feminist politics and human nature.* Totowa, NJ: Rowman and Allanheld.

Jarvik, L. (1990). Role reversal: Implications for therapeutic intervention. *Journal of Gerontological Social Work, 15*(1), 23–24.

Jilek, W. (1974). *Salish Indian mental health and cultural change.* Toronto: Holt, Rinehart and Winston.

Jilek, W. (1981). Anomic depression, alcoholism and a culture-congenial Indian response. *Journal on Studies of Alcohol, 9*(Suppl.), 159–170.

Jilek, W. (1982). *Indian healing: Shamanic ceremonialism in the Pacific Northwest today.* Surrey, BC: Hancock House.

Jintrawet, U., & Harrigan, R. C. (2003). Beliefs of mothers in Asian countries and among Hmong in the United States about the causes, treatments, and outcomes of acute illnesses: An integrated review of the literature. *Issues in Comprehensive Pediatric Nursing, 26*(2), 77–88.

John, R. (1988). The Native American family. In C. Mindel, R. Habenstein, & R. Wright (Eds.), *Ethnic families in America* (pp. 325–363). New York: Elsevier.

Johnson, L. B., & Jenkins, D. (2004). Coming out in mid-adulthood: Building a new identity. *Journal of Gay and Lesbian Social Services, 16*(2), 19–42.

Johnston, R. C. (2000). In L.A.'s Koreatown, a Relentless Focus on Schooling. *Education Week, 19*(28), 20–21.

Jones, L. (1983). Appalachian values. In B. Ergood & B. E. Kuhre (Eds.), *Appalachia: Social context, past and present* (pp. 101–105). Dubuque, IA: Kendall/Hunt.

Jones, L., & Brunner, W. E. (1994). *Appalachian values* (1st ed.). Ashland, KY: Jesse Stuart Foundation.

Kameoka, V. A. (2005). The influence of Sekentei on family caregiving and underutilization of social services among Japanese caregivers. *Social Work, 50*(2), 111–118.

Kart, C., & Kinney, J. (2001). *The realities of aging: An introduction to gerontology.* Boston: Allyn and Bacon.

Keith, J. (1982). *Old people as people.* Boston: Little, Brown.

Kernberg, O. F. (1985). *Internal world and external reality: Object relations theory applied.* New York: J. Aronson.

Kernberg, O. F. (2002). Unresolved issues in the psychoanalytic theory of homosexuality and bisexuality. *Journal of Gay and Lesbian Psychotherapy, 6*(1), 9–27.

Kershaw, S. (2000). Living in a lesbian household: The effects on children. *Child and Family Social Work, 5*(4), 365–371.

Kim, I. J. (2004). A century of Korean immigration to the United States: 1903–2003. In I. J. Kim (Ed.), *Korean-Americans: Past, present and future* (pp. 13–37). Elizabeth, NJ: Hollym International.

Kim, J. Y., & Sung, K. (2000). Conjugal violence in Korean American families: A residue of the cultural tradition. *Journal of Family Violence, 15*(4), 331–345.

Kim, Y. O. (1995). Cultural pluralism and Asian-Americans: Culturally sensitive social work practice. *International Social Work, 38*(1), 69–78.

Kirk, J., & Miller, M. (1986). *Reliability and validity in qualitative research.* Beverly Hills, CA: Sage.

Kitano, H. H. L. (1988). The Japanese American family. In C. H. Mindel, R. W. Habenstein, & R. Wright, Jr. (Eds.), *Ethnic families in America* (pp. 258–275). New York: Elsevier.

Kocarek, C. E., & Pelling, N. J. (2003). Beyond knowledge and awareness: Enhancing counselor skills for work with gay, lesbian, and bisexual clients. *Journal of Multicultural Counseling and Development, 31*(2), 99–112.

Koenen, K. C., Stellman, J. M., Stellman, S. D., & Sommer, J. I. (2003). Risk factors for course of posttraumatic stress disorder among Vietnam veterans: A 14-year follow up of American Legionnaires. *Journal of Consulting and Clinical Psychology, 71*(6), 980–986.

Koetting, M. E. (2004). Beginning practice with preoperative male-to-female transgender clients. *Journal of Gay and Lesbian Social Services, 16*(2), 99–104.

Krestan, J., & Bepko, C. (1980). The problem of fusion in the lesbian relationship. *Family Process, 13*(3), 277–289.

Krill, D. F. (1976). Existential psychotherapy and the problem of anomie. In F. L. Turner (Ed.), *Differential diagnosis and treatment in social work* (pp. 728–748). New York: Free Press.

Krill, D. (1978). *Existential social work.* New York: Free Press.

Krill, D. (1979). Existential social work. In F. L. Turner (Ed.), *Social work treatment: Interlocking theoretical approaches* (2nd ed., pp. 147–175). New York: Free Press.

Kung, W. W. (2003). Chinese Americans' help seeking for emotional distress. *Social Service Review, 77*(1), 93–109.

Lamberg, L. (2000). Military psychiatrists strive to quell soldiers' nightmares of war. *Journal of the American Medical Association, 292*(13), 1539–1540.

Langle, A. (2001). Old age from an existential-analytical perspective. *Psychological Reports, 89,* 211–215.

Langle, A. (2004). Objectives of existential psychology and existential psychotherapy: Answering Paul Wong's editorial. *International Journal of Existential Psychology & Psychotherapy, 1*(1), 99–102.

Lantz, J. (1975). *Relationship enrichment needs of gay and lesbian couples: A phenomenological study.* Unpublished manuscript.

Lantz, J. (1978). *Family and marital therapy.* New York: Appleton-Century Crofts.

Lantz, J. (1987). The use of Frankl's concepts in family therapy. *Journal of Independent Social Work, 2*(2), 65–80.

Lantz, J. (1989). Meaning in profanity and pain. *Voices, 25*(1), 34–37.

Lantz, J. (1990). Existential reflection in marital therapy with Vietnam veterans. *Journal of Couples Therapy, 1*(1), 81–88.

Lantz, J. (1991a). Franklian treatment with Vietnam veteran couples. *Journal of Religion and Health, 30*(2), 131–138.

Lantz, J. (1991b). Heart and soul. In E. Tick & S. Sabom (Eds.), *Healing a generation: The Vietnam experience* (pp. 89–91). New York: Guilford Press.

Lantz, J. (1992a). Meaning, nerves and the urban-Appalachian family. *Journal of Religion and Health, 31*(2), 129–139.

Lantz, J. (1992b). Using Frankl's concepts with PTSD clients. *Journal of Traumatic Stress, 5*(3), 485–490.

Lantz, J. (1993). *Existential family therapy.* Northvale, NJ: Jason Aronson.

Lantz, J. (1995). Frankl's concept of time: Existential psychotherapy with couples and families. *Journal of Contemporary Psychotherapy, 25*(2), 135–144.

Lantz, J. (1996). Basic concepts in existential psychotherapy with couples and families. *Contemporary Family Therapy, 18*(4), 535–548.

Lantz, J. (1997). Reflection, meanings and dreams. *International Forum for Logotherapy, 20*(2), 95–103.

Lantz, J. (1998). Recollection in existential psychotherapy with older adults. *Journal of Clinical Geropsychology, 4*(1), 45–53.

Lantz, J. (1999). Heidegger's brightness as a responsibility of the therapist in existential family therapy. *Contemporary Family Therapy, 21*(1), 29–43.

Lantz, J. (2000a). Existential psychotherapy with Vietnam veteran couples: A twenty-five year report. *Contemporary Family Therapy, 22*(1), 19–37.

Lantz, J. (2000b). Franklian psychotherapy: Treatment elements and dynamics. *International Forum for Logotherapy, 23*(1), 17–23.

Lantz, J. (2000c). *Meaning centered marital and family therapy: Learning to bear the beams of love.* Springfield, IL: Charles C. Thomas.

Lantz, J. (2000d). Phenomenological reflection and time in Viktor Frankl's existential psychotherapy. *Journal of Phenomenological Psychology, 3*(2), 220–231.

Lantz, J. (2001). Depression, existential family therapy and Viktor Frankl's dimensional ontology. *Contemporary Family Therapy, 23*(1), 19–32.

Lantz, J. (2002). Existential psychotherapy: What endures? *Voices, 38*(1), 28–33.

Lantz, J. (2004). Worldview concepts in existential family therapy. *Contemporary Family Therapy, 26*(2), 165–178.

Lantz, J., & Alford, K. (1995). Existential family treatment with an urban-Appalachian adolescent. *Journal of Family Psychotherapy, 6*(4), 15–27.

Lantz, J., & Frazer, P. (1996). Existential psychotherapy with migration crisis couples. *Crisis Intervention and Time-Limited Treatment, 3*(2), 155–163.

Lantz, J., & Greenlee, R. (1990a). Existential social work with Vietnam veterans. *Journal of Independent Social Work, 5*(1), 39–52.

Lantz, J., & Greenlee, R. (1990b). Logotherapy and the Vietnam veteran. *International Forum for Logotherapy, 13*(2), 115–188.

Lantz, J., & Gregoire, T. (2000a). Existential psychotherapy with couples facing breast cancer: A twenty-year report. *Contemporary Family Therapy, 22*(3), 315–327.

Lantz, J., & Gregoire, T. (2000b). Existential psychotherapy with Vietnam veteran couples: A twenty-five year report. *Contemporary Family Therapy, 22*(1), 19–37.

Lantz, J., & Gregoire, T. (2003). Couples, existential psychotherapy, and myocardial infarction: A ten year evaluation study. *Contemporary Family Therapy, 25*(4), 367–379.

Lantz, J., & Gyamerah, J. (2002a). Art in short-term existential psychotherapy. *Journal of Brief Therapy, 1*(2), 155–162.

Lantz, J., & Gyamerah, J. (2002b). Existential family trauma therapy. *Contemporary Family Therapy, 24*(2), 243–256.

Lantz, J., & Harper, K. (1989). Network intervention, existential depression and the relocated Appalachian family. *Contemporary Family Therapy, 11*(3), 213–223.

Lantz, J., & Harper, K. (1990). Anomic depression and the migrating family. *Contemporary Family Therapy, 12*(2), 153–163.

Lantz, J., & Harper, K. (1991). Using poetry in logotherapy. *The Arts in Psychotherapy, 18*(4), 341–345.

Lantz, J., & Harper, K. (1992). Stories and tales in logotherapy with urban Appalachian families. *Contemporary Family Therapy, 14*(6), 455–466.

Lantz, J., & Lantz, J. (1989). Meaning, tragedy and logotherapy with the elderly. *Journal of Religion and Aging, 5*(1), 43–51.

Lantz, J., & Lantz, J. (1991). Franklian treatment with the traumatized family. *Journal of Family Psychotherapy, 2*(1), 61–73.

Lantz, J., & Lantz, J. (1992). Franklian psychotherapy with adults molested as children. *Journal of Family Psychotherapy, 2*(1), 61–73.

206 References

Lantz, J., & Lantz, J. (2001). Trauma therapy: A meaning centered approach. *International Forum for Logotherapy, 24*(2), 68–76.
Lantz, J., & Lenahan, B. (1976). Referral-fatigue therapy. *Social Work, 21*(3), 239–240.
Lantz, J., & Pegram, M. (1989). Cross cultural curative factors and clinical social work. *Journal of Independent Social Work, 4*(1), 55–68.
Lantz, J., & Raiz, L. (2003). Play and art in existential trauma therapy with children and their parents. *Contemporary Family Therapy, 25*(2), 165–177.
Lantz, J., & Raiz, L. (2004). Existential psychotherapy with older adult couples: A five year treatment report. *Clinical Gerontologist, 27*(3), 39–54.
LaRowe, K. (2004). *Compassion fatigue.* Retrieved February 2, 2006, from http://www.breathofrelief.com/compassionfatigue.html
Larson, E. B., & Imai, Y. (1996). An overview of dementia and ethnicity with special emphasis on the epidemiology of dementia. In D. Gallagher-Thompson (Ed.), *Ethnicity and the dementias* (2nd ed., pp. 9–20). Bristol, PA: Taylor & Francis.
Lee, D., & Saul, T. (1987). Counseling Asian men. In M. Scher, M. Stevens, G. Good, & G. Eichenfield (Eds.), *Handbook of counseling and psychotherapy with men* (pp. 180–191). Beverly Hills, CA: Sage.
Lee, E. (2004). In the name of the family: Gender and immigrant small business ownership. In I. J. Kim (Ed.), *A century of Korean immigration to the United States: 1903–2003* (pp. 121–149). Elizabeth, NJ: Hollym International.
Leon, A. M., & Dziegielewski, S. F. (1999). The psychological impact of migration: Practice considerations in working with Hispanic women. *Journal of Social Work Practice, 13*(1), 69–82.
Leung, P., & Cheung, K. M. (2001). Competencies in practice evaluations with Asian American individuals and families. In R. Fong & S. Furuto (Eds.), *Culturally competent practice: Skills, interventions and evaluations* (pp. 426–437). Boston: Allyn and Bacon.
Leung, P., Erich, S., & Kanenberg, H. (2005). A comparison of family functioning in gay/lesbian, heterosexual and special needs adoptions. *Children and Youth Services Review, 27*(9), 1031–1044.
Lifton, R. (1973). *Home from the war.* New York: Simon and Schuster.
Lincoln, C. E. (1999). *Race, religion, and the continuing American dilemma.* New York: Hill & Wang.
Lincoln, Y., & Guba, E. (1985). *Naturalistic inquiry.* Beverly Hills, CA: Sage.
Lindy, J. (1988). *Vietnam: A casebook.* New York: Brunner-Mazel.
Linzer, N. (2004). An ethical dilemma in elder abuse. *Journal of Gerontological Social Work, 43*(2/3), 165–173.
Liss, M., Hoffner, C., & Crawford, M. (2000). What do feminists believe? *Psychology of Women Quarterly, 24*(4), 279–284.
Locke, D. C. (1992). *Increasing multicultural understanding.* Newbury Park, CA: Sage.
Lum, D. (2004). *Social work practice and people of color: A process-stage approach.* Pacific Grove, CA: Brooks/Cole.
Lyon, G. E. (1990). *Come a tide.* New York: Orchard Books.
Mackie, C. (1997). *Think about it. The African-American engineer in the 21st century: A burden, challenge, and opportunity.* Retrieved June 15, 2005, from http://www.black-collegian.com/african/thinkaboutit.shtml
MacPherson, M. (2001). *Long time passing.* Bloomington, IN: Indiana University Press.

Maddox, G. L. (1963). Activity and morale: A longitudinal study of selected elderly subjects. *Social Forces, 42*(2), 195–204.

Mann, J. (2003). Appalachian subculture. *The Gay & Lesbian Review, 10*(5), 19–21.

Mapp, I. (2005). Hispanic families in the United States with deaf and hearing impaired children. In E. P. Congress & M. J. Gonzalez (Eds.), *Multicultural perspectives in working with families* (pp. 267–287). New York: Spring.

Maramaldi, P. & Naleppa, M. J. (2003). Late adulthood. In E. D. Hutchison (Ed.), *Dimensions of human behavior* (pp. 291–435). Thousand Oaks, CA: Sage.

Marcel, G. (1952). *Man against humanity.* London: Harvell Press.

Marcel, G. (1963). *The existential background of human dignity.* Cambridge, MA: Harvard University Press.

Marcel, G. (1973). *Tragic wisdom and beyond.* Evanston, IL: Northwestern University Press.

Marino, G. (2004). *Basic writings of existentialism.* New York: Modern Library.

Masters, W. H., Johnson, V. E., & Kolodney, R. C. (1995). *Human sexuality* (6th ed.). New York: HarperCollins.

May, R. (1977). *The meaning of anxiety.* New York: Norton.

May, R. (1986). *The discovery of being: Writings in existential psychology.* New York: Norton.

May, R., & Yalom, I. (2005). Existential psychotherapy. In R. J. Coirsini & D. Wedding (Eds.), *Current psychotherapies* (pp. 269–298). Belmont, CA: Brooks/Cole.

Mayo, Y. (1997). Machismo, manhood, and men in Latino families. In E. P. Congress (Ed.), *Multicultural perspectives in working with families* (pp. 181–197). New York: Spring.

Mays, B. (2003). As the "schoolmaster of the movement," he shaped generations of men. *Nation, 277,* 26–29.

McDowell, J., & Stewart, D. (1996). *Handbook of today's religions* (2nd ed.). Nashville, TN: Thomas Nelson.

McGoldrick, M., Giordano, J., & Pearce, J. K. (1996). *Ethnicity and family therapy.* New York: Guilford Press.

McGuiness, C. (1989). *Aging in America.* Washington, DC: Congressional Quarterly.

McPhatter, A. R. (1997). Cultural competence in child welfare: What is it? How do we achieve it? What happens without it? *Child Welfare, 76*(1), 255–278.

McQuade, S. (1989). Working with Southeast Asian refugees. *Clinical Social Work Journal, 17*(2), 162–176.

Mengel, T. (2004). Supplementary elements of a comprehensive existential psychology: A response to Paul T. P. Wong's editorial, "Existential Psychology for the 21st Century." *International Journal of Existential Psychology & Psychotherapy, 1*(1), 107–108.

Miller, L. (2003). Family therapy of terroristic trauma: psychological syndromes and treatment strategies. *American Journal of Family Therapy, 31*(4), 257–280.

Min, P. G. (1988). The Korean American Family. In C. Mindel, R. Habenstein, & R. Wright (Eds.), *Ethnic families in America* (pp. 199–229). New York: Elsevier.

Montague, A. (1964). *Man's most dangerous myth: The fallacy of race* (4th ed.). Cleveland, OH: World Publishing.

Montalvo, F. J. (2004). Surviving race: Skin color and the socialization and acculturation of Latinas. *Journal of Ethics and Cultural Diversity in Social Work, 13*(3), 25–43.

Moody, H. (2002). Should we ration health care for older people? In H. Moody, *Aging: Concepts and controversies* (4th ed.), Walnut Creek, CA: Pine Forge Press.

Moon, B. (1990). *Existential art therapy: The canvas mirror.* Springfield, IL: Charles C. Thomas.

Moore, J., & Pachon, H. (1985). *Hispanics in the United States.* New York: Little, Brown.

Moore, P. J. (2003). The Black church: A natural resource for bereavement support. *Journal of Pastoral Counseling, 38,* 47–57.

Morikawa, S. (2001). The significance of Afrocentricity for non-Africans: Examination of the relationship between African Americans and the Japanese. *Journal of Black Studies, 31*(4), 423–436.

Moses, A., & Hawkins, R. (1982). *Counseling lesbian women and gay men.* Columbus, OH: Charles Merrill.

Mumford, A. (2001). Marketing working mothers: Contextualizing earned income tax credits within feminist cultural theory. *Journal of Social Welfare and Family Law, 23*(4), 411–426.

Murguia, A., Peterson, R. A., & Zea, M. C. (2003). Use and implications of ethnomedical health care approaches among Central American immigrants. *Health & Social Work, 28*(1), 43–53.

Mwanza (1990). *Afrikan naturalism.* Columbus, OH: Pan Afrikan Publications.

Nagel, J., & Snipp, M. (1993). Ethnic reorganization: American Indian social, economic, political, and cultural strategies for survival. *Ethnic and Racial Studies, 16*(2), 203–235.

Naleppa, M. J., & Reid, W. J. (2002). *Gerontological social work.* New York: Columbia University Press.

NARA. (1999). *President Clinton and Vice President Gore: Supporting Native Americans' economy.* National Archives and Records Administration. Retrieved July 5, 2005, from http://www.clinton2.nara.gov/WH/Accomplishments/natacc99.html

NASW. (2000). *Code of ethics.* Washington, DC: NASW.

NASW National Committee on Racial and Ethnic Diversity. (2001). *NASW standards for cultural competence in social work practice.* Retrieved August 30, 2006, from http://www.socialworkers.org/sections/credentials/cultural_comp.asp

National Center for Health Statistics. (2005). *Life expectancy hits record high.* Hyattsville, MD: Center for Disease Control, U.S. Department of Health and Human Services. Retrieved April 15, 2005, from http://www.cdc.gov/nchs/pressroom/05facts/lifeexpectancy.htm

National Institute on Aging. (2006, April 25). *Alzheimer's disease fact sheet.* Retrieved May 1, 2006, from http://www.nia.nih.gov/Alzheimers/Publications/adfact.htm

Neal, B. E. (2000). Native American women. In M. C. Julia (Ed.), *Constructing gender: Multicultural perspective in working with women* (pp. 157–176). Belmont, CA: Wadsworth/Thomson Learning.

Neeley, C. (2005). Gay men and lesbians in rural areas. In N. Lohmann & R. Lohmann (Eds.), *Rural social work practice* (pp. 232–254). New York: Columbia University Press.

Nes, J., & Iadicola, P. (1989). Toward a definition of feminist social work: A comparison of liberal, radical, and socialist models. *Social Work, 34*(1), 12–21.

Newman, B. M., & Newman, P. R. (2003). *Development through life: A psychosocial approach* (8th ed.). Belmont, CA: Thomson/Wadsworth Learning.

Nilmanat, K., & Street, A. (2004). Search for a cure: Narratives of Thai family caregivers living with a person with AIDS. *Social Science & Medicine, 59*(5), 1003–1010.

Norwich, J. O. (1966). *Revelations of divine love.* London: Penguin.

Oberhauser, A. M. (2005). Scaling gender and diverse economies: Perspectives from Appalachia and South Africa. *Antipode, 37*(5), 863–874.

Obermiller, P., & Maloney, M. (1991). Living city, feeling country: The current status and future prospects of urban Appalachians. In B. Ergood & B. Kuhre (Eds.), *Appalachia: Social context, past and present* (3rd ed., pp. 133–138). Dubuque, IA: Kendall/Hunt.

Obermiller, P. J., & Howe, S. R. (2000). *Urban Appalachian and Appalachian migrant research in greater Cincinnati: A status report.* Retrieved March 1, 2006, from http://www.uacvoice.org/workingpaper16.html

O'Brien, S. (1996). *Bureau of Indian Affairs.* Retrieved July 10, 2005, from http://college.hmco/history/readerscomp/naind/html/na_004900_bureauofidi.htm

O'Brien, T. (1998). *The things they carried.* New York: Broadway Books.

O'Dell, S. (2000). Psychotherapy with gay and lesbian families: Opportunities for cultural inclusion and clinical challenge. *Clinical Social Work Journal, 28*(2), 171–182.

Oliver, M., & Shapiro, T. (1996). *Black wealth, White wealth.* New York: Routledge.

Olson, T. (2004). The mountain melting pot: Appalachia's diverse ethnic and racial groups. In M. Evans, H. George-Warren, & R. Santelli (Eds.), *The Appalachians: America's first and last frontier* (pp. 10–19). New York: Random House.

Palmer, M. G. (2004). Compensation for Vietnam's Agent Orange victims. *International Journal of Human Rights, 8*(1), 1–15.

Parker, L. (2003). A social justice model for clinical social work practice. *Affilia, 18*(3), 272–288.

Park Ethnography Program. (2006). *African American heritage and ethnography.* U.S. Department of the Interior/National Park Service. Retrieved November 15, 2006, from http://www.cr.nps.gov/ethnography/aah/aaheritage/histContextsD.htm

Payne, M. (2005). *Modern social work theory.* Chicago: Lyceum Books.

PBS. (1999). *Children of the camps.* Retrieved November 5, 2006, from http://www.pbs.org/childofcamp/history/timeline.html

PBS. (2005). *Hidden Korea.* Retrieved October 25, 2005, from http://www.pbs.org/hiddenkorea/religion.htm

Perez-Stable, E. J. (1987). *Issues in Latin American care.* Newbury, CA: Sage.

Perry, B. J., Burston, A., Murray, C., Mooney-Somers, J., Stevens, M., & Golding, J. (2003). Children with lesbian parents: A community study. *Developmental Psychology, 39*(1), 20–33.

Poku, N. K., & Whiteside, A. (2006). Introduction, 25 years of living with HIV/AIDS: Challenges and prospects. *International Affairs, 82*(2), 249–256.

Poon, M. K.-L. (2004). A missing voice: Asians in contemporary gay and lesbian social service literature. *Journal of Gay and Lesbian Social Services, 17*(3), 87–106.

Popielski, K. (1990). Universal truths. *International Forum for Logotherapy, 13*(1), 49–50.

Popple, P. R., & Leighninger, L. (2002). *Social work, social welfare, and American society* (5th ed.). Boston: Allyn and Bacon.

Portella, E. (2000). Cultural cloning or hybrid cultures? *UNESCO Courier, 52*(4), 9.

Potocky-Tripodi, M. (2002). *Best practices for social work with refugees and immigrants.* New York: Columbia University Press.

Powell, P. A. B. (2000). The Lord in Black skin. *Christianity Today, 44*(11), 50–56.

Prince, J. (1999). Black single mothers and the politics of oppression: Efforts to effect change. In C. L. Schmitz & S. S. Tebb (Eds.), *Diversity in single-parent families: Working from strength* (pp. 107–130). Chicago: Lyceum Books.

Ramirez, R. R., & Cruz, P. de la. (2002). The Hispanic population in the United States, *March 2002. Current population reports,* P20-545. Washington, DC: U.S. Census Bureau.

Reicherzer, S. (2005). Coming out and living across the life span. In D. Comstock (Ed.), *Diversity and development* (pp. 161–183). Belmont, CA: Brooks/Cole.

Riemenschneider, A., & Harper, K. V. (1990). Women in academia: Guilty or not guilty? Conflict between caregiving and employment. *Initiatives, 53*(2), 27–35.

Ritchie, L. H., Ritchie, P. N., & Dietz, B. E. (2001). Clarifying the measurement of activity. *Activities, Adaptation, and Aging, 26*(1), 1–21.

Robinson, B. A. (2003, January 17). *De-criminalizing same-sex behavior.* Retrieved February 15, 2006, from http://www.religioustolerance.org/hom_laws2.htm

Robinson, B. A. (2005, December 11). *Criminalizing same-sex behavior.* Retrieved March 15, 2006, from http://www.religioustolerance.org/hom_laws1.htm

Rodriguez, G. (2005). Why we're the new Irish. *Newsweek, 145*(22), 35.

Rogers, C. (1980). *On becoming a person.* New York: Bantam Dell.

Rose, S. J., & Hartmann, H. I. (2004). *Still a man's labor market: The long-term earnings gap.* Retrieved February 2, 2006, from http://ww.iwpr.org/Publications/pdf.htm

Ruchlin, H. S., & Morris, J. N. (1991). Impact of work on the quality of life of community-residing young elderly. *American Journal of Public Health, 81*(4), 498–500.

Russell, K., Wilson, M., & Hall, R. (1993). *The color complex: The politics of skin color among African Americans.* New York: Doubleday.

Saleeby, D. (1999). *The strengths perspective in social work practice* (2nd ed.). New York: Longman.

Sandner, D. (1979). *Navaho symbols of healing.* New York: Harcourt, Brace and Jovanovich.

Savarese, V. W., Suvak, M. K., King, L. A., & King, D. W. (2001). Relationships among alcohol use, hyperarousal, and marital abuse and violence in Vietnam veterans. *Journal of Traumatic Stress, 14*(4), 717–732.

Scannapieco, M., & Jackson, S. (1996). Kinship care: The African American response to family preservation. *Social Work, 41*(2), 190–197.

Schaefer, R. T. (1998). *Racial and ethnic groups* (7th ed.). New York: Longman.

Schiele, J. H. (1996). Afrocentricity: An emerging paradigm in social work practice. *Social Work, 41*(3), 284–294.

Schope, R. D., & Eliason, M. J. (2004). Sissies and tomboys: Gender role behaviors and homophobia. *Journal of Gay and Lesbian Social Services, 16*(2), 73–97.

Schriver, J. M. (2004). *Human behavior and the social environment* (4th ed.). Boston: Pearson.

Schulz, R., & Salthouse, T. (1999). *Adult development and aging: Myths and emerging realities* (3rd ed.). Upper Saddle River, NJ: Prentice Hall.

Schwartz, W. (2003–2004). The Asian and Pacific Islander population in the U.S. *ERIC Digest.* Retrieved October 15, 2005, from http://www.ericdigests.org/2003-4/asian.html

Scott, W. J. (1992). PTSD and Agent Orange: Implications for a sociology of veterans' issues. *Armed Forces & Society, 18*(4), 592–612.

Shapiro, R. (2004). *The demographics of aging in America.* Retrieved April 4, 2006, from http://www.prcdc.org/summaries/aging/aging.html

Sheehy, G. (1982). *Pathfinders: Overcoming the crisis of adult life.* New York: Bantam Books.

Shernoff, M. (1984). Family therapy for lesbian and gay clients. *Social Work, 29*(4), 393–396.

Simmons, T., & O'Connell, M. (2003). *Married-couple and unmarried-partner households: 2000* (Census 2000 Special Reports, CENSR-5). Washington, DC: U.S. Census Bureau, U.S. Government Printing Office.

Simpson, R. (2004). Journalism and trauma: A long overdue conjunction. *Nieman Reports, 58*(2), 77–79.

Sniderman, P. M., & Piazza, T. (2002). *Black pride and Black prejudice.* Princeton, NJ: Princeton University Press.

Sohng, S. S. L., & Song, K.-H. (2004). Korean children and families. In R. Fong (Ed.), *Culturally competent practice with immigrant and refugee children and families* (pp. 81–99). New York: Guilford Press.

Spindler, G., & Spindler, L. (1971). *Dreamers without power: The Menomini Indians.* New York: Holt, Rinehart and Winston.

Stein, E. (1964). *On the problem of empathy.* The Hague: M. Niijhoff.

Strauss, A., & Corbin, J. (1990). *Basics of qualitative research: Grounded theory procedures and techniques.* Thousand Oaks, CA: Sage.

Strauss, A., & Corbin, J. (1998). Grounded theory methodology. In N. K. Denzi & Y. S. Lincoln (Eds.), *Strategies of qualitative inquiry* (pp. 158–183). Thousand Oaks, CA: Sage.

Sue, D. W., & Sue, D. (2003). *Counseling the culturally diverse: Theory and practice* (4th ed.). New York: Houghton Mifflin.

Sue, S. (1994). Mental health. In W. S. Nolan, D. T. Zane, D. T. Takeuchi, & K. N. J. Young (Eds.), *Confronting critical health issues of Asian and Pacific Islander Americans* (pp. 266–288). Thousand Oaks, CA: Sage.

Szapocznik, J., & Hernandez, R. (1988). The Cuban American family. In C. Mindell, R. Habenstein, and R. Wright (Eds.). *Ethnic Families in America.* New York: Elsevier.

Takaki, R. (1993). The success of Asian Americans has been exaggerated, in part, to criticize other minority groups. In R. Takaki (Ed.), *A different mirror: A history of multicultural America* (pp. 414–417). Boston: Little, Brown.

Tan, S., & Dong, N. J. (2000). Psychotherapy with members of Asian American churches and spiritual traditions. In P. S. Richards & A. E. Bergin (Eds.), *Handbook of psychotherapy and religious diversity* (pp. 421–444). Washington, DC: American Psychological Association.

Tick, E. (1989). *Sacred mountain: Encounters with the Vietnam beast.* Santa Fe, AZ: Moon Bear Press.

Tick, E. (2005). *Fallen leaves, broken lives.* Retrieved June 20, 2006, from http://www.utne.com/cgi-bin/udt/im.display.printable?client.id=utne&story.id=11508

Tillich, P. (1952). *The courage to be.* New Haven, CT: Yale University Press.

Timberlake, E. M., & Chipungu, S. S. (1992). Grandmotherhood: Contemporary meaning among African American middle-class grandmothers. *Social Work, 37*(3), 216–222.

Tobin, J., & Freidman, J. (1983). Spirits, shamans, and nightmare death: Survivor stress in a Hmong refugee. *American Journal of Family Therapy, 53,* 439–448.

Tomaine, S. (1991). Counseling Japanese Americans: From internment to reparation. In C. Lee & B. Richardson (Eds.), *Multicultural issues in counseling: New approaches to diversity* (pp. 189–206). Alexandria, VA: American Association for Counseling and Development.

Tong, B. (2004). Race, culture, and citizenship among Japanese American children and adolescents during the internment era. *Journal of American Ethnic History, 23*(3), 3–40.

Torres, V. (2004). The diversity among us: Puerto Ricans, Cuban Americans, Caribbean Americans, and Central and South Americans. *New Directions for Student Services, 105,* 5–16.

Torrey, E. (1986). *Witchdoctors and psychiatrists.* New York: Harper and Row.

Towle, C. (1952). *Common human needs.* Silver Spring, MD: National Association of Social Workers.

Tran, T. V. (1988). The Vietnamese American family. In C. H. Mindell, R. Habenstein, & R. Wright (Eds.), *Ethnic families in America* (pp. 276–299). New York: Elsevier.

Trujillo, A. (2000). Psychotherapy with Native Americans: A view into the role of religion and spirituality. In P. S. Richards & A. Bergin (Eds.), *Handbook of psychotherapy and religious diversity* (pp. 445–466). Washington, DC: American Psychological Association.

Tully, C., & Nibao, J. (1979). Homosexuality: A social worker's imbroglio. *Journal of Sociology and Social Welfare, 7*(3), 154–168.

U.S. Census Bureau. (2000a). *Projections of the resident population by race, Hispanic origin, and nativity.* Retrieved July 15, 2006, from http://www.census.gov/population/projections/nation/summary

U.S. Census Bureau. (2000b). *Qt-P6: Race alone or in combination and Hispanic and Latino.* Retrieved June 16, 2005, from http://factfinder.census.gov

U.S. Census Bureau. (2004a). *Global population profile: 2002* (No. Report WP/02). Washington, DC: U.S. Census Bureau.

U.S. Census Bureau. (2004b, March 18). *U.S. interim projections by age, sex, race and Hispanic origin.* Retrieved July 15, 2005, from http://www.census.gov/ipc/www/usinterimproj

Van den Bergh, N. & Cooper, L. (1986). *Feminist visions for social work.* Silver Spring, MD: National Association of Social Workers.

Van den Bergh, N., & Crisp, C. (2004). Defining culturally competent practice with sexual minorities: Implications for social work education and practice. *Journal of Social Work Education, 40*(2), 221–238.

Vanfraussen, K., Ponjaert-Kristoffersen, I., & Brewaeys, A. (2003). Family functioning in lesbian families created by donor insemination. *American Journal of Orthopsychiatry, 73*(1), 78–90.

Vega, W. A., & Alegria, M. (2001). Latino mental health and treatment in the United States. In M. Aguirre-Molina, C. W. Molina, & R. E. Zambrana (Eds.), *Health issues in the Latino community* (pp. 179–208). San Francisco: Josey-Bass.

Voss, R. W., Douville, V., Soldier, A. L., & Twiss, G. (1999). Tribal and shamanic based social work practice: A Lakota perspective. *Social Work, 44*(3), 228–241.

Walsh, B., & Middleton, R. (1984). *The transforming vision: Shaping a Christian worldview.* Downers Grove, IL: Intervarsity Press.

Weaver, H. N. (1998). Indigenous people in a multicultural society: Unique issues for human services. *Social Work, 43*(3), 203–211.

Weaver, H. N. (1999). Indigenous people and the social work profession: Defining culturally competent services. *Social Work, 44*(3), 217–225.

Weiss, B. P. B. (1989). Culturally appropriate crisis counseling: Adapting an American method for use with Indochinese refugees. *Social Work, 34*(3), 252–254.

Weller, J. E. (1965). *Yesterday's people: Life in contemporary Appalachia.* Lexington: University of Kentucky Press.

Wertz, F. (1982). The findings and value of a descriptive approach to everyday perceptural process. *Journal of Phenomenological Psychology, 13*(1), 169–195.

White, M. (1995). *Re-authoring lives: Interviews and essays.* Adelaide, South Australia: Dulwich Centre.

Wiley, A., & Rappaport, J. (2000). Empowerment, wellness and the politics of development. In D. Cicchetti, J. Rappaport, I. Sandler, & R. Weissberg (Eds.), *The promotion of wellness in children and adolescents* (pp. 59–99). Thousand Oaks, CA: Sage.

Williams, J. (1983). The mental foxhole: The Vietnam veteran's search for meaning. *American Journal of Orthopsychiatry, 53,* 4–17.

Williams, J. (1987). *Eyes on the prize: America's civil rights years.* New York: Penguin.

Williams, M. (2004). Elizabeth A. Flynn: Feminism beyond modernism. *Women's Studies, 33*(4), 561–564.

Winbush, G. B. (1996). African-American health care: Beliefs, practices, and service issues. In M. C. Julia (Ed.), *Multicultural awareness in the health care professions* (pp. 8–22). Needham Heights, MA: Allyn and Bacon.

Winbush, G. B. (2000). African American women. In M. C. Julia (Ed.), *Constructing gender: Multicultural perspectives in working with women* (pp. 11–34). Belmont, CA: Wadsworth/Thomson Learning.

Wolf, R. S. (2000). The nature and scope of elder abuse. *Generations, 42*(1), 6–12.

Wong, M. (1988). The Chinese American family. In C. Mindel, R. Habenstein, & R. Wright (Eds.), *Ethnic families in America* (pp. 230–257). New York: Elsevier.

Wong, P. T. P. (2004). Existential psychology for the 21st century. *International Journal of Existential Psychology & Psychotherapy, 1*(1), 1–2.

Wright, D. E. (2001). *I'ma tell ya like that: African American blueswomen and multiple jeopardy.* Retrieved June 20, 2005, from http://hipertextos.mty.itesm.mx/num2delane.html

Wright, S. (1985). An existential perspective on differentiation/fusion: Theoretical issues and clinical applications. *Journal of Marital and Family Therapy, 11*(1), 35–46.

Yalom, I. (1980). *Existential psychotherapy.* New York: Basic Books.

Yee, B. W. K. (1990). Gender and family issues in minority groups. *Generations, 14*(3), 39–42.

Yeo, G. (1996). Background. In D. Gallagher-Thompson (Ed.), *Ethnicity and the dementias* (2nd ed., pp. 3–7). Bristol, PA: Taylor & Francis.

Yick, A. G. (2000). Predictors of physical spousal/intimate violence in Chinese American families. *Journal of Family Violence, 15*(3), 249–267.

Zaharlick, A. (2000). Southeast Asian-American women. In M. C. Julia (Ed.), *Constructing gender: Multicultural perspectives in working with women* (pp. 177–204). Pacific Grove, CA: Brooks/Cole.

Zane, N., Morton, T., Chu, J., & Lin, N. (2004). Counseling and psychotherapy with Asian American clients. In T. B. Smith (Ed.), *Practicing multiculturalism* (pp. 190–214). Boston: Pearson.

Zastrow, C., & Kirst-Ashman, K. K. (1997). *Understanding human behavior and the social environment.* Chicago: Nelson-Hall.

Zavodny, M. (2003). *Race, wages, and assimilation among Cuban immigrants.* Atlanta, GA: Federal Reserve Bank of Atlanta.

Index

Japanese Americans, 181–182
loss and, 188
Mexican Americans, 182
myths associated with, 182–184
Native Americans, 181
overview of, 177–179
Vietnamese Americans, 182
Emigrate, defined, 131
Empathetic availability
holding and, 31–32
telling and, 33
Empowerment, 6, 21
Enthnocentrism, 15
Essence worldview, 38
Ethnicity, defined, 15
Ethnomedicine, 110
Existence worlview, 38–39
dimensions of, 39
Existential frustration, 132
Existential guilt, overcoming, 61
Existential helping elements
for African American clients, 89–90
cross-cultural curative factors and, 29–36
for elderly clients, 191–192
Hispanic American clients and, 54–57
holding, 29
honoring, 29
individual reality and, 30
mastering, 29
telling, 29
for traumatized clients, 61–65
for Vietnam Veteran clients, 100
Existentialism
concepts of, for social work practice, 36–39
social work practice and, 27–29
Existential psychology, defined, 28
Existential realization, 9
Existential trauma therapy, 38–39
Existential vacuum, 132

Families, African American, role flexibility in,
85–88
Familism, 50
Family networks, Native American clients and,
75–76
Feminism
cultural, 151
defined, 148

radical, 150–151
socialist, 149–150
Feminist perspectives, 148–151. *See also* Women
clients
cultural feminism, 151
liberal feminism, 149
radical feminism, 150–151
socialist feminism, 149–150
Feminist social work, principles of, 153–154
Feminist therapy, 152
Folklore, in Appalachia, 140–141
Folk medicine
in Appalachia, 140–141
Asian American clients and, 110
Foucault, Michel, 28
Frankl, Victor, 5, 32, 35, 36–37, 60–61, 86, 132

Gay, lesbian, bisexual, and transsexual (GLBT)
clients
coming out issues and, 170–171
cross-cultural competencies for working with,
163–166
gay and lesbian families with children and,
173–174
HIV/AIDS and, 169–170
homophobia and, 161–163
overview of, 159–161
social work with, 163–168
transgender/gender reassignment and, 171–
173
Gay couples, marital therapy with, 166–168
Gay rights movements, 161
Gender identity, 171
Gender identity disorders, individuals with, 159–
160
GLBT clients. *See* Gay, lesbian, bisexual, and
transsexual (GLBT) clients
Grounded theory, 1–2
Guilt, existential, overcoming, 61

haan, 115
Handshakes, Native American clients and, 74
Heidegger, Martin, 28, 38
Helper attractiveness, 5, 33
Helping environment, establishing, for trauma-
tized clients, 65
Hinduism, 109

About the Authors

Karen V. Harper-Dorton, MSW, MA, PhD, is professor of social work in the Division of Social Work at West Virginia University and serves as director of the Beatrice Ruth Burgess Center for West Virginia Families and Communities. She earned her PhD in social work from Ohio State University, where she later served on the faculty. She has published more than seventy scholarly works and is also the coauthor of *Working with Children, Adolescents, and Their Families* (2002). In addition to her work in existential family therapy and cross-cultural social work practice, Professor Harper-Dorton has a passion for project development and is an expert grant writer and the recipient of more than thirty grant awards. Currently, her work focuses on rural families, child welfare, and cross-cultural competencies. She enjoys poetry, piano, classical music, and gardening.

Jim Lantz, MSW, PhD, earned his degrees from Ohio State University. He served as director of the Midwest Existential Psychotherapy Institute, co-director of Lantz and Lantz Counseling Associates, and professor in the College of Social Work, Ohio State University. Over the years, he studied with such pioneers in existential psychotherapy and family therapy as Ernest Andrews, Viktor Frankl, Virginia Satir, and Carl Whitaker. Professor Lantz was a graduate of the Viktor Frankl Institute of Logotherapy and the Cincinnati Family Therapy Institute. Professor Lantz is recognized for more than 125 publications and four books that extend the practice of Viktor Frankl's logotherapy and existenzanalyse to students and practitioners in clinical settings and in social work practice In addition to his work, Jim Lantz enjoyed camping, fishing, poetry, jazz, classical music, Tae kwon Do, and being with his wife and son.

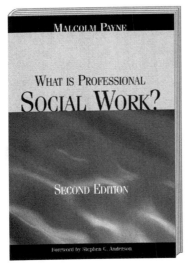